IN THE GRIP OF FREEDOM:
LAW AND MODERNITY IN MAX WEBER

Faith in the utility and value of legal rights informs the political common sense of our age. *In the Grip of Freedom* examines the relationship between Max Weber's *Sociology of Law* and his analysis of the structure and meaning of modern society. The interpretation of legal phenomena plays a prominent role in Weber's account of the development of the West and in his conception of the rationalism of modern social arrangements. In this study, Cary Boucock looks at Weber's social and political thought in the context of developments in Canada following the 1982 enactment of the Canadian Charter of Rights and Freedoms – namely, the movement towards a rights-oriented nation, where broad social issues are routed through the courts, and the political self-understanding of the citizen becomes increasingly tied to a conception of the individual as a rights-bearing subject.

Boucock goes beyond conventional assessments of Weber's legal theory and its applicability to understanding contemporary legal developments. He explores the significance of Weber's sociology of law theories within the larger compass of his sociological thought and illustrates the significance of Weber's sociology for interpreting the social and legal practices of our time.

CARY BOUCOCK is Assistant Professor in the Department of Sociology and Anthropology at Concordia University.

# IN THE GRIP
# OF
# *Freedom*

## LAW AND MODERNITY
## IN MAX WEBER

Cary Boucock

UNIVERSITY OF TORONTO PRESS
Toronto Buffalo London

© University of Toronto Incorporated 2000
Toronto Buffalo London
Printed in Canada

ISBN 0-8020-4804-8 (cloth)
ISBN 0-8020-8342-0 (paper)

Printed on acid-free paper

**Canadian Cataloguing in Publication Data**

Boucock, Cary
    In the grip of freedom : law and modernity in Max Weber

Includes index.
ISBN 0-8020-4804-8 (bound)    ISBN 0-8020-8342-0 (pbk.)

1. Weber, Max, 1864–1920 – Contributions in sociological jurisprudence.
2. Sociological jurisprudence.    3. Civil rights – Canada.    I. Title.

K370.B68 2000        340'.115        C00-930768-0

This book has been published with the help of a grant from the Humanities
and Social Sciences Federation of Canada, using funds provided by the
Social Sciences and Humanities Research Council of Canada.

The University of Toronto Press acknowledges the financial assistance to its
publishing program of the Canada Council for the Arts and the Ontario Arts
Council.

University of Toronto Press acknowledges the financial support for its
publishing activities of the Government of Canada through the Book
Publishing Industry Development Program (BPIDP).

He who clings to a law does not fear the judgement that reinstates him in an order he believes in. But the keenest of human torments is to be judged without a law. Yet we are in that torment. Deprived of their natural curb, the judges, loosed at random, are racing through their job. Hence we have to try to go faster than they, don't we? And it's a real madhouse. Prophets and quacks multiply; they hasten to get there with a good law or a flawless organization before the world is deserted.

Albert Camus, *The Fall*,
Trans. Justin O'Brien

# Contents

# Acknowledgments

In the long course of creating this book I have incurred a number of intellectual debts. In particular, I would like to thank Anthony Giddens, Patrick Baert, Alan Hunt, and Mark Mason for their advice and timely encouragement. Finally, I would like to acknowledge the support of my family.

# Abbreviations

ES  *Economy and Society: An Outline of Interpretive Sociology*, ed. Guenther Roth and Claus Wittich (London, 1978).

FMW *From Max Weber: Essays in Sociology*, trans. and ed. H.H. Gerth and C. Wright Mills (London, 1948).

GARS *Gesammelte Aufsätze zur Religionssoziologie* (Tübingen, 1920–21).

GASS *Gesammelte Aufsätze zur Soziologie und Sozialpolitik* (Tübingen, 1924).

GEH *General Economic History*, trans. Frank H. Knight (New Brunswick, N.J., 1981).

MSS *The Methodology of the Social Sciences*, trans. and ed. Edward A. Shils and Henry A. Finch (New York, 1949).

PE  *The Protestant Ethic and the Spirit of Capitalism*, trans. Talcott Parsons (London, 1930).

RK  *Roscher and Knies: The Logical Problems of Historical Economics*, trans. Guy Oakes (London, 1975).

ST  *Weber: Selections in Translation*, ed. W.G. Runciman, trans. Eric Matthews (Cambridge, 1978).

# IN THE GRIP OF FREEDOM:
## LAW AND MODERNITY IN MAX WEBER

# Introduction: Law and Modernity in Max Weber

In the world of sociological theory there has been a renewed interest in Max Weber's social and political thought over the past ten to fifteen years.[1] Today, because of its profound breadth and insight into the modern condition, Weber's scholarly legacy is widely considered to be the most influential social thought of the era. Though his sociology of law is less well-known than other areas of Weber's work, it has garnered a respectable proportion of scholarly attention, particularly since the early 1980s. Since the breakdown at that time of a certain post–Second World War ideological consensus in the advanced capitalist democracies, the forms and uses of law in the welfare state have become problematical and intensely debated. One response to this state of agitation has been to return to and reassess the classical social theories of law.

Despite the renewed engagement with Weber, attempts to contextualize his legal thought within the larger compass of his sociology, particularly through his interpretation of the structure and meaning of modernity, remain rare.[2] Standard investigations of Weber's sociology of law tend to isolate it from the larger corpus of his work, a tendency that reflects a more general problem of integration between the sociological study of advanced capitalist societies and theorization of the social dimensions of their legal culture.

Nevertheless, the central figures of classical social theory – Marx and Durkheim, as well as Weber – all advanced theories about the role of law in the constitution of modernity.[3] Weber's interpretation of legal phenomena plays a central role in both his account of the development of the West and his conception of the rationalism of modern social arrangements. As Talcott Parsons once remarked, Weber's conception of 'formal legal rationality' is perhaps the core of his substantive sociology of modernity.[4] In other words, it is difficult to overstress the significance that Weber accords to norms of the legal type in the development of the West's 'specific and peculiar rationalism.'

In Weber's comparative-historical sociology of the great world civilizations, the modern West is distinguished by the specific and thoroughgoing legal-rational character of its structures of power and domination. As we shall see, this rationality is manifest in the desubstantivized and positivistic character of modern social norms; in the impersonal, objectified, and adiaphorous character of modern social arrangements; in the socially unencumbered and atomistic character of modern conceptions of personhood; and in the predominance of social conduct oriented by purposeful, means-ends calculation.

Here I should add a somewhat apologetic but important note about 'jargon.' Specialized terminology is unavoidable today: it is both the virtue and bane of modern scholarship, as formal domains of knowledge become ever more specialized, complex, and differentiated, much like the societies with which they reflexively engage. In every field of expertise, specialized terminology provides a necessary shorthand for referring to complex, multifaceted phenomena, but also renders communication between experts, let alone experts and non-experts, increasingly difficult. Even worse, the larger picture of how things fit together tends to get lost in the specialized focus. But with some forbearance from the reader, unfamiliar terms (I promise) will acquire more clarity as this study proceeds.

Deficiencies in standard treatments of Weber's sociology of law are undoubtedly attributable, at least in part, to the overall character of his work. Though his importance and influence as one of the founders of modern sociology is undeniable, lacking an overarching, systematic, and explicit theoretical perspective, the nature and aims of his scholarship remain much disputed.[5] Weber left an enormous and highly fragmented corpus, ranging in character from the encyclopedia of analytical tools found in *Economy and Society* to more narrowly focused comparative-historical sociologies of religion, music, the city, and, of course, law.[6] Whatever the reasons, while commentators usually emphasize the importance of 'rationalism' and 'rationalization' in Weber's account of the origins and cultural specificity of the West, few have comprehensively examined his legal thought within the broad framework of his sociology of modernity. Certainly, none have given

the relationship between formal legal rationality and individual autonomy the attention it deserves. The present study redresses these over-
sights, not merely for the sake of scholarly score-setting on Weber's
behalf, but also to illustrate the power that Weber's sociological vision
retains for us today.

There is an underlying unity in Weber's social and political thought,
a unity that can be discerned if his interpretation of modernity is
viewed in terms of the problematic relationship between individual
autonomy and formal legal rationality. For Weber, the significance of
formal legal rationality is tied to its promotion and protection of individual autonomy. In fact, the theme of the problematic relationship
between the formal legal rationality of modern social arrangements
and the subjective experience of modern 'freedom' runs like a red
thread throughout Weber's social and political thought.

Integrating Weber's sociology of law within his work as a whole
enables us to retrieve the classical project of examining law as a key
element in the constitution of modernity.[7] Weber's writings on law represented an attempt to identify the distinctive features of the legal traditions of the West and to relate them to the unique features of modern
economic and political structures of power, and thus to modern conceptions of personhood. This aim lies behind his efforts to describe the
relationship between the emergence of constitutive features of modernity and the rise of purposive contracts, the gradual replacement of
special (group and local) law with uniform national rules, the growth
of an autonomous legal profession, and ultimately, the rationalization
of legal thought and the legalization of social power.

Most studies of Weber's sociology of law – in fact most studies of the
law in general – tend to frustrate theorization of the social dimensions
of law in modern society. Standard analyses frequently take as their
object a formal legal rationality considered exclusively in terms of the
legal thought of jurists conducted in specialized institutional settings.
'Law' is consequently separated from society in a way that falsifies the
complex imbricated relationship between legal and social norms: 'law'
is not an epiphenomenal structure regulated by ideal or material interests alone, nor is 'society' the other of a controlling and unitary law.

The standard approach to Weber's sociology of law not only tends to
neglect the relationship of formal legal rationality to the general structure of modern economic and political arrangements, it also fails to
discern the formal legal rationality of everyday social relations, including those that transpire outside of specifically legal settings. Yet this is

precisely the inner significance of Weber's conception. The postulates of formal legal equality and economic mobility and their concretization through the early modern formal legal rationalization of economic and political structures of power not only 'paved the way for the destruction of all patrimonial and feudal law in favour of abstract norms and hence indirectly of bureaucratization' but also 'made it possible for the capitalist to use things and men freely' (ES, 1209). The purposive rationality so characteristic of modern social conduct – that is, action oriented to calculation of profit or observance of rules without regard for particular persons – is correlative of the legal norms embodied in modern structures of authority, and the automation of modern power in general.

A secondary dividend of an interpretive approach centred on the theme of formal legal rationality and individual autonomy is that it offers an effective heuristic device for theorizing the salient features of contemporary patterns of legal domination. By drawing on a general sociological account of modern structures of economic power and political authority I hope to illustrate the way in which formal legal rationality refers not only to the character of modern modes of adjudication but also describes the ideal-typical character of modern social arrangements and their related conceptions of personhood. More controversially, by extrapolating from Weber's account of legal domination I will argue that the trajectory of legal development from the period of nineteenth-century industrial capitalism to the twentieth-century expansion of regulatory law, with its process of expanded legalization – as well as the seemingly antithetical more recent explosion of rights claims and litigation – can be shown as manifestations of a general developmental trend identified and explained by Weber's interpretation of modernity.

By pursuing this line of argument and linking the significance of Weber's concept of formal legal rationality to his account of the origins and developmental tendencies of modern society, this book also runs against the grain of conventional assessments of Weber's legal theory and its applicability to contemporary legal developments. Weber's conception of modern legal rationality has typically been dismissed as too formalistic and positivistic to be of any more than limited relevance to the study of the advanced capitalist democracies of the West.[8]

Paradigmatic of this orthodoxy is the argument advanced by the influential German social theorist and philosopher, Jürgen Habermas. According to Habermas, Weber's depiction of modern society in terms

of the increasing salience of formal (instrumental) rationality is apposite to modern economic and political structures of power (capitalism
and bureaucracy) but overdrawn when applied to the modern legal
order – an argument advanced in order to exempt the ethical dimensions of modern society from an all-embracing instrumental rationalization.[9] Following Habermas's terminology, the 'logic' of modern
legal order may indeed imply a substantive post-traditional morality.
Nonetheless, Weber's conception of formal legal rationality remains
apposite to the 'dynamic' of an unfolding reality in modern societies,
which ideology critique does not make disappear. It is argued here that
his vision of law and modernity reveals good reasons for questioning
our ever-growing and increasingly exclusive reliance on the normative
rationality of modern law as a means of enhancing the individual
sense of 'freedom,' of countermanding the narrow technical and
instrumental rationalities that entangle individuals in modern social –
and especially economic and political – arrangements.

Weber's conception of formal legal rationality does emphasize
the formalistic and positivistic orientation of modern legal norms.
Although the emphasis derives from an earlier liberal jurisprudence
characteristic of late nineteenth century liberal modernity, this intellectual affiliation should not discredit the sociological significance of
Weber's conception. Given the rationality of modern economic and
political structures of power that evince mastery and control through
depersonalization and objectification of social arrangements, and the
concomitant predominance of purposive-rational conduct oriented
towards the instrumentalism of profit calculation and the consistency
of rule-observance, the specific character of modern rationalism *is* formalistic and positivistic. These characteristics are tied not only into the
pattern of social arrangements but also to the form of modern conceptions of personhood. Perhaps Weber recognized that legal organization
and its pattern of operation in modern society are not exempt from formalism and positivism, but rather very much at the heart of it. A critique that focuses on the contradictions and limitations of Weber's
conception of modern legal rationality is somewhat misleading, since
the contradictions and limitations inherent within Western society,
including its legal systems, are what Weber's ideal-types explore.

Weber engaged in sociological research because of his desire to
understand the character and destiny of his own society. My interpretation of Weber's social and political thought is similarly oriented to
explaining the uniqueness of contemporary legal forms and, thereby,

the continued relevance of the conceptual typologies he devised for the interpretation of the structure and meaning of modernity. Here, a sociological perspective on law means viewing the law in a wider social context, alert to the relations between legal development and wider social changes and the interactions of law with the ostensibly non-legal social environment. The mania for control and organizational discipline continues unabated in our culture. Paradoxically, this tendency is a structural concomitant of our deepest beliefs in the validity of individual autonomy and the efficacy of self-realization, at least as such beliefs have historically been actualized. This is the sense in which modern legal domination turns out to mean, in Wolfgang Mommsen's memorable phrase, 'the utmost freedom through the utmost domination.'[10] The explication of the significance of formal legal rationality in Weber's social and political thought undertaken here provides a trenchant model of the nexus between control and freedom, rationality and autonomy, that lies at the centre of our civilization. The nationalistic, authoritarian culture of the German mandarins of Weber's world seems remote from us in many respects. But the ambiguities and contradictions that arise from the realization of the 'rational society' form a broad bridge between his world and our own.

Chapter 1 argues that Weber's interpretation of the structure and meaning of modern social arrangements is centred on a legalistic conception of rationalism. Rationality is not a normative concept in Weber's thought, but merely refers to those various features of any mode of living that become ordered and systematized over time. In this sense, 'rationality' has existed in numerous forms, in various societies, throughout history. It is the 'specific and peculiar' form of rationalism of the modern West that Weber seeks to isolate and specify. The meanings of this modern rationalism are well summarized by Rogers Brubaker:

> modern capitalism is defined by the rational (deliberate and systematic) pursuit of profit through the rational (systematic and calculable) organization of formally free labor and through rational (impersonal, purely instrumental) exchange on the market, guided by rational (exact, purely quantitative) accounting procedures and guaranteed by rational (rule-governed, predictable) legal and political systems. Ascetic Protestantism is characterized by rational (methodical) self-control and by the rational (purposeful) devotion to rational (sober, scrupulous) economic action ...[11]

On the one hand, this systematic, calculable, instrumental, exact, quantitative, rule-governed, and predictable rationalism relates to the objective and impersonal quality of modern structures of economic and political power, epitomized by the capitalist market and the bureaucratic organization of the state; on the other hand, this deliberate, methodical, purposeful, sober, scrupulous, efficacious, and consistent rationalism is related to a cultural system that presupposes a fundamental distinction between knowledge of facts and judgments of value, and the importance of planful intentionality in the attribution of meaning or normative significance to the 'facts' of the world. My analysis of the philosophical unity behind Weber's interpretation of modern social arrangements is indebted to Anthony Kronman's exemplary study, particularly Kronman's reading of 'value-positivism' and his concept of 'will-centred individualism.' Weber's neo-Kantian epistemology and theory of personality presuppose what Kronman calls a 'positivistic theory of value' and a 'will-centred conception of personhood.'[12] I depart from Kronman, however, with respect to his exclusive reliance on Weber's methodological writings for the derivation of the philosophical suppositions of Weber's social thought.[13] Weber's work 'matures' with his studies of religious rationalization, where he discerns a world-historical process of rationalization and disenchantment that poses specific ethical consequences for the modern individual.[14] This is the deeper root of Weber's value-positivism. Modern structures of power and authority reflect an openness to human goal-setting and a facility for individual purposive, planful action. As I argue, the conceptual nexus between the pure means-ends rationality of modern social arrangements and the desubstantive, positivistic character of modern values reflects, in different but analogous ways, the moral significance of individuals as value-creators in a post-traditional world, a world denuded of 'objective' value by disenchantment and secularization of the normative power of the actual and the metaphysical.

Chapter 2 illustrates how the formal rationality of social arrangements and the normative power of individual choice converge in Weber's conception of formal legal rationality. Modern legal rationality, in all of its manifestations, promotes a particular form of individual autonomy. The two characteristic dimensions of modern rationalism – the objective and impersonal quality of a rationalism oriented to control and mastery and the normative power of choice and consent which it presumes – derive from the positive and public, and the formal and autonomous character of formally rational law. The formalism of legal relations maximizes the predictability and calculability of social arrangements, while the positivity of legal norms locates the derivation of legitimacy in correct enactment and individual consent. Both dimensions of the modern legal order facilitate individual autonomy defined in terms of the capacity for purposive-rational, free-choice behaviour. Thus modern social arrangements manifest transparency to reason, inner distance from emotions, and orientation to control and prediction, paralleling the positive, formal, and autonomous qualities of modern legal rationality.

The contribution of formal legal rationality to the modern experience of 'freedom' is epitomized by the planful, self-regarding social conduct facilitated by the institution of 'purposive' contractual association. The relationship between economic and legal rationalization is revealed by the centrality of such contractual relations and transactions in modern society. Yet the distinction that Weber draws between formal legal rationality and the substantive realization of autonomy and the substantive validation of authority points to ambiguities in the legal guarantee of freedom. A fundamental imaginary signification of modernity, one might argue, has been emancipation and self-realization through control of self and other. The formal legal rationality of economic and political structures of power eliminates the ad hoc, contingent, and ascriptive systems of authority of traditional civilization, greatly enhancing the possibilities for individual self-determination. However, Weber underscores the contribution of formal legal rationality to a qualitative and quantitative increase in the authoritarian-hierarchical domination that most people experience in their lives, especially in the realm of work. This peculiar relationship between individual autonomy and modern rationalism also parallels the interdependence of autonomy and discipline in the personality type of the Protestant inner-worldly ascetic, which in Weber's view formed the basis of modern conceptions of selfhood.

Legal rationality emancipates individuals from the 'eternal yesterday' of customary norms and the stultifying moral proximity of traditional 'community,' but it replaces old forms of personal domination with new impersonal ones that do not offer the consolations of belonging and direction once imparted to individual life by the community scenario. Under legal domination, individuals are disencumbered of ascriptive ties and restrictive considerations for others, but they are also dispossessed of various social connexions and existential certainties. In 'the grip of freedom,' modern individuals are both allowed and obliged to create their 'selves,' regardless of whether or not they possess the resources to do so. Weber anatomizes the structural homology between the formal legal rationality of modern social arrangements and the individual experience of freedom, but then proceeds to emphasize the dehumanizing consequences of legal rationalization. Ultimately, he endorses formal legal rationality, but there is no triumphant affirmation of the superiority of the modern West in his work. Weber's judgment is tempered by a remorseless probity about the limitations of a merely formal promotion and protection of individual autonomy and an awareness of the endemic social contradictions created by the tensions between formal and substantive rationality in modern social arrangements. In Mommsen's words, Weber is the 'liberal in despair'[15]

In Chapter 3, I offer an interpretation of Weber's account of modernity that highlights the parallels between his interpretations of the development of capitalism and its origins in a value-rational transformation of traditional economic institutions (the Protestant ethic thesis) and the development of modern law and its origins in a value-rational belief in a higher law. By identifying the parallels between Weber's explanations of legal and economic rationalization, I confront the orthodox critique of his account of legal rationalization as a process of increasing formalization and positivization. Paradigmatic of such critiques is that offered by Habermas, who argues that, by linking the progressive institutionalization of purposive-rational action orientations to a process of merely formal legal rationalization, Weber's sociology of law contradicts his account of the formation of modernity, in which the Protestant ethic *and* the modern legal system successfully institutionalize a distinctively modern, post-traditional moral consciousness, providing a value-rational anchoring for purposive-rational action orientations.[16]

Yet, in Weber's developmental history of modern law, although the formal rationalization of law was originally driven by certain ideal interests, and although the formalization and positivization of law originally represented a value-rational transformation of traditional, patrimonial patterns of law, subsequent legal rationalization is more or less directed by the rationalization of material, particularly economic, interests. Thus, the developmental history of modern law parallels the rise of modern capitalism vis-à-vis the relationship between ideal interests and an increasingly autonomous process of formal rationalization. The controversial implication of Weber's developmental history, I argue, is that the direction of legal rationalization in present-day Western democracies (towards expanded legal regulation alongside enhanced rights-consciousness) is only superficially reflective of the kind of normative rationality that concerns Habermas (i.e., a broad form of reason capable of counterbalancing the narrow rationality of political and economic organizations and enhancing the individual sense of freedom), but substantively correlative with the ideal interests of the autonomous economic development of capitalism (i.e., the right 'to use things and men freely' in the pursuit of one's own economic interests).

In Chapter 4, I extrapolate Weber's developmental history of legal rationalization in order to outline the salient features of contemporary legal domination, namely, the modern dyarchy of legal rights and legal rules, the representative institutional forms of which are the rights-oriented polity and the regulatory-administrative state.[17] Here, the potential value of Weber's legal thought for understanding the world we live in begins to crystallize. Although the early stages of the formal legal-rational reconstitution of social arrangements were, one might say, unambiguously freedom-enhancing, with subsequent stages of legal development, formal legal rationality, particularly in its hypertrophic manifestations, becomes itself an impediment to the real-ization of individual autonomy.

The wide extension of social relations in time and space created by modern institutions, though freeing individuals from the constraints of the locale, also exposes them in an unprecedented degree to the unin-tended consequences of economic and political activities conducted far and near. Because of the complex functional interdependence between individuals and groups, the links between actions and their conse-quences tend to be invisible to participants in these activities. When disengaged individuals feel caught up in a threatening tangle of un-willed and incomprehensible dependencies one increasingly prevalent response is to attempt to reinforce autonomy through extension of the legal rationalities of control and distance. But the more individuals attempt to defend their autonomy exclusively through the assertion of rights and the use of law, the more complex and extended organiza-tions must become in order to support and sustain the enhanced level of social disengagement and delocalized impersonality created by the resultant increase in the legal rationality of society.

Again, this is the sense in which modern legal domination means 'the utmost freedom through the utmost domination.' For it is a striking feature of modern societies that they offer a powerful promise of freedom at the same time as they implicate individuals in a formidable array of functional interdependencies and economic insecurities. This theme of rationalization and disenchantment undergirds much of Weber's interpretation of the relationship between legal rationality and individual autonomy. In modern societies, as David Trubek argues, people are caught between structured but meaningless realms of instrumental action and meaningful but private and transitory experiences that preserve some sense of the experience of freedom.[18] As the scale of social, economic, and political organization of modern societies has become more complex, individuals have become ever more entangled in a formidable array of obligations and dependencies, while ever less attached by collective forms of identity.[19]

The contestation and restructuring of 'organized modernity' which has been observable for the past few decades seem to point in the direction of a new 'neo-liberal' or 'extended liberal modernity.'[20] These contemporary changes are signalled, inter alia, by the sense of crisis that has attached to key aspects of modern society – such as the crisis of the social welfare state and the dismantling of Keynesian-style economic management, and the (re)emerging stress upon 'entrepreneurial culture' and the 'enterprising self.'[21] This surprising revival of liberal cultural forms only underscores the continuing relevance of Weber's thought. The new, increasingly global economy of 'extended liberal modernity,' with its entrepreneurial culture and renewed emphasis on the 'enterprising self,' represents further dissolution of the modes of collective, political rule-making with regard to key sets of social practices, particularly those which attempt to extend political regulation over economic activities. As Weber's account of modernity would suggest, over the course of development of modern society, an ethic of community and tradition has slowly been supplanted by an ethic of individuality and claims of right. The sociological factors behind this development are clear: the transition from hierarchical social structures reflecting unified substantive norms to multiple social structures based on reciprocity and exchange; gradual loss of influence of church and family as means of structuring interpersonal relations; urbanization and industrialization which, by encouraging the division of labour, have multiplied contractual relations of all types. Behind this growing functional interdependence of increasingly atomized strangers, I argue, is the 'developmental dynamic' of legal rationalization – albeit, a legalization that varies in effect depending upon its strategic relationship to economic accumulation: in this instance, the expansion of legal rights and the detachment of entangled individuals, and the flood of legal rules and the entanglement of detached selves.

My inclusion of legal rights and the rights-oriented polity within the framework of Weber's conceptions of formal legal rationality and legal-rational domination is controversial. Sociologists are accustomed to thinking of the administrative-regulatory dimension of modern legal domination within Weberian terms. But for most commentators, the post–Second World War absorption of individual rights into the political arena and the consequent alteration of patterns of authority in the Western capitalist democracies appear to contradict the formalization and positivization dynamic of Weber's developmental history of modern law. In other words, the rise of the rights-oriented polity appears to represent a substantive rationalization of the structures of authority in these societies, and thereby a deeper institutionalization of individual autonomy, which contradicts Weber's pessimistic prognostications of increasing formal-rational discipline and diminishing individual freedom.[22]

But as I demonstrate in Chapter 5, the pattern and functioning of individual rights as institutionalized in the rights-oriented polity – namely Canada since the advent of the Charter of Rights and Freedoms – exhibits the same pattern of formalization and positivization described in Chapter 4. Although the constitutional adjudication of individual rights in Canada is a comparatively recent phenomenon (post-1985), the Canadian modification of the British legacy of parliamentary supremacy by extension of judicial powers of review and the trend towards a rights-oriented society provides, I contend, a perspicuous example of the dynamic of legal rationalization, which can be detected more generally, but less obviously, in most advanced capitalist democracies.

Faith in the value and utility of legal rights forms the political common sense of our age; legal rights tend to be unambiguously associated with the substantive protection and promotion of individual autonomy. But it is one thing to argue for the value of individual rights per se; quite another to simply accept the way in which such rights have been institutionalized and litigated as their inevitable concomitant. However laudable individual rights are – and as Weber remarks, 'it is a gross self-deception to believe that without the achievements of the age of the Rights of Man any one of us, including the most conservative, can go on living his life' (ES, 1403) – their importance and value in contemporary political culture should not inhibit critical reflection on the manner in which they are institutionalized and litigated, or on the way in which they function in contemporary society.[23] For as my interpretation of the contemporary relationship between individual autonomy and formal legal rationality suggests, the enhancement of individual autonomy through the assertion and litigation of individual rights may result in the counterintuitive consequence of expanding the web of functional interdependencies that instigated such litigation in the first place. The growth of legal rights-asserting forms of individualism and the concomitant rise of judicial forms of political power are part and parcel of a larger pattern of legal rationalization. In the long run, the rights-oriented polity may actually contribute to a qualitative and quantitative increase in our sense of entanglement and domination.

Chapter 6 deals with Weber's theory of modern politics and the question of what options may be available to us, if the idea of freedom is to be taken seriously. Notwithstanding its many shortcomings, an important point made in Weber's political thought, the implications of which have not received the attention they deserve, is that, although contributing immeasurably to the historical enhancement of the experience of freedom, formal legal rationality possesses inherent limits which, when exceeded, produce countertendencies detrimental to the substantive realization of individual autonomy. The countertendencies of legal rationalization stem from the kinds of influence that the 'thin reason' of modern social arrangements inappropriately exerts over the setting of 'values,' supposedly a matter of individual choice and consent in the liberal universe, and therein over the shaping if not stunting of responsible modern selfhood.

The rationalism of modern social arrangements is about control, objectification, and routinization. In effect, this kind of rationalism is a thin form of reason that shapes social conduct along the lines of an instrumentalism of technical or monetary calculations and a consistency of rule-observance: a society dominated by thin forms of reason, Weber feared, tends to inculcate the 'shallow-willing' personalities of techno-managerial 'specialists without spirit.' Of course, Weber did not object to the institution of the modern 'free' market, for he viewed this economic sphere as an important arena for entrepreneurial expression of individual innovation. The problem is that the rationalization of economic structures of power involves the inexorable growth of ever larger economic organizations and concentrations of corporate wealth, which tend to diminish the market freedom of entry-level entrepreneurs. The rationalization of political and especially economic structures of power means that individuals increasingly work within large organizations, which routinize action and constrain individually differentiated conduct.

Given Weber's propensity for pessimism, this picture of the modern world is undoubtedly overdrawn. The important point is this: despite its undeniable practical efficacy in organizational efficiencies and the creation of wealth, the thin reason of modern social arrangements *is unable to tell us to what end the power to control and manipulate things ought to be directed.* According to Weber's theory of value, rational analysis cannot validate judgments of value. The correlate of this theory of value is the proposition that rational social arrangements cannot supply values; they can only function as a means to the furtherance of pregiven values. Weber believed that the most pressing problems of social life, even those economic and social policy issues that involve some technical dimension, are not purely problems of finding the most rational means to a predetermined end, but rather problems relating to general cultural values that must be subjected to debate.

What Weber feared was that, given the cultural prestige of cognitive-instrumental modes of problem articulation and resolution and the premium placed on purposive-rational action orientations, modern societies are constitutionally predisposed to approach the question of 'what shall we do and how shall we live' in terms of the thin reason of techno-managerial expertise. The expanding political role of judiciaries in rights-oriented societies, and the legalization of political conflict which results from the pursuit of broad social goals through the courts, represents yet another aspect of this bureaucratic tendency. For as Weber controversially argues, and analysis of Canadian Charter adjudication demonstrates, legal rationality is a thin form of reason which is 'rational' only within a narrow ambit of formal rule application and the 'technical' language of legal discourse. When courts are drawn into disputes involving policy-oriented interpretation of constitutional rules, the task of defining broad social goals becomes effectively depoliticized. Value-choices are surreptitiously disguised as legally determinate readings and creative modes of norm-enactment that legitimately operate through representative institutions are usurped by non-elected legal experts and jurists. The depoliticization of value-setting knits very well with the more general depoliticization of social goals and priorities in modern society, particularly where issues of the market economy are concerned.

Given the historical link between the modern experience of freedom and the control-through-objectification orientation of the formal legal rationality of social arrangements, it is not surprising that the freedom-threatening countertendencies generated by the dynamic of legal rationalization are likely to provoke legal-rational strategies for protecting and promoting individual autonomy via more control and better organization. The gap between the powerful promise of freedom in modern society and the substantive experience of discipline and dependency has fuelled demands for enhanced legal protection and the promotion of individual autonomy. However, as the case study of the rise of the rights-oriented polity in Canada will illustrate, these strategies do not address the modern sources of individual powerlessness – domination in the workplace and insecurities generated by the capitalist market – and may actually amplify the countertendencies of hypertrophic rationalization.

Weber argues that the central issue of modern politics must be expressed in terms of how best to subordinate the techno-managerial concern with utility and profit to the political function of defining the ends that power is to serve. As a counterbalance to formal legal rationality he recommends the vitalistic resources of strong leaders at the helm of large economic and political organizations. These superficial authoritarian tendencies reflect political concerns specific to Wilhelmine Germany and early twentieth century anxieties about the potential political irresponsibility of the 'masses,' and even of the German middle-classes. But Weber's political thought carries a more profound message, which is rooted in his interpretation of modernity. Perhaps the individual experience of freedom within the 'tremendous cosmos of the modern economic order' is more likely to be enhanced by strengthening the political value-setting capacity of individuals through a process of substantive democratization of both political and economic institutions than by further promoting a process of legal rationalization that purposefully isolates individuals and discourages meaningful social community.

In any event, the conflict between formal and substantive rationality remains germane to understanding present-day social problems and addressing the political issues they create. For instance, the systemic problem of balance between the formal logic of calculations based upon profit and efficiency in the market and substantive moral con-

*distribution*               *damages*

cerns for socially beneficial and environmentally benign economic development will provoke continued conflict over the regulation and deregulation of economic activity, not to mention more global concerns regarding the effects of technological intensification on the environment and the quality of human life. *These are structural contradictions within modernity itself.*

This study reveals a critical and existential dimension of Weber's thought notably absent in the standard presentations of his sociology of law. More importantly, it illustrates that, whatever shape solutions to modern social problems might take in the future, Weber can help us to formulate the questions that our situation should raise. Sociologically, what kinds of personhood are shaped by legal-rational domination and what forms of freedom are facilitated by the progressing legalization of power and authority? Politically, are efficiency and profit to be the ultimate and only goals that determine the course of social development? These questions lie at the heart of Weber's social and political thought.

# CHAPTER ONE

# The 'Specific and Peculiar Rationalism of Western Culture'

The significance of formal rationality and value-positivism, and their inner relationship, is key to understanding the meaning of legal-rational domination in Weber's thought. Formal rationality represents a modality of control and mastery involving the objectification and depersonalization of modern social arrangements. The rationality of modern economic and political structures of power is purely formal precisely because the means-ends relationship of economic or political action is no longer determined by traditional, emotional, or evaluative orientations. It is instead forged according to the calculation of efficiency or profit accumulation. The corollary to the formalization of the means-ends rationality of modern social arrangements is the 'positivity' of modern norms. With the diminution of the normative power of tradition and revelation, the validity of the rationality of social arrangements has become increasingly tied to its capacity to effectuate a particular kind of autonomy for individuals. The purely formal rationality of economic and political arrangements instates individual choice and consent as the basis of modern 'normative power.'

## 1. The Formal Rationality of Modern Economic and Political Arrangements

In Weber's view, the structure and meaning of the modern West is tied to its 'specific and peculiar rationalism' (PE, 26). But what precisely is 'rationalism'? In only a few pages of the *Protestant Ethic*, one learns from Weber's characterization of modern capitalism and its ethic of professional vocationalism that 'rational' means deliberate, systematic, calculable, impersonal, instrumental, exact, quantitative, rule-governed, predictable, methodical, purposeful, sober, scrupulous, efficacious, intelligible, and consistent (PE, 26).

To refine our conception of rationalism we can examine Weber's famous typology of social action. Basically, Weber argues, sociology studies the patterns of regularity that emerge in social action. Employing the usual distinction between 'means' and 'ends,' Weber identifies three fundamental ways in which social actions develop patterns of regularity: due to evaluative, traditional, and rational orientations (ES, 24–5). Social actions are influenced by evaluative orientations when driven by emotions, or oriented to the elaboration and establishment of fixed ends.[1] They are influenced by traditional forces when directed by habit or custom. What Weber calls 'purposive-rational' action, however, is either determined by the methodical attainment of pregiven ends through the increasingly precise calculation of adequate means, or by the methodical ordering of activities according to fixed rules and routines. According to this typology, the patterns of regularity exhibited by modern social relations are increasingly the result of purposive-rational orientations.

Another important element of Weber's conception of rationalism is illustrated by his distinction between formal and substantive rationality, the clearest articulation of which appears in his categories of economic action. According to Weber, the formal rationality of economic action increases with the degree of calculability of means and ends: the more means and ends are susceptible to quantification and comparison, the more formally rational the action becomes. The highest level of formal rationality is exemplified in purposive-rational social action where an individual chooses first a particular end based on cost analysis, or by ranking various ends in terms of priority, and then the most efficacious means for achieving it. The hallmark of formal rationality is thus calculation and the most technically perfect means of orienting economic activity is through 'calculation in terms of money' (ES, 86). This conception of formal rationality can be applied to social relations and arrangements as well. In a hypothetical bus service between Toronto and Montreal, for instance, the route between the two points, the frequency of service, and its number and location of points of ingress would represent the 'system' qualities, or the formal rationality of the linkage between the means and ends of transportation.

Conversely, economic action is formally irrational to the extent that action is taken without calculating the advantages or disadvantages incurred through the use of various means for achieving a given end. The highest level of formally irrational action is exemplified by affectual social action where an individual chooses a particular means or end based on a whim, or in response to some adventitious 'sign.' Thus, the hallmark of formal irrationality is incalculability. If the route and/or the schedule of our hypothetical bus service depended upon the driver's mood or the particular travel requests of the passengers, that service would become highly arbitrary and unpredictable, hence formally irrational in character. It would be impossible to calculate beforehand how long the journey to Montreal would take.

Substantive rationality is measured by the degree to which an economic action satisfies ultimate values or needs. Concepts of substantive rationality 'measure the results of the economic action, however formally "rational" in the sense of correct calculation they may be, against these scales of "value-rationality" or "substantive goal rationality"' (ES, 85–6). The hallmark of substantive rationality is thus the fulfilment of ultimate values or needs derived from ethical, political, utilitarian, hedonistic, egalitarian, or whatever, scales. The substantive rationality of the bus service would be represented by its 'purpose,' namely the conveyance of travellers from Toronto to Montreal.

Conversely, economic action is substantively irrational to the extent that ultimate values or needs are not satisfied. The apocryphal story of the bus that, in order to maintain its strict schedule, avoided picking up any passengers at all is a perfect example of a substantive irrationality resulting from the triumph of the means of transportation rationality over the purpose of conveying passengers.

The essence of Weber's distinction between 'formal' and 'substantive' aspects lies in the extent to which the action is part of a system of activities that is internally self-sufficient. The essence of the distinction between 'rational' and 'irrational' relates to the manner in which the materials of the system, its rules and procedures, are utilized. For example, the use of money to quantify and compare the merits of various courses of action based on their costs represents a highly formal action system: all the rules and information necessary to the decision-making process are available within the system; decision making need not refer to any external criteria or values at all. In terms of the example of the bus, the less picaresque the journey to Montreal, and the more it is organized with the aim of getting people from Toronto to Montreal as efficiently as possible, the greater the formal rationality of the system. A maximum degree of calculability of predictability of service would be achieved if the bus travels directly and regularly from A to B, non-stop. Substantive systems are characterized by their reference to external criteria, in particular, to religious, ethical, or political values. For instance, if the bus was scheduled not to operate on the Sabbath, the logic of this arrangement would have nothing to do with the internal means-ends configuration of the system, but would represent instead a response to a value external to transportation itself.

In Weber's view, modern social arrangements represent historically unparalleled examples of formal rationality, such as the 'instrumental' profit-calculus of capitalist enterprise and the 'methodical' rule-observance of bureaucratic organization. One of the fundamental claims of Weber's substantive sociology is that modernity erodes 'unthinking acquiesence in customary ways as well as devotion to norms consciously accepted as absolute values.' This rationalization of action, involving 'deliberate adaptation to situations in terms of self-interest,' is related to the inexorable increase in the formal rationalization of social arrangements in general (ES, 30).

## 1.1 Capitalism and the Instrumental Calculus of Profit

The eternal substantive economic function of any society is the satisfaction of human need through the production of wealth and its exchange between persons. The creation and distribution of wealth in premodern societies, for example, were enmeshed within the network of rights and obligations surrounding the manorial pattern of land ownership and 'the complicated mutual dependence of the proprietor and the peasant' (GEH, 92).[2] The structure of social organization meant that economic relations and the 'economy' as such did not exist as a differentiated 'subsystem' of the overall social order. Because economic relations were locked into traditional modalities of power, the means of creating wealth could not develop and change without threatening the material interests of the establishment. As long as economic activity remained embedded within other social institutions and enmeshed within the heterogeneous web of traditional patterns of everyday life, productive and distributive activity was subject to the pressures of innumerable non-economic social norms (such as kinship duties, religious beliefs, royal prerogatives, and the jurisdiction of manorial estates which, in the East Prussian homeland of the Junker landowners, survived well into Weber's own lifetime (GEH, 92–111)). The norms that directed traditional economic activity were not aimed at enhancing and developing the economic order per se; they were instead oriented towards the maintenance and reproduction of non-economic institutions and social arrangements.

As Weber illustrates in his 1894 study of the 'Developmental tendencies in the situation of East Elbian rural labourers,' attempts to introduce methods of modern production into communities where they had been unknown frequently foundered upon traditional attitudes towards economic activity.[3] For example, employers introduced piece rates to provide the workers a remunerative incentive for increasing their productivity; if they worked harder they could increase their earnings well above what they had previously received. But the results were frequently counterintuitive for employers: with the implementation of such schemes the amount of work done actually decreased. The traditionalistic workers did not think in terms of maximizing their daily wages; they considered only how much work must be accomplished at the new rate in order to meet their customary needs. As Weber remarks, 'a man does not "by nature" wish to earn more and more money, but simply to live as he is accustomed to live and to earn as much as is necessary for that purpose' (PE, 60). This traditionalistic attitude towards work reflects the premodern subordination of the economic order within non-economic institutional and cultural frameworks.

According to Weber, the crucial feature of modern capitalism, distinguishing it from all previous economic orders, is the way in which it implements the eternal substantive economic function of all societies (the satisfaction of human needs) via a thoroughgoing application of means-ends calculation to the question of choice in the organization and exploitation of finite economic resources. The formal rationality of the modern economic order represents the emancipation of economic decision making from the constraints imposed by traditional and evaluative concerns of a non-economic nature. The application of means-ends instrumental rationality to the provision of material needs effectuated, in contemporary parlance, the 'disembedding' of an economic system from non-economic social arrangements.[4] The gestation of the economy as a system of human activities, independent of the whole universe of traditional interlocking dependencies of the land-based economy, eventually created a self-contained and (more or less) self-regulating economic totality, governed solely by the logic of supply, demand, and the circulation of goods. Modern capitalism was the world's first economic *system*, a system that has become ever more differentiated, developing according to its own internal logic.

The specific rationalism of modern capitalism is reflected in the instrumental orientation of economic actors and the rational calculability of both the total production process and the overall legal and administrative environment of economic activity.[5] Exchange in the market has been the prototype of all rational activity. With the kind of social action that takes place in the exchange market, Weber argues, 'participants do not look toward the persons of each other but only toward the commodity; there are no obligations of brotherliness or reverence, and none of those spontaneous human relations that are sustained by personal unions. They all would just obstruct the free development of the bare market relationship, and its specific interests serve, in their turn, to weaken the sentiments on which these obstructions rest' (ES, 636). The structure of social action in market exchange elicits the subjective disposition to act on the basis of impersonal calculation oriented to the acquisition of profit. Money provides the most technically perfect technology for carrying out economic calculations (ES, 86). Subjectively rational (instrumental) market transactions are thus guided by objectively rational (quantitative) calculations. Economic action in the market is a paradigm of formally rational activity because it is unrestrained by considerations of tradition and sentiment, and typically determined only by deliberate and calculated pursuit of profit without regard for particular persons. As Weber writes, 'the market is fundamentally alien to any type of fraternal relationship' (ES, 637).

Of course, market exchange and monetary calculation have existed for centuries in most cultures. In premodern economic orders, however, the purposive-rational behaviour typical of the market exchange was severely restricted by customary and evaluative attitudes: the notion of a 'free' market unbounded by 'ethical norms' has represented 'an abomination to every system of fraternal ethics' (ES, 637). What is historically unique about modern capitalism is that the self-interested purposive-rational action once confined within a narrowly defined sphere of market exchange has been progressively extended to the organization of the production process and the legal and administrative environment as well. In the process, the traditional and ethical restraints that once circumscribed the sphere of market activity have slowly been eliminated and replaced by 'purely economic and rational' regulations (ES, 639). The free development of the market according to its own autonomous tendencies has finally completely reversed the age-old subordination of the economic order to the social: today, education, politics, scientific research, and so forth, are geared increasingly to the expansion of the economy.

The rational calculability of the total production process of modern capitalism is secured through the 'complete appropriation of all material means of production by owners' (ES, 161) – that is, the extension of a centralized, legally assured control over the workplace, tools, machinery, sources of power, raw materials – and 'the expropriation of the individual worker from ownership of the means of production' (ES, 137). The disciplined control of workers in particular and the calculability of the labour element of the production process in general are accomplished, not through slavery or vassalage, but under a system in which labour is formally 'free,' yet economically compelled to sell its services on the market (GEH, 277). The institution of formally free wage labour permits the rationalization of economic production towards increased efficiency and calculability: it allows the employer 'to select the labor force according to ability and willingness to work,' while the risk of dismissal becomes an important incentive for the employee to maximize productivity (ES, 163).

The separation of workers from the means of production and the process of functional differentiation in general characterizes not only the capitalist form of economic production but also the organization of the modern state, army, church, university, and so forth and is linked with the broader process of rationalization that Weber subsumes under the concept of bureaucracy (ES, 223, 980–3). Weber argues that this separation results partly from the fact that modern production processes are typically too large, too expensive, or too sophisticated to be controlled by individual workers and partly from the advantages of greater efficiency of centrally organized activity. The process of functional differentiation goes hand-in-hand with the exploitation of technical knowledge, 'especially the mathematical and experimentally exact natural sciences with their precise rational foundations' (ST, 338).[6] The exact calculability of economic structures of power and the regulation of life in general are thereby enhanced. The technical-scientific apparatus that supports these developments has the general effect of fostering a 'rationalist and antitraditionalist spirit' in society at large.[7] Capitalism is profoundly at odds with traditionalism. New kinds of acquisition and enterprise endanger social order or meet religious and ethical objections because they threaten the sanctity of tradition, which is the basis of legitimacy for patrimonial forms of political authority (ES, 1094).

The calculability of the legal and administrative environment is also crucial to modern capitalism. As Weber frequently elaborates, 'market behavior is influenced by rational, purposeful pursuit of interests,' where individual transactions are undertaken with the expectation of reciprocity in accordance with the formal inviolability of rational legal procedures (ES, 636). 'Industrial capitalism must be able to count on the continuity, trustworthiness and objectivity of the legal order, and on the rational, predictable functioning of legal and administrative agencies' (ES, 1095). Similarly, modern capitalism is deeply affected by arbitrariness. Judicial decisions made on the basis of revelation, a sense of equity in each case, or the 'unpredictability and inconsistency on the part of court and local officials, and variously benevolence and disfavor on the part of the ruler and his servants' lack the procedural and political predictability required by capitalism (ibid.). The rationalization of economic structures of power is thus intimately connected with the rationalization of political structures of power, the legal order and government administration.

In summary, the organizational features of modern capitalism – purposive-rational economic action involving a technically perfected form of capital accounting and continuous market struggle for profit-making, bureaucratically organized enterprises employing free labour, the functional differentiation of labour tasks, and a predictable legal and administrative environment – all contribute to the precise control of the human and non-human elements in the overall economic process.

## 1.2 Bureaucracy and the Methodical Observance of Rules

Another important aspect of the 'specific and peculiar rationalism' of modern social arrangements is illustrated in Weber's conception of modern bureaucracy. The rationalism of modern power and authority, Weber argues, is exemplified by the structure of bureaucracy. The two key features of modern bureaucracy, which make it an exemplary instance of legal-rational domination, are its impersonal formalism and its technical efficiency.

The heart of bureaucratic rationalism is regulation of administrative activity through observance of abstract, impersonal rules. The structure of the bureaucratic organization is highly articulated and its functioning differentiated by a tightly meshing matrix of formal, impersonal rules. For example, the jurisdiction of each agency is articulated by formal rules; within an agency, individual offices are arranged hierarchically with internal relationships codified; the distribution of authority, duties associated with each position, and procedures for carrying out duties follow formal, abstract, general rules; the official does not own her office; the resources of the organization are distinct from those of the official; official tasks are divided into functionally distinct spheres and organized on a continuous regulated basis; official work is conducted according to technical abstract rules that can be applied to all conceivable fact-situations which might fall into the jurisdiction of the agency; administration is based on written records. In short, Weber argues, the essence of modern bureaucracy is the reduction of management to abstract rules. Bureaucracy provides a marked contrast with the regulation of relationships through individual privilege and the bestowal of favours, which prevailed in premodern structures of political power (ES, 958).

Impersonal formalism also inheres in the character of authority that bureaucratic organizations embody. Bureaucratic domination is based on legal authority. Officials exercise authority according to an impersonal bond to a generally defined 'duty of office'; official duty is fixed by rationally established norms, that is, norms that are purposefully thought out and enacted in a procedurally correct manner; the obedience of individuals subject to the administrative apparatus is due not to the person holding the office but to the impersonal order of which the official is a representative (FMW, 299). In short, the hallmark of the legal authority behind the rationalism of bureaucratic organization is the performance of duty 'according to *calculable rules* and "without regard for persons"' (ES, 975). Just as the rationalization of economic structures of power involves an increasing degree of purposive-rational action oriented to the acquisition of profit without regard for persons, so the rationalization of political structures of authority involves an increasing degree of purposive-rational action oriented to rules, without regard for particular persons and detached from sentimental or evaluative considerations. The impersonal, rule-governed character of the bureaucratic agency is complemented by its reliance on technical-professional expertise. As Weber notes, bureaucratic organization involves 'domination through knowledge' in lieu of habit, guesswork, or caprice (ibid.). As the technical and economic bases of modern social life become increasingly sophisticated, a premium is placed on political and business administration that draws from the resources of specialized technical expertise.

A second key feature of Weber's depiction of modern bureaucratic organization is his emphasis on its superior technical efficiency and the calculability of the results it can obtain. Weber argues that the decisive reason for the advance of bureaucratic organization in the modern world is its purely technical superiority over other forms of organization: 'The fully developed bureaucratic apparatus compares with other organizations exactly as does the machine with the non-mechanical modes of production. Precision, speed, unambiguity, knowledge of the files, continuity, discretion, unity, strict subordination, reduction of friction and of material and personal costs – these are raised to the optimum point in the strictly bureaucratic administration' (ES, 973). This quasi-mechanical efficiency 'makes possible a particularly high degree of calculability of results' (ES, 223). Both the capitalist market and mass democracy are deeply affected by the arbitrary and discretionary administration of political resources. Economic incentives for development depend upon the predictability of investment return, and the formal equality of all persons places a premium on the non-discretionary administration of political resources. The economic and political bases of modern life thus require the high degree of calculability of processes and predictability of results provided by the rational rules of modern bureaucratic organization and, ultimately, by the legal-rational structure of the modern state.

The rationalism of both the capitalist economic order and the bureaucratic organization are oriented towards mastery and control over nature and society, as evidenced by the importance of the calculability of operations and the predictability of outcomes. The theme of control over things in the world, control over other people, and mastery of the self pervade Weber's discussions of the rationalism specific to the modern world. His analysis of the relationship between personality and social structure in the *Protestant Ethic* emphasizes the 'elective affinity' between a new ethos of rigorous self-control derived from Puritanism and a new form of vocational discipline (ES, 556). Modern capitalism involves detailed mastery over the whole process of production, including the rational conditioning and training of individual work performances. In turn the controllability of economic production is interrelated with the bureaucratic organization's efficient control over information and the knowledgeable administration of resources.

The power to manipulate things offered by the formal rationality of capitalism and bureaucracy is achieved through the objectification and depersonalization of modern structures of power and authority (ES, 601). Market transactions between strangers are paradigmatic of formally rational social relations. The bureaucratic official works according to rules without regard for individual persons; economic action is likewise oriented to the calculation of profit without regard for particular persons. The formal rationality of economic arrangements liberates the linking of economic means and ends from 'ethical requirements' that inhibit the technical efficiency and controllability of economic action (ES, 585). Similarly, as Weber's depiction of bureaucratic rationality illustrates, modern structures of authority are also objectified and depersonalized worlds of instrumentally organized activities. In contrast to forms of administration based upon personal authority, the formal rationality of bureaucracy eliminates from official business 'all purely personal, irrational, and emotional elements which escape calculation' (FMW, 216). Resources can then be administered and controlled with quasi-mechanical efficiency.

The theme of control and mastery through objectification and depersonalization, however, represents only one side of Weber's interpretation of the significance of the 'specific and peculiar rationalism of Western culture.' To understand how the various institutions of modernity fit together into a meaningful whole, we must also examine the conception of 'subjective' rationality that these institutions presuppose. The formal rationality and control-orientation of modern social arrangements presuppose the 'positivistic' character of modern values and the normative power of choice and consent in modern conceptions of personhood. This positivistic theory of value and will-centred conception of personhood can be elucidated and systematized through examining Weber's 'existential' epistemology and conception of human action.[8]

## 2. Weber's Existential Epistemology

A basic postulate of Weber's conception of modernity is that, because of the ineluctable disenchantment of the world, the foundations for a unified religious or metaphysically based modern world view have been destroyed. In ages before ours, 'absolute values' connected with the various characteristics of the age could exist. For instance, social arrangements were once believed to be God-willed. In such traditional world-views, Weber argues, the tensions between value-spheres were hidden from human awareness: the 'true,' the 'good,' and the 'beautiful' were identical. Galileo's discovery of the moons around Jupiter with his newly invented telescope was proscribed by the Catholic

Church because his findings contradicted scriptural interpretation of cosmic order and thus were *morally* wrong. In Galileo's time, cognitive and moral relations to the world were not yet differentiated. But the rationalization and disenchantment of our relations to the world 'have then pressed towards making conscious the *internal and lawful autonomy* of the individual spheres; thereby letting them drift into those tensions which remain hidden to the originally naive relation with the external world' (FMW, 328).

In Galileo's day, factual statements and moral judgments were believed to coincide. But the demagification or disenchantment and systematization of our relations to the world expose first the tensions between cognitive and moral spheres and subsequently – perhaps ultimately – their complete independence. In contrast to Galileo's time, modern value-spheres are highly differentiated from one another (truth, goodness, and beauty) and highly formalized internally (science, morality, and aesthetics). In place of unity and harmony of value-spheres, today we experience irresolvable conflict between them. As Weber remarks, 'it is commonplace to observe that something may be true although it is not beautiful and not holy and not good' (FMW, 148).

The corollary of this differentiation of value-spheres is the subjectification of values and normative power. The differentiation of value-spheres erodes the belief that social arrangements are part of quasi-natural order. Once social arrangements lose this absolutist character of inevitability the problem of value-contingency emerges. In a sense, the notion of 'value' as something distinct from the 'factual' characteristics of a given social milieu is only articulated when the normative power of the actual begins to weaken. This loss of the transcendental rooting that previously secured the 'objectivity' and unity of values transfers the problem of meaning-contingency (and ultimately the contingency of social arrangements) to the responsibility of human action. Once faith in 'objective' values has been broken and the world has been emptied of 'mysterious incalculable forces' mastery of the consequent disenchanted cosmos of natural causality through human calculation becomes a primary imaginary signifier of human consciousness. With the eclipse of the notion of a God-willed cosmos, the world no longer contains inherent impediments to human will. The assumption that 'the world itself places no fundamental restrictions on human beings' calculating and dominating will,' Weiss argues, 'implies ... just as fundamentally that from this world no points of reference can be derived for "objectively" binding meanings and values.'[9]

Kant exposed the problematic nature of the metaphysical basis of all traditional unified world-views. The difficulty of grounding a religious world-view in a metaphysics that claims cognitive adequacy to the world, he argues, is that there are as many possible worlds as there are modes of apprehending them. His response was to ground ethical imperatives in the structure of individual ethical life itself. This solution points in the direction of all subsequent analyses of religion, which, though perhaps rejecting Kant's narrowly rational ethics, have been forced to ground religion in various interpretations of the human situation rather than some hypostatized conception of the correct order of things. Once the symbolization of the conditions of human existence is no longer authoritatively anchored by a conception of the 'objective,' there are as many answers to the 'questions' of human existence as there are individual experiences and perspectives. As Robert Bellah remarks, the premodern Western world of heaven and earth rooted in a religiously based conception of the cosmos has been replaced by 'an infinitely multiplex world,' and modern life 'has become an infinite possibility thing.'[10]

The 'enchanted' relationship that once existed between individuals and the world in traditional civilizations involved a faith in some kind of 'objective' meaning that was rationally expressed in a religious or metaphysically based world-view. In the modern world, 'objectivities' of all kinds have been demystified through a process of rationalization and disenchantment and no longer possess an authoritative hold. If, as Weber argues, modernity is characterized by the impossibility of linking conceptions of 'objective value' with any features of the world, what forms of understanding might be available to the sociologist?

In a celebrated essay on the relationship between Weber and Marx's social thought, Karl Löwith argues that Weber's disenchantment thesis forms the ultimate presupposition behind the 'logical structure' of his methodology and 'cognitive style.'[11] The 'ideal-type,' for instance, illustrates what could be called Weber's existentialist epistemology or 'cognitive style.' A corollary of the disenchantment of the world is the inherent meaninglessness and heterogeneous character of 'reality.' Weber writes, 'as soon as we attempt to reflect about the way in which life confronts us in immediate concrete situations, it presents an infinite multiplicity of successively and coexistently emerging and disappearing events, both "within" and "outside" ourselves' (MSS, 72). Whereas Kant argues that 'categories of understanding' that ordered this plethora of phenomena were 'synthetic *a priori*' – that is, they inhered ontologically in the nature of human subjectivity – Weber extends the implications of disenchantment one step further, arguing in effect that the categories of understanding are themselves histori- cally generated conceptual schemata. Given this cognitive style, one might say that Weber's orientation to the world was unremittingly sec- ular and sober in character.

Since an indefinite number of conceptual taxonomies of reality are possible, sociological concepts such as 'capitalism,' 'bureaucracy,' 'for- mal rationality,' even psychological concepts such as 'mental illness,' are ultimately 'constructivist' or 'nominalist' in character. In a world that provides no points of reference for deriving 'objective' interpreta- tions of its characteristics, the 'ideal-type' is a cognitive device that allows the sociologist to design research concepts according to the val- ues that he/she considers of heuristic value to the investigation (MSS, 90). Thus, for instance, the ideal type of modern 'bureaucracy' is designed to highlight features of modern bureaucracy most relevant to the future of an individualistic liberal culture, namely, the problem of subordination and discipline within large-scale organizations and the effects of these organizations on society as a whole.[12]

In addition, ideal-types resist cementing into 'objectivities' by virtue of the attention they draw to their own 'constructedness.' Weber's nominalism represents an acknowledgment that if the various charac- teristics of the modern world have been voided of objective meaning, then the 'logical structure' of investigation must perforce maintain a cognitive 'open-mindedness' to the world. 'Open-mindedness' means being alert for belief in false 'objectivities.' Weber writes, 'The *objective* validity of all empirical knowledge rests exclusively upon the ordering of the given reality according to categories which are *subjective* in a spe- cific sense, namely, in that they present the *presuppositions* of our knowledge and are based on the presupposition of the *value* of those *truths* which empirical knowledge alone is able to give us' (MSS, 110). Hence Weber's criticism of liberal belief in the 'progress' of Western civilization as an attempt to provide a secular but nevertheless objec- tive meaning for human destiny once it has been voided of religious content (RK, 229, n. 81), or equally for the Marxian historical material- ism of his day, which imputed ultimate factors behind social processes and general 'laws' of historical development (ST, 257–62). Weber's 'nominalist' cognitive style, his existential epistemology, is also con- ceptually congruent with his political theory, which sought to resist the

routinizing tendencies of modern social order by stressing the conflictive character of politics and the indeterminacy of values.

## 2.1 The Positivistic Character of Modern Values

Weber's theory of value follows logically from his existential epistemology. As a result of the historical or contingent character of cogni-
tion and symbolization, conceptual schemata of interpretation become
relative to the perspective of particular value-standpoints and commitment to specific 'givens.' Consequently, modern forms of 'knowledge'
become differentiated into logically distinct spheres of understanding
and evaluation. Kronman's discussion of the Socratic method provides
a good illustration of the way in which Weber's cognitive style in general and his theory of value in particular represent a departure from
'premodern' correlates, in terms of the differing relationships they presuppose between understanding and evaluation and the differing conceptions of personhood they assume.

The Socratic method, Kronman argues, represents a cognitive style
in which understanding is identical with evaluation. For Socrates,
knowledge is a necessary and sufficient condition for virtue, and hence
for right conduct. The object of virtue for Socrates was to put the soul
into a 'good' condition, the attainment of which would be concordant
with individual happiness. This condition was universal: the specific
and identifiable condition of the soul that produces this state of happiness does not vary. According to this view, people have different conceptions of good only because they are ignorant of its true nature. Once
an accurate understanding of the nature of the goodness of the soul is
acquired, disagreements about what goodness consists in will disappear. Knowledge of goodness is a necessary and sufficient condition
for holding the 'right' values. Thus, it is ignorance which explains why
people lead different sorts of lives and seek happiness in different
ways.[13]

By contrast, Weber's epistemology argues the absolute logical heterogeneity of understanding and evaluation, of empirical propositions and normative orientations (MSS, 51–8). The separation of
understanding and evaluation is exemplified by his conception
of 'value-freedom' [Wertfreiheit]. 'Value-freedom' means that sociological research attempts to understand social life from the standpoint of
the values that individual actors attach to their actions but, at the same
time, deliberately abstains from adopting the normative commitments

of those being studied. The sociologist tries to see the world as others do without accepting their values as correct. Weber's methodology argues that it is possible for a sociologist to understand the normative commitments of those being studied without adopting their values as normative criteria of the investigation. This form of detached empathy does not impair our ability to understand the structure of someone else's value commitments; it does not render the values of others unintelligible. Nor does this detachment mean that the sociologist's own values play no role in the choice and definition of problems for study. On the contrary, what the concept of 'ideal-type' expresses, and what Weber repeatedly emphasizes, is the extent to which the sociologist's own values are a lens that shapes both the investigation and the choice of subject matter. Indeed, to engage in sociological research at all reflects a particular value-commitment to the enterprise of sociology as a discipline. Nevertheless, the peculiar form of detached empathy that characterizes sociological investigation illustrates the logical heterogeneity of knowing and evaluating.

The divergence of Weber's existential epistemology from the Socratic method, Kronman argues, also illustrates differing conceptions of 'value.' In the Socratic view, a person acquires knowledge of values in the same manner as any other form of knowledge: through an act of intellectual vision. In this view, the basic task of moral life is the attainment of 'clarity': if one can obtain a view of the world unclouded by ignorance, then, seeing what is 'true,' one will find oneself disposed to do the 'right thing.' For Weber, however, a person's understanding of the world may influence his values – that is, a person's knowledge is sometimes a *necessary condition* of his values.' But given that the disenchanted world offers no points of reference for deriving the 'right' way of acting, knowledge of the world is never a *sufficient condition* for holding a particular value or set of values.'[14]

According to Weber's 'positivistic' theory of value, whatever a person's knowledge or beliefs may be, an additional and distinct act of choice is always required to render some perspective or aspect of the world a 'value.' Although Weber argues that values are the product of choice, he does not mean to imply that the values people hold are simply the product of choice and consent. Obviously, in many if not most situations, such values have been 'preselected' by a multitude of sociological and psychological processes. But Weber's positivistic theory of value argues that, ultimately, the status of a value, the fact that a particular norm happens to be a value for someone, can only be accounted for in terms of the volitional bestowal of meaning.[15]

The logical heterogeneity of knowing and evaluating, the disjunction of facts and values, assumes cardinal significance in Weber's account of modern structures of power and authority in general. In traditional civilizations, the values people hold are supplied either by the 'fate of ascription' or revelation. Weber argues that, in a disenchanted, post-traditional world, where 'objectivities' of all kinds have been demystified, the basis on which persons hold particular values must ultimately rest on individual choice. The Socratic conception of knowledge reflects an essentialist notion of rationality as something implanted in human nature and unitary in structure. In this view, to be rational basically involves self-adjustment to an ideal cosmic pattern, which is itself conceived in static and unitary terms. With secularization and the disenchantment of the world, 'value' must be viewed ultimately as the product of an individual posit, that is, a deliberate choice or decision on the part of the individual. With disenchantment, values can no longer inhere in the factual order of the world: 'we cannot learn the *meaning* of the world from the results of its analysis, be it ever so perfect' (MSS, 57). Rather, values, ideals, and 'the general views of life and the universe which move us so forcefully' must be viewed as the fruit of choice.

Like Marx and Nietzsche, Weber holds that God, certainly in the Old Testament sense of the Supreme Law-Giver, is absent. But he is less confident in attributing responsibility for what he sees as a strange and tragic event fated to happen in the modern world (PE, 182).[16] In other words, although Weber argues that modern values are 'positive' in character because of the disenchantment of 'objective' value in the modern world, the exact logical relationship between the 'existential' and the 'epistemological' dimensions of his social and political thought is ambiguous. But if the process of disenchantment and the differentiation of value-spheres are irreversible world-historical phenomena, the positivity of values is in a sense the universal endpoint of an age-old process of civilizational development, and not merely a historical peculiarity of modern, Western cultural values.

## 2.2 The Normative Power of Individual Choice and Consent

Weber's social thought contains what might be called a 'philosophical anthropology,' that is, a conception of those characteristics that distinguish social action as specifically *human* conduct.[17] Human action is distinguished from the causal order of the world in terms of its 'meaningfulness,' 'rationality,' and 'autonomy' – that is, to the extent that action is deliberately and consciously guided by a plan of our own design. When extended to the organization of an individual's life as a whole, these features of human conduct converge in Weber's will-centred concept of 'personality.'[18]

A primary assumption in Weber's sociology is that individuals possess and conform to certain motives by which their action is coordinated. Humans create their social environment from their cultural values and this activity can be understood through the reference of individual action to the meanings that motivate it. To understand an individual's particular course of action, one must uncover the particular values or ends by which it was motivated. The motives individuals possess for choosing particular values or ends, Weber acknowledges, may be conditioned by physiological, behaviourial, or even geographical factors. In addition, 'in the great majority of cases,' 'actual action goes on in a state of inarticulate half-consciousness or actual unconsciousness of its subjective meaning' (ES, 21). Nevertheless, he argues, the more individual conduct is determined by the meanings that individuals posit or acknowledge, the more characteristically 'human' their action becomes.

Human action is distinguished from nature and thus 'meaningful' to the extent that it is 'rational' – that is, deliberately and consciously guided by a plan of the individual's own design. Although 'irrationality' and 'unpredictability' may be important features of human behavior and experience, they do not represent the primary attributes of what is distinctively human (RK, 97 and 192–3). The meaningfulness and rationality of ideal-typically 'human' action are also linked with the experience of 'freedom' or autonomy that humans uniquely possess. As Weber writes, 'we associate the highest measure of an empirical "feeling of freedom" with those actions which we are conscious of performing rationally – i.e., *in the absence of physical and psychic "coercion," emotional "affects" and "accidental" disturbances of the clarity of judgement,* in which we pursue a clearly perceived end by "means" which are the most adequate in accordance with the extent of our knowledge' (MSS, 124–5). For Weber, the more human action is deliberately oriented to self-chosen goals the more it embodies human autonomy.

The meaning, rationality, and autonomy of particular human actions has an additional significance for Weber when extended to the organization of individual life as a whole. In this context, they converge in Weber's conception of 'personality.' A meaningful, rational, and autonomous personality involves a systematic integration of individual actions into a unified life pattern based on certain fundamental values, that is, the coherence of an individual's ends and values and the constancy over time with which these ends and values are pursued. As Weber states, 'personality' 'entails a constant and intrinsic relation to certain ultimate "values" and "meanings" of life, "values" and "meanings" which are forged into purposes and thereby translated into rational-teleological action' (RK, 192).

According to Weber, the achievement of 'personality' demands the deliberate, planful, systematic integration of individual actions into a unified life pattern based on volitionally assigned meaning. An individual must become a 'personality' to live a life informed by reason. To become a personality, the individual must commit himself to 'a series of ultimate decisions in which the soul chooses the meaning of its own existence' (MSS, 18). But this commitment, which lies at the foundation of personality and thus of every rational life, cannot itself be guided by any supra-individual conception of 'reason.'

The value-creating activity of the individual will is clearly at the heart of Weber's conception of personality. 'Personality' becomes an object of our knowledge only through a process of self-revelation and objectification. If 'personality' were identical to an immediate experience called 'will,' then, like animals fully situated in the causal order of nature, we would be non-existent to ourselves, *for we would lack a knowledge of our own will.*[19] Persons, however, are specifically human because they are both 'outside' and 'of' the world at the same time; conversely, they are both 'outside' and 'of' *themselves* as well.[20] As Weber writes, 'when one begins to think, *first-person* experiences are replaced by reflection upon third-person experiences which are conceived as an "object"' (RK, 166). To apprehend aspects of the world, sensations or experiences must be made into objects. This applies to individual self-awareness as well: we must first objectify ourselves before we can begin to view ourselves as a phenomenon to be understood.[21] In this process of objectification, the 'infinite multiplicity of successively and coexistently emerging and disappearing events' 'within' ourselves and 'out' in the world acquire 'perspectives and interrelationships that were not "known" in the experience itself' (MSS, 178). The dignity and coherence of the 'personality' lies in the fact that there exist values about which it organizes its life. As Weber writes, individual personalities are 'synthetically produced by a value relationship' (RK, 183); 'we' are a 'complex of "constant motives"' (ibid., 152).

Weber was well aware that most human behaviour falls below the threshold of the conscious and deliberate; people quite often fail to reflect upon the purposes of their actions while actually performing them. In addition, he was aware that, although some individuals do on occasion make meaning for themselves and their fellows, the capacity to effectuate the 'will' and thereby develop 'personality' in its full depends largely upon the social resources at the disposal of particular individuals. Most individuals are dependent on their social and cultural context for their ultimate values; individual 'will' exists in a social situation not of its own making.

Nevertheless, the point that Weber's will-centred conception of personality argues is that, in a post-traditional, disenchanted world, individual choice unavoidably assumes new moral significance as a value-creating and personality-forming activity. Within the world-view presupposed by the Socratic epistemology discussed above, the basic moral task of life is to put one's soul in the right condition through the progressive elimination of the ignorance that obscures comprehension of the cosmic order. Although this goal may require an active effort over a long period of time, Kronman argues, 'the goal itself should be conceived as an essentially *passive* state or condition in which the soul looks at the world in an unclouded way and, seeing what is true, finds itself disposed to do the right thing *without an intervening act of choice.*'[22] Here, individual will is subordinate to the normative boundaries that have their foundation in the world.

By contrast, according to Weber's existential epistemology and positivistic theory of value, values must ultimately be posited rather than found, and to choose values people are guided by reason rather than technique. For there is no straight-forward way of deciding among the variety of possible value commitments. This does not mean that a rational way of life must ultimately be founded upon the 'irrational' suppositions of moral choice.[23] Rather, a substantively rational way of life perhaps inheres in some historically evolving human moral capacity.[24] Choice has a central moral significance for Weber: it is conscious, deliberate, and personality forming. Weber argues that the clearest knowledge of values can never be more than a preparation for the act of choice that alone binds a value to the person. In this view, values do not have their foundation in the world, as Socrates claims, but in the choosing subject. Of course, as Habermas's theory of communicative action correctly points out, Weber's theory of value involves a liberal philosophy of consciousness that ignores the intersubjective and communicative dimensions of the process of individual choice making – a deficiency that inheres within the liberal cultural system itself. But Löwith argues that in Weber's theory of value the positive element in the modern loss of faith in something that goes beyond the given, the modern loss of moral certitude, is a gain in personal autonomy expressed as the pure responsibility of the individual towards himself.[25]

## 3. The Conceptual Nexus of Formal Rationality and Value-Positivism

The formal rationality of modern social arrangements represents a modality of control and mastery involving the objectification and depersonalization of political and economic structures of power and authority. At the heart of Weber's concept of formal rationality is the idea of correct calculation of operations and prediction of results. Both modern capitalism and bureaucratic organization are rationalized on the basis of rigorous control, the former directed towards the calculation of profit, the latter towards consistent observance of formal rules, both contributing to the purposeful achievement of economic and political ends. This elimination of evaluative and affectual concerns underscores an important feature of modern rationalism: the rationality of modern social arrangements is purely *formal*. In principle, it expresses no substantive value-preference.

The corollary to the merely formal rationality of modern social arrangements is the positivity of modern values and the normative power of individual choice. In the Socratic world-view, the normative power for setting values resides in the boundary-setting capacity of the world, which provides the points of reference for deriving 'objectively' binding meanings and values. Once the world no longer performs this value-setting function, the problem of individual choice enters the formulation of values. In the Socratic view, our capacity for knowledge plays a fundamental role in moral life; in Weber's view, the power of creative choice is central to the moral dimension.

Weber's conception of personality argues the central moral significance of the value-creating activity of individual will, and hence the normative power of choice. The great discovery of the Reformation was that connection with the cosmic 'centre' of life was already prefigured in the 'conscience' of the individual. This brought the act of revelation into every single person and saddled the individual with the responsibility of choice for 'ultimate meanings' that the Church had previously borne. The shift from God-willed hierarchy to the centrality of individual will has been paradigmatic of the gradual concentration of normative power within the individual.

The unifying principle linking the politics and economics, as well as the law and science, of the modern world is a rationality premised on the fundamental tension between description of facts and judgments of value, and therefore, a fundamental tension between efficient linking of means with ends and the selection of ends in themselves. As Brubaker argues, the 'end' towards which formal rationality is oriented is not really an 'end' at all, but a *'generalized means'* open to the goal-setting of individuals, and thereby indiscriminately facilitative of 'the purposeful pursuit of all substantive ends.'[26]

The calculability and predictability of formally rational social arrangements thus represents the structural concomitant of purposeful, planful individual conduct within the economic and political spheres of modern society. In contrast to premodern social arrangements, which only facilitated those social actions that harmonized with the substance of God-willed hierarchy, the formal rationality of modern social arrangements is purely instrumental and 'meaningless.' Because of this formal rationality, modern social arrangements in principle furnish maximum scope for the individual pursuit of substantive ends that they themselves determine. With the diminution of the normative power of tradition and revelation, the basis of validity behind the structure of social arrangements has become increasingly tied to their capacity to respect individual choice and consent. The formal rationality of social arrangements and the normative power of individual choice converge in Weber's concept of formal legal rationality. The relationship between individual autonomy and the control-orientation of social arrangements, the positivity of values and the 'empty' formal rationality of economic and political structures of power, is articulated in Weber's focal conception of modern legal rationality.

# The 'Specific and Peculiar Rationalism' of Modern Authority: The Problematic Relation between Modern Freedom and Domination

In different but analogous ways, the rationalism of the capitalist market economy and of bureaucratic forms of organization (and by implication, all the supportive institutions of modern society) represents forms of control and mastery involving rigorous calculation of the means-ends relationships of economic and political activity. Mastery and control are obtained through the exploitation of knowledge, particularly technical expertise, but more generally through the objectification and depersonalization of social arrangements. The rationalism of modern social arrangements and the conceptions of individualism prevalent to modern society presuppose, first, a fundamental distinction between knowledge of 'facts' and judgments of 'value,' and second, the importance of intentionality in the attribution of meaning to the 'facts' of the world. The corollary to this positivistic theory of value and will-centred conception of personhood is that modern structures of power and authority reflect an openness to human goal-setting and facilitate purposive, planful action. The relationship between modern social arrangements and value-positivism converges in the 'specific and peculiar rationalism' of modern legal thought and, more generally, of the legal structure of modern power and authority.

## 1. Weber's Typology of Legal Rationality

Weber's sociology of law was directed to explication of the specific and peculiar rationalism of the modern Western legal order, 'the ways and consequences of the "rationalization" of the law, that is the development of those juristic qualities which are characteristic of it today' (ES,

775–6). In order to assess the growth and direction of rationalization in legal development, Weber employs the typology shown in Figure 1 (ES, 656–8):

|  | *formal*<br>(*means*) | *substantive*<br>(*ends*) |
|---|---|---|
| *irrational* | magical<br>(e.g., revelation, ES, 761) | contextual<br>(e.g., khadi justice, ES, 845) |
| *rational* | procedural<br>(e.g., Roman Law, ES, 976–8) | objective norms<br>(e.g., Natural law, ES, 868–71) |

Figure 1
Typology of Legal Rationality

This typology is notoriously beguiling: simple in appearance, but actually quite difficult to explicate systematically.[1] Like the typology of economic rationality discussed in the previous chapter, Weber's categories of legal rationality indicate two axes of differentiation: the distinction between formal and substantive rationality and that between rationality and irrationality (ES, 85–6 and 656–8). Just as the formal rationality of economic action increases with the degree to which means and ends become susceptible to calculation – that is, quantitative comparison – so the formal rationality of law-making and law-finding increases as means that can be controlled by the intellect are employed. The epitome of formally rational economic action is the comparative cost-analysis of particular courses of action; the epitome of formally rational legal thought is the logical analysis of unambiguous legally relevant general characteristics of the facts of the case at hand. The more the administration of legal norms is governed by general rules or principles, as opposed to the unique circumstances of each case, the more 'rational' it is. Thus formal rationality refers to the systematic character of legal order; the legal order is rational to the extent that 'it represents an integration of all analytically derived legal propositions in such a way that they constitute a logically clear, internally consistent, and, at least in theory, gapless system of rules, under which, it is implied, all conceivable fact situations must be capable of being logically subsumed lest their order lack an effective guaranty' (ES, 656). As opposed to being 'a featureless conglomeration of ethical and legal duties, moral exhortations and legal commandments' (ES, 810), the rational legal order effects a logical distinction between legal and extralegal norms. The calculability of law is directly related to the organizational clarity and comprehensiveness (gapless quality) of its order.

Conversely, legal thought is formally irrational 'when one applies in lawmaking or lawfinding means which cannot be controlled by the intellect, for instance when recourse is had to oracles or substitutes therefor' (ES, 656), for this introduces unpredictability into the lawmaking and law-finding process, rendering the outcome of judicial decisions difficult to predict or calculate. For example, oracular adjudication is relatively unpredictable. Because the magical power that speaks through the oracle is assumed to be fundamentally superior to humans, there is no reason to doubt the ethical propriety of the judicial decision, and hence no reason to provide explanations for a given decision. As Kronman writes, 'only when the law ceases to be considered an oracular pronouncement of a divine power and comes to be viewed, instead, as a product of deliberate human legislation, can the problems of its organization and content be regarded as ones that human beings are competent to solve.'[2] Once the administration of legal norms is demystified, judicial decisions must be accompanied by reasonable explanations. Since humans err, justifications must be framed that are intelligible to the litigants themselves. Reason-giving is thus an important step in the 'disenchantment' of law.

Analogous to Weber's description of substantively rational economic action, the substantive rationality of legal thought increases with the satisfaction of 'objective norms' applied generally to all cases – that is, ultimate values or needs derived from moral or political commitments but unrelated to the rules and principles of the legal order itself. Legal thought is substantively rational if 'the decision of legal problems is influenced by norms different from those obtained through logical generalization of abstract interpretations of meaning. The norms to which substantive rationality accords predominance include ethical imperatives, utilitarian and other expediential rules, and political maxims' (ES, 657).

Conversely, legal thought is substantively irrational 'to the extent that decision is influenced by concrete factors of the particular case as evaluated upon an ethical, emotional, or political basis rather than by general norms' (ES, 656). For example, primitive legal thought locates the juristic meaning of events in their extrinsic or tangible characteristics. In contrast, legal rationality involves the logical analysis of meaning as opposed to the tangible perception of 'sense-data' (ES, 657). With the modern logical interpretation of meaning, the external characteristics of a particular fact situation merely provide an evidential base for discovering the existence of purposive human attitudes. With primitive law and procedure, Weber writes,

> there is a complete unconcern with a notion of guilt, and, consequently, with the idea of degrees of guilt reflecting inner motivations and psychological attitudes. He who thirsts for vengeance is not interested in motives; he is concerned only with the objective happening of the event by which his desire for vengeance has been aroused. His anger expresses itself equally against inanimate objects, by which he has been unexpectedly hurt, against animals by which he has been unexpectedly injured, and against human beings who have harmed him unknowingly, negligently, or intentionally (ES, 647–8).

Connecting this to Weber's methodological suppositions, particularly his theory of value, in modern legal rationality what is legally relevant (i.e., 'values') does not inhere in the external characteristics of a given case (i.e., the 'facts'), but rather, must be read from the purposive conduct of individuals.

## 2. The 'Specific and Peculiar Rationalism' of Modern Law

The concept of formal legal rationality comprises the core of Weber's substantive sociology of modern law. Just as the degree of formal rationality of economic action increases with the calculability of means and ends, so the calculability of judicial decision making increases with the clarity and generality of legal rules. Weber's conception of legal rationality thus parallels his account of the more general process of rationalization behind modernity: increasing formal rationalization generally means increasing knowledge, impersonality, and control.

From his typology of legal thought Weber identifies three different senses in which, by virtue of its 'specific and peculiar rationalism,' modern law is distinguished from traditional law. First, with respect to the quality of legal norms, he draws a distinction between legal systems that rest to some degree on 'magical' thinking – that is, a legal order which allegedly expresses and addresses substances possessing intrinsic meaning, in which 'values' are thought to connect with various factual attributes of the social order – and those legal systems that make a logical separation between values and facts, substance and meaning. Second, Weber distinguishes between legal systems with general, abstract, and predictable rules and those that involve particularistic, adventitious decisions. Finally, with respect to legal authority, Weber distinguishes between legal systems that separate law from morality and politics and those which merge them. Modern law is thus 'rational' for Weber in terms of the positivism of legal norms (the mode of norm creation: its positive and formal character), the formalism of legal relations (the formal qualities of the legal order: its general and autonomous character), and, finally, the 'legalism' of modern structures of authority (the type of justice which this legal order realizes).

## 2.1 The positivism of legal norms

In the broadest sense, any recurring mode of interaction among individuals and between groups represents a normative order. Weber distinguishes between normative orders based upon 'subjective' principles, such as traditional or affectual beliefs, and orders based upon 'objective' principles, such as 'convention' and 'law' (ES, 33–4). He distinguishes further between convention and law through, first, the manner in which such 'objective' norms are *administered*: 'an order will be called ... *law* if it is externally guaranteed by the probability that physical or psychological coercion will be applied by a *staff* of people in order to bring about compliance or avenge violation' (ES, 34). For example, in contrast to legal norms, subjective norms are 'characterized by the very absence of any clearly defined coercive apparatus.'

Second, Weber distinguishes 'objective' normative orders by modes of *validity*:

> if furniture movers regularly advertise at the time many leases expire, this uniformity is determined by self-interest. If a salesman visits certain customers on particular days of the month or the week, it is either a case of customary behavior or a product of self-interested orientation. However, when a civil servant appears in his office daily at a fixed time, he does not act only on the basis of custom or self-interest which he could disregard if he wanted to; as a rule, his action is also determined by the validity of an order ... (ES, 31)

A normative order is constituted by the manner in which actors orient their actions according to their subjective belief in the validity of the order (ES, 33). Unfortunately, Weber seems to conceptualize 'convention' as a 'subjective' form of normative order, that is, one which lacks formal principles of validity and modes of administration (actually, he is somewhat inconsistent on the issue, for example, cf. ES, 34 and ES, 320). However, an enormous cosmos of 'conventions' have multiplied throughout the twentieth century which subject individuals to the 'rational' discipline of the human 'sciences' (e.g., medicine, psychiatry, and education). These specifically non-legal (sometimes quasi-legal) conventions do indeed, to paraphrase Weber, claim 'objective' principles of validity and possess delimited groups of persons who continuously hold themselves ready for the special task of coercion through physical or psychological means (ES, 320).[3]

At any rate, Weber's sociological approach to law is concerned with the fact that people view legal norms as evaluative standards, or expect them to be viewed this way by others, and are thus led to modify their conduct in some observable fashion.

With customary law, there is no sharp distinction between facts and norms. The factual regularities of conduct that arise from custom or habituation are the source for laws of conduct. In customary law, Roberto Unger argues, 'the issue of what in fact happens can never be kept clearly separate from the question of what ought to be done.'[4] Thus, customary law is neither 'positive' nor 'public'; its nonpublic quality means that it is common to the whole society, rather than associated with a government that stands apart from society. In this form of domination, the normative order is morally integrated with the tissue of everyday life, and since the legal order runs continuous with custom, the family, the neighbourhood, and the tribe are its guardians.

Customary law is also nonpositive: 'originally there was a complete absence of the notion that rules of conduct possessing the character of "law", i.e., rules which are guaranteed by "legal coercion", could be intentionally created as "norms"' (ES, 760). Although the utility of legal norms for resolving disputes and binding behaviour to a 'valid' order may have been recognized, legal norms were still not conceived as the products of, or subject matter for, human enactment. Rather, their 'legitimacy' 'rested upon the absolute sacredness of certain usages as such ... As "tradition" they were, in theory at least, immutable' (ES, 760).[5] In summary, in a society that holds people together through a collection of partially articulated, largely tacit, customary rules, general norms are not considered the subject matter of human creation, nor is their administration the responsibility of a government body distinguished from the society at large. Law exists as a collection of nonpositive, nonpublic rules.

The increasing intervention into human conduct of enacted norms, Weber argues, is yet another component of 'that process of rationalization and association whose growing penetration into all spheres of social action we shall have to trace' (ES, 333). With the increasing division of labour and growing structural complexity of societies based on customary law, social relations present problems of order that require human control; the factual regularities of what people do is perceived to diverge from what they should do. The division of labour, for instance, erodes the basis for an inclusive set of shared beliefs: separate social classes can no longer rely upon a shared community of perceptions and ideals, shared expectations of what should be done. In this scenario the normative order becomes problematic, and regulatory law must be devised to cope with the development of unconventional situations for which customary law provides no guidance. Regulatory law consists of explicit rules established and enforced by an identifiable government. Regulatory law is deliberately imposed by rulers and administrators rather than spontaneously generated by society. Thus, regulatory law is distinguished from customary law by its public and positive qualities.

Despite the positive and public qualities of regulatory law, its validity remains largely dependent on the presumptive legitimacy of traditional norms. The validity of traditional normative order inheres in the pre-existing structure of the world and is thus prior to human volition. Individuals are assigned a place within this order by the circumstances of their birth, their economic station, and so forth. As Weber argues, under this structure of traditional domination even voluntarily created social relations were patterned after and assimilated within the 'natural' relations that appear in the biological household. This assimilation requirement reveals the belief that only 'natural' characteristics could be 'legitimate.'

What decisively separates modern from traditional social orders is the break with the age-old belief in the normative power of the natural and the actual.[6] The structure of economic and political organization characteristic of the modern West reveals the public and positive qualities of its normative order. This formally rational law is distinctively modern in that legislation consists in deliberate enactment of new legal norms and procedures whereby norms are created are themselves governed by posited legal norms. Legal-rational bureaucracies administer laws acknowledged to be deliberate creations of human beings. These laws are valid insofar as they are promulgated in accordance with a normative structure that is itself deliberately enacted. Here, legal rationality refers to the extent to which legal norms are controlled by the intellect. Within the modern rational legal order one can in theory devise and implement legal norms according to human convenience. In contrast, primitive mechanisms of dispute resolution employ magical means; conversely, religious-metaphysical ends are rationalized in sacred law (ES, 790).

Underlying Weber's conception of modern legal order is the central philosophical presupposition of a 'positivistic' theory of value. According to this theory, the 'fruit of the tree of knowledge' is the inescapable awareness that the value-judgment of 'every single important activity and ultimately life as a whole' is the product of an 'ultimate decision' that cannot be rationally determined in the narrow sense of the term (MSS, 18). A person's knowledge or beliefs are sometimes a necessary condition of his or her values but not per se a sufficient precondition for preferring one value rather than another. In the absence of norms 'revealed' in a religious or charismatic fashion, 'given' by custom or usage, or 'deduced' by natural law (which, as we shall see, Weber did not consider a tenable option in the twentieth century), legal norms must perforce be 'enacted.'

Whereas the exercise of power through customary and regulatory law seeks to legitimate authority by appealing to norms assumed to be intrinsic to the world, legal rational authority must appeal to criteria of justification established by human will. Legal-rational authority explicitly embraces what all forms of domination exemplify, that, ultimately, the normative order is an artifact of human valuation. According to Weber's positivistic theory of value, values are the product of enacted preference; legal rational authority similarly rests upon an appeal to norms that have been deliberately enacted, and whose binding force is believed to derive from the very fact of their enactment in accordance with procedures that are themselves enacted.

## 2.2 The Formalism of Legal Relations

In addition to its positive and public qualities, the modern Western legal order is distinguished from all other historical forms of legal normativity by its commitment to being general and autonomous. A unique feature of the Western legal order is the high degree of functional differentiation of elements which it exhibits. Intrajuristically, formal distinctions exist between substantive and procedural law (i.e., between 'rules of law to be applied in the process of law-finding and rules regarding that process itself' (ES, 654)), between discerning questions of law and ascertaining questions of fact (i.e., specialized procedures regarding the examination of witnesses, the admission of evidence, etc. (ES, 811)), and, finally, between law-making and law-finding (i.e., between the setting of general rules and the application of those rules in particular cases). Thus, the mode of establishing legal norms is rational and deliberate; the mode of applying legal norms to particular cases is rational and predictable; legal norms are formal to the extent that they are general principles involving no reference to substantive ends or values; and legal norms are systematically related to one another so as to constitute a 'logically clear, internally consistent, and, at least in theory, gapless system of rules under which, it is implied, all conceivable fact situations must be capable of being logically subsumed' (ES, 656).

The legal structure of modern authority also exhibits a high degree of functional differentiation of elements. There are conceptual separations between 'the "state", as an abstract bearer of sovereign prerogatives and the creator of "legal norms"' and the 'personal "authorizations" of individuals,' between the '"objective" legal order' and 'the "subjective rights" of the individual which it guarantees,' and finally between the public law, which 'regulates the interrelationships of public authorities and their relationships with the "subjects,"' and the private law, which 'regulates the relationships of the governed individuals among themselves' (FMW, 239).

The conceptual differentiations that formal rationality instates are thematically analogous: they establish the 'generality' of the legal order, its formal coherence, uniformity, comprehensiveness and 'objectivity,' and its 'autonomy' vis-à-vis customary values, material interests, and so forth. The autonomy of the legal order has several senses.[7] First, legal rules are substantively autonomous from nonlegal beliefs and norms. This independence of the legal and the nonlegal contrasts profoundly with traditional normative order. Often in 'Asiatic civilizations,' for example, 'religious prescriptions were never differentiated from secular rules and ... the characteristically theocratic combination of religious and ritualistic prescriptions with legal rules remained unchanged. In this case, there arose a featureless conglomeration of ethical and legal duties, moral exhortations and legal commandments without formalized explicitness, and the result was a specifically *non-formal* type of law' (ES, 810). Second, the legal order is institutionally autonomous to the extent that rules are applied by specialized institutions whose main task is adjudication. This separation of adjudication from the legislative and administrative arms of the state is the cornerstone of liberal constitutionalism. The separation of the public order of the state from the private sphere of the individual corresponds to the legal and physical separation of official and private life – that is, the separation of the bureaucrat, worker, or official, from the means of administration, production, and authority. As Weber argues, nonownership of the means of 'production' is not indicative simply of capitalistic enterprise; it is a principle of formalistic impersonality that characterizes modern structures of power and authority as a whole. Third, modern law is methodologically autonomous in that legal reasoning has a method and style that differentiates its explanations and justifications from those of, say, scientific, religious, political, or economic discourses. Finally, modern law is occupationally autonomous in that legal institutions are staffed by a special profession defined in terms of its prerogatives and its training in specialized legal argument.

The modern legal order is also distinguished by the 'generality' of law-making and uniformity in the application of law. Regulatory law, for example, may consist of rules that apply to general categories of persons and acts and thus have a wide range of application. Alternatively, the rules may be designed to target a narrowly defined group or to apply to a special situation. The decisive difference between the premodern regulatory law of patrimonial states and modern law is that generality in the former is merely a consequence of political expedience. As Unger writes, in the law of patrimonial states 'there are no commitments to generality in law-making and to uniformity in adjudication that must be kept regardless of their consequences for the political interests of the rulers.'[8]

The high degree of formal rationality in modern law is reflected in its positive and public and, especially, in its autonomous and general qualities. This formal legal rationality is essential to the liberal constitutional state. Through it, the legal system functions, to use Unger's expression, like a 'balance wheel of social organization.'[9] Unger's metaphor of the balance wheel mechanically regulating the complex movement of modern social relations fits felicitously with Weber's association of the modern legal system with a 'technically rational machine' (ES, 811). Both connect legal generality and autonomy with legal predictability and control. Weber's 'juridical formalism' and Unger's 'rule of law ideal' are defined by the interrelated notions of neutrality, uniformity, and predictability. The procedures of legislating, administrating, and adjudicating legal rules are differentiated to avoid favouring or punishing particular groups or individuals and to prevent officials employing public power for private ends. In short, they are intended to ensure the impersonality of power. In turn, the routine and stable qualities of legal order contribute substantially to the modern experience of freedom. Juridical formalism 'guarantees to individuals and groups within the [legal] system a relative maximum of freedom, and greatly increases for them the possibility of predicting the legal consequences of their actions' (ES, 811).

In principle, the 'rule of law' has nothing to do with the particular contents of legal norms, only their form. The substantive contents of legal order are in a sense supplied by individual preference. For instance, the modern individual is legally guaranteed the formal freedom to arrange contractual relationships according to personal choice. As the French Civil Code of 1804 proclaims with epigrammatic aplomb, 'a contract properly concluded holds the place of law for those who have made it.'[10] Of course, in practice the contractual freedom an individual effectively possesses is limited by the material resources he or she can summon. Contractual freedom represents an increase in situational freedom yet introduces new forms of coercion. Nevertheless, the features of modern formal law that underwrite contractual freedom reflect the conceptual distinction between the naturally acquired and the deliberately created. As opposed to the prescription of concrete duties and substantive precepts, modern law through negative restriction legitimates the purposive individual creation of new social relations and valuations.

## 2.3 The Legalism of Modern Authority

According to Weber's theory of authority, a stable social order cannot be maintained indefinitely by the power of physical force or material interests alone. There is, he argues, a basic human need to perceive the order of things as somehow 'intelligible,' and this need can never be met by merely pragmatic orientations to a given constellation of material interests (FMW, 275). Structures of domination, insofar as they are stable, depend upon the legitimacy of their claims to command and to be dutifully obeyed. To add to the tasks of legitimation that must be borne by all social orders, there is an 'existential' dimension to the problem of validity as well:

> the fates of human beings are not equal. Men differ in their states of health or wealth or social status or what not. Simple observation shows that in every such situation he who is more favored feels the never ceasing need to look upon his position as in some way 'legitimate,' upon his advantage as 'deserved,' and the other's disadvantage as being brought about by the latter's 'fault.' That the purely accidental causes of the difference may be ever so obvious makes no difference (ES, 953).

The unequal distribution of human fortune, which all but the most simple social orders tend to create and perpetuate, must be given a practical-ethical justification. The distribution of fortunes must be shown to conform with a coherent normative conception of some kind, that is, it must be shown to make ethical sense.

An inequality of fortunes is sanctioned de facto by all social orders. Weber's theory of authority asks when and why do people obey the powers that be, especially when such authority inevitably contributes to existing inequalities of fortune (FMW, 78)? The subjective meaning of the various reasons why social actors would accept an authority and thus obey its commands are divided by Weber into four ideal-typical patterns of legitimation.[11] Thus, Weber defines structures of domination by the type of normative framework through which they derive validity. A social order may be viewed as legitimate by virtue of: i) tradition: valid is that which has always been (traditional law); ii) faith: valid is that which is newly revealed or exemplary (revealed law); iii) value-rational faith; valid is that which has been deduced as an absolute (natural law); and iv) positive enactment: valid is that which either derives from a voluntary agreement of the interested parties or is imposed by an authority that is held to be legitimate in accordance with some established agreement (ES, 36).

Traditional domination is based on 'the authority of the "eternal yesterday", i.e. of the mores sanctified through the unimaginably ancient recognition and habitual orientation to conform' (FMW, 79). Here, the basis of obedience to authority is the duty to individual incumbents as holders of traditionally legitimated offices or roles, such as patriarchs or princes. The typical structure of administration is patrimonial and hereditary principles form the major factor determining the structure and content of the political order.

It is characteristic of patriarchical and of patrimonial authority, which represents a variety of the former, that the system of inviolable norms is considered sacred; an infraction of them would result in magical or religious evils. Side by side with this system there is a realm of free arbitrariness and favour of the lord, who in principle judges only in terms of 'personal,' not 'functional,' relations. In this sense, traditionalist authority is irrational (FMW, 296)

By contrast, legal domination is based on 'the belief in the validity of legal statute and functional "competence" based on rationally created *rules*' (FMW, 79). The validity ascribed to the social order is based on positive enactment which is believed to be legally correct – that is, it derives from 'a voluntary agreement of the interested parties' and/or is 'imposed by an authority which is held to be legitimate and therefore meets with compliance' (ES, 36). The basis of obedience to authority is impersonal, owed not to individuals or offices but to the 'system.'

According to Weber, the principle form of legitimacy in modern associational society is the belief in legality, compliance with enactments that are 'fixed by *rationally established* norms, by enactments, decrees, and regulations, in such a manner that the legitimacy of the authority becomes the legality of the general rule, which is purposely thought out, enacted, and announced with formal correctness' (FMW, 299).

Thus, the validity of modern social arrangements is based on legally correct enactment. This system of domination obtains its legitimacy from the existence of a system of rationally enacted legal rules that designate powers of command. These jurisdictional competencies are exercised in accordance with the rules; the rules also specify the agency and the procedures by which they can be legitimately altered. Authority is legitimate insofar as it is exercised in accordance with these rules. Rationally created and systematically ordered rules not only define the legitimate function of state administration but are also at the base of all stable authority in modern society, including large business enterprises.

The relationship between individual autonomy and formal legal rationality is central to Weber's sociology of modern law: the formal legal rationality of modern structures of power and authority provides a relative maximum of 'freedom' to individuals. But what forms of freedom are facilitated by the legalization of modern structures of power and authority? What features of modern legal domination and legitimacy promote this experience of freedom?

## 3. Individual Autonomy and Formal Legal Rationality

Behind the implementation of the formal rationality of modern social arrangements and the subjective rationality of modern value-orientations (the will-centred conception of personhood and the positivistic theory of value), the origins of modernity lie, on the one hand, in the fragmentation of the premodern non-equivocal and all-encompassing normative order and, on the other, in the increasing functional differentiation and autonomization of premodern life-orders. Both processes, which Weber describes in terms of the differentiation of value-spheres and life-orders, occasioned the demise of traditional structures of domination and the rise of legal-rational domination.

The legal-rational reconstitution of modern social arrangements involves a 'formalization' of social arrangements and a 'positivization' of values. The formalization of social arrangements represents an emancipation of individuals from the kind of social considerations imposed under the personal structures of traditional domination. The characteristic feature of a formalized social relation is the way in which the actor's attention becomes detached from the personal, substantive qualities of interactions with others and is oriented instead to the impersonal rules of the interaction itself.

The positivization of values contributes to individual autonomy in two ways. First, it refers to the basis of modern norms in deliberate enactments, or posits, rather than 'found' or 'revealed' aspects of the world. The normative order of modern legal domination is thus radically desubstantive in the sense that, being 'human-willed,' it lacks grounding in moral 'givens' or 'absolutes.' The legitimacy of formally correct enactment is rooted in the modern authority of individual choice and consent. Second, positivization refers to the fact that the ends and purposes expressed by the orientations of individual social action fall increasingly within the horizon of individual calculation. The paradigmatic example of positivization of value is the growing social permeation of purposive-rational action, which lies at the heart of the modern experience of 'freedom' – at least in its historically instantiated forms discussed here.

### 3.1 The Legal-Rational Reconstitution of Normative Power

Weber defines the various possible structures of domination according to the principles of legitimacy that they ideal-typically presuppose and depend upon for symbolic validation. The legitimation principles behind premodern structures of domination, based as they are on notions of the magical, the sacred, and the meta-human, assume that normative power inheres within the order of the 'world.' In traditional structures of domination, normative power flows from the presumptive validity of historical and revealed facts. By contrast, the basis of legitimacy under legal·domination, Weber argues, is formally correct enactment.

Weber's formalistic and positivistic conception of modern authority has disturbed many critics. What is most striking about his definition of the modern principle of legitimation is its tautological character: the legitimacy of legal rules is based on their conformity with the existing legal order, and this order is in turn justified by its enactment in accordance with the procedural requirements of the legal order. Legality appears to be legitimacy per se. Weber's view of legal domination as a form of machinery seems such a bloodless phenomenon: impersonal, technical, and remote. Lawrence Friedman writes, 'it is easy to understand why tradition should be so tough and tenacious, encrusted as it is with historical experience and enforced by powerful bonds of culture; it is easy to see how the passion and magic of charismatic authority make it irresistible. But what sustains the *basic* rules of the modern state? What is the source of the power of law?'[12]

Modern governments, in connection with the capitalist economy, assume complex technical tasks that do not lend themselves to charismatic, customary, or naked expressions of authority. They require routine, predictable, and calculable methods, bureaucratic administration and organization that follow definite 'objective' rules. The particular accomplishment of the positivization of the legal order, Habermas agrees, 'consists in *displacing* problems of justification, that is, in relieving the technical administration of the law of such problems over broad expanses.' But, he argues, procedural fidelity alone fails to provide a sufficient justificatory backing for the basic rules of legal domination.[13]

To understand the inner significance of Weber's formal and positive definition of modern authority we must relate it back to the kind of individual autonomy that modern legal domination makes possible. The modern experience of freedom is based on the legal reconstitution of normative power. This positivization of values involves both the elimination of ascriptive norms and the opening of value-setting to individual choice.

The highly formal character of modern authority is indicative of the extent to which modern legal domination has broken free of all references to the magical, the sacred, and the meta-human. Traditional structures of domination, where the legitimacy of authority is based upon the normative power of faith or of 'that which has always been,' correspond to essentialist and teleological conceptions of the relationship between humans and the world. In traditional forms of domination what 'ought to be' is undifferentiated from what 'truly is.' The premodern individual was defined in relation to the social and cosmic whole; individuals followed *externally* defined purposes and were linked *a priori* to a pre-existing order. In contrast to our modern preoccupation with *self*-fulfilment, the emphasis was on the individual's fulfilment of socially defined purposes.

The emergence of the modern conception of the individual as an autonomous moral agent, and the logical dichotomy of 'is' and 'ought' that Weber's positivistic theory of value embraces, is linked to the disintegration of traditional domination and the collapse of the teleological-theistic conceptions of normative power. Individuals are gradually disengaged from the external definition of purposes by divine law, natural teleology, hierarchical authority – this is the sense in which modernity 'empties' the human condition. Structures of domination legitimated on the basis of tradition and revelation are endowed with a sense of inevitability and naturalism. With the disenchantment of metaphysical-theistic world-views, norms are desubstantivized, 'values' are differentiated from 'facts,' that is, particular social arrangements and conceptions of order are drained of metaphysical necessity and exposed as historically contingent products of human action. The collapse of a non-equivocal and all-encompassing normative order and the resulting controversialization of social authority destroys the normative substance, the sense of weight and direction in life, that individuals once derived from their social location in the immutable 'chain of being.'

As a result of the dissolution of historical substantive modes of boundary setting and rule making with regard to key sets of social practices, ever more generalized and desubstantivized definitions of justification have been required to legitimate set norms. The most universal and formal definition of justification possible in the modern world is that of individual choice. As Karl Löwith argues in his famous interpretation of Weber's existential epistemology 'today only the "individual", the self-sufficient single person, is true and real and entitled to existence, because "objectivities" of all kinds have been demystified (through rationalization) and no longer have any independent meaning.'[14]

The highly formal and desubstantive character of legal domination reflects the emancipation of legal norms from the external authority of nonlegal norms. Detached from substantive criteria of 'reason' or 'nature' and conceptions of universally binding human 'good' or 'purpose' the legitimacy of legal norms is now measured in terms of procedural correctness and legal self-consistency. The formal and desubstantive character of legal domination represents an enormous amplification of consciously selected norms; the formal rationality of modern law allows the legal system to function as an instrument for realizing, in principle, almost any goal or purpose, as long as it has been properly enacted. As Bendix writes, under legal-rational authority, 'any norm may be enacted as law with the claim and expectation that it will be obeyed by all those who are subject to the authority of the political community.'[15]

In addition to the elimination of ascriptive norms, the legal reconstitution of normative power involves the positivization of values: the opening of value-setting to individual choice and consent. According to Weber, the world-historical process of disenchantment culminates with the recognition that the world does not provide any fundamental normative boundaries to the willing and striving of humans. An age freed from dogmatic dependence on traditional or revealed norms must rely on its own spontaneous self-legislation to determine its agenda.[16] Weber's fundamental epistemological supposition, which he believes ties into this disenchanted condition, is that the growing recognition and awareness of the 'underdetermined' quality of reality makes it increasingly implausible to treat moral judgments as factual statements.[17] Questions about the 'ends' of human life, or the content of the 'good life' become, from a public standpoint, systemically open to debate and revision, for morality and law can no longer be derived or justified in terms of any substantive supra-individual reference. In this modern scenario individual choice and consent acquire a new moral significance, both in relation to the new autonomy individuals acquire for choosing the ends to which they orient their lives, and the methods by which deliberately enacted norms are legitimated.

Legal rational domination holds a privileged position in Weber's political sociology because it alone accords with his assessment of modernity as 'self-grounding.' In contrast to traditional structures of domination, where normative power flows from a belief in the inherent meaning of historical facts or revelation, modern authority is based on intentionally posited rules. Weber interprets legal domination as part of a modern cultural system that presumes the positivity of values and a will-centred conception of personhood – that is, a fundamental differentiation of knowledge of facts and judgments of value, and the importance of intentionality in the attribution of meaning to the 'facts' of the world.[18]

The concept of formal legal rationality represents, for Weber, all those attributes of the modern legal system that acknowledge in its forms and procedures that it is nothing more than an authoritatively posited set of norms, administered by a special staff. Of course, in Weber's view, all forms of domination reflect the historical legacy of particular patterns of human willing. What differentiates modern legal-rational authority from premodern traditional authority, however, is its self-consciousness about the nature and origin of norms. Every structure of authority, regardless of the legitimation principle on which it is based, is a product of normative evaluation, of an imposition of meaning-giving value on a morally neutral world. But only legal authority recognizes and incorporates the role of human volition within its 'cognitive style.' The importance of deliberate enactment of positive norms places humans at the centre of things, by assuming that values have legal import only insofar as they are related to purposive human attitudes. The modern legal system is a self-acknowledged artifact of human planning, a rational technical apparatus manipulable for the achievement of posited social ends.

The basis of modern authority in procedurally correct enactment relates to the modern normative importance of individual choice and consent. The core of legal authority is impersonal and procedural. Modern authority does not rest upon a conception of entitlements to specific substantive goods, nor does it mandate a particular set of social arrangements. Rather, modern authority, as Weber defines it in terms of formally correct enactment, rests on an idea of process. What the importance of impersonal procedures signifies is that the form of modern laws is always the same. Only the substantive content of law changes. The problem of value-rationality is solved by divorcing legal forms and procedures from legal content. While the form of law remains 'objective' and unchanging, the particular content of legal norms is an issue of value-preference that can only be determined through individual choice. The provision of legal content is a legislative responsibility that people delegate to legislators through the electoral process. Impersonal procedures are instruments for measuring and aggregating the choice of legal content; procedures are ways of arriving at decisions that, in some orderly way, will reflect what people choose. Legal authority rests upon the assumption that norms are made and not discovered. Just as the 'meaning' of the world can only be established by human volition, so the legitimacy of every binding norm in modernity is linked to its deliberate imposition by humans on a morally neutral world.

The history of modernity is marked by worries over its feasibility manifest in attempts to limit the meaning and application of its primary significations: individual autonomy and rational mastery. While the modern concept of the individual is universal in principle, attempts have been made to contain its impact within collectively controllable limits. Thus, for example, in the nineteenth century large portions of the population, the working class in particular and women in general, were deemed unfit for the responsible utilization of their autonomy. As modernizers have worked at the elimination of these boundaries to the application of the rule of individual choice, intentionally or not, a fuller social permeation of the concepts of modernity has resulted in an increasing disembedding of social relations based on customary norms and an emergent awareness of the cultural constructedness of norms in general.

Thus, although modernity has hitherto depended, culturally, and economically, on innumerable limits to the actualization of the organizational logic of individual choice and consent, its developmental history points unmistakeably in one direction: in modernity, the individual is the only point of reference for 'objectively' binding meanings or values. Ultimately, individuals are the only 'true' and 'real' objectivities. The ever more widely extended application of this principle represents a 'positivization' of values. The legal reconstitution of normative power in terms of procedurally correct enactment facilitates individual autonomy by recognizing the importance of intentionality and the individual positing of value preferences.

## 3.2 The Legal-Rational Reconstitution of Social Arrangements

Legal domination contributes to individual autonomy through the institutionalization of purposive-rational action within modern economic and political spheres. In Weber's view, the paradigmatic legal form of this kind of autonomy is the voluntary 'purposive' contract. Most interpretations of Weber's analysis of contractual association emphasize the functional relationship between contractual freedom and the capitalist market. But I wish to argue the significance of the institution of contract in terms of its relationship with the conception of knowledge and personhood that Weber believes underlie the modern sociological embodiment of individual autonomy.

In correspondence with his distinction between traditional and legal-rational authority, Weber contrasts 'status' and 'purposive' contractual agreements (ES, 672–4). Nowhere is the relationship between the purely formal rationality of legal order and the volitional origin of specific legal contents more apparent than in the characteristically modern institution of the 'purposive' contract [*Zweck-Kontrakt*], which contrasts with the 'status' contract of traditional structures of domination (ES, 672).

Traditional authority, Weber argues, is culturally and economically rooted in patrimonial relations of the household, where associations and 'rights' conferred upon individuals are largely determined by family membership, that is, by natural attributes belonging to the individual 'independently of his own acts of consociation' (ES, 669). As the example of marriage illustrates, the social identity of those who enter a status contract can be greatly transformed, for the status contract, Weber explains, 'involve[s] a change in what may be called the total legal situation (the universal position) and the social status of the persons involved' (ES, 672). The parties to a status contract believe that a successfully concluded agreement will in one way or another transform their identities and thus reconfigure their whole social existence. With a status contract, a person can 'become somebody's child, father, wife, brother, master, slave, kin, comrade-in-arms, protector, client, follower, vassal, subject, friend, or, quite generally, comrade' (ibid.). By contrast, the purposive contract presupposes the idea of the individual as a person who exists independently of the particular attributes that may be added or subtracted as a result of contractual arrangement. At the foundation of most status contracts is a belief in the normative validity of customary or 'natural' associations (such as networks of kinship), and reliance on magical or divine powers to consecrate the contracted bond (the marriage ceremony today remains a symbolic expression of the status contract).

A hallmark of modernity is the pervasive role of purposive contracts in the constitution of social relations. The distinction between premodern status contracts and modern purposive contracts implies differing conceptions of the status of values and the role of individuals in their creation. While status contracts imply natural or quasi-natural relationships patterned after the household or kinship community, purposive contracts refer to artificial relationships planfully created.

Through purposive contractual relationships individuals acquire rights through choice and consent. The legal order 'grants to an individual *autonomy* to *regulate* his *relations with others* by his own transactions' (ES, 668). The legitimacy of purposive contracts reflects the normative power of individual choice: the new social orientation created by the contract has no intrinsic legal meaning; its significance derives entirely from the intentions and purposes of the contracting parties. The distinction between premodern status contracts and modern purposive contracts reflects a contrast between the normative import of the naturally acquired and the deliberately created. The movement from status to purposive contractual associations signifies the increased importance, indeed centrality, of individual choice and its subsidiary form, consent, in the creation and validation of modern social relations. The legal enforcement of purposive contracts provides individuals with the kind of control over the purposes of their social conduct that is associated with the modern experience of 'freedom.'

Of course, the movement from status to purposive contractual relations also reflects the rise of the capitalist economic system: purposive contracts 'neither [affect] the status of the parties nor [give] rise to new qualities of comradeship but [aim] solely, as, for instance, barter, at some specific (especially economic) performance or result' (ES, 673). The archetypical purposive contract is the quantitative, qualityless, abstract, and usually economically conditioned agreement (ES, 674). Purposive contracts are 'the legal reflex of the market orientation of our society' (ES, 672).

The movement from status to purposive contractual relations is another barometer of the increasing formal rationality of the normative order in general. The legal facilitation of purposive contracts entails a comprehensive restructuring of social relations in terms of impersonality and rule-governance. The key feature of Weber's distinction between traditional and modern (legal) domination is the contrast between personal and impersonal forms of authority. Under traditional domination, social relations are stamped by the predominance of assumption and discretion. The hallmark of every 'personal' structure of authority – for instance, the traditional employment relationship between master and servant – is its inherently ambivalent character. The apprentice blacksmith, for example, could influence his master in a way which is impossible for a clerk in a bureaucratically structured multinational corporation. But personal relations of this type were also highly unpredictable: social proximity possesses awesome potential not only for love, self-sacrifice, and care but also for hatred, envy, and cruelty.

By contrast, modern legal domination is impersonal. This impersonality is not an accidental feature of modern social arrangements, but part and parcel of the way in which legal domination instates individual autonomy. Unlike the 'closed' cultural community of traditional civilization, where members are bound together in personal, affectively suffused, hierarchical relationships, modern society consists of an 'open' association of anonymous individuals who, connected by purposive rather than status contractual relations, freely pursue their own self-regarding aims and purposes. The role of legal domination in the construction of this modern social scenario involves the refurbishment of a 'public' space in which the social proximity of personal relations in a community is replaced by impersonality and distance between strangers.

The constitution of the property-owning legal subject as a bearer of economic 'rights' represented one of the first legal guarantees of individual 'freedom.' The rationalization of economic arrangements entailed by the institution of this early modern form of individual autonomy, namely, the reconstitution of social relations in terms of impersonality and rule-governance, is paradigmatic of the general and ongoing relationship between the formal legal rationality of modern social arrangements and the legal guarantee of 'freedom.' With the rationalization of economic arrangements, relations among individual commodity owners were subjected to a legal regulation tailored to strategically acting legal persons who enter into purposive contracts with one another. The formal rationalization of economic arrangements represented an opening of the economic sphere to the unchallenged rule of means-ends calculation and free-choice behaviour. In a sense, the rationalization of the economic sphere created a 'training ground' for the practice of individual autonomy, a sphere in which individuals could formulate their own purposes free from arbitrary political interference or noneconomic ethical considerations. From the eighteenth century onwards, the liberty and rights originally connected with the economy and the ownership of wealth were slowly extended to other spheres of social life and deepened to inhere in the very core of modern selfhood.

The growing importance of purposive contracts as a source of legal rights is linked, firstly, with the expansion of market exchange as a form of economic organization and, secondly, with the emergence of the liberal-constitutional state. Since the nineteenth century, the imagery of voluntary contractual association has been an important organizing principle in the 'public sphere' of economic action and political relations. Modern economic arrangements, for example, replace ascriptive occupational ties to indentured servitude, apprenticeship, and the like with formally free labour. Thus modern individuals can choose their occupations as part of the overall self-planning of their lives. In other words, they have more control over the *ends* of their lives. In a formal sense, modern societies are to an historically unprecedented degree comprised of voluntaristic arrangements which, in principle, offer individuals a virtually unlimited choice of ends towards which they may orient their actions. In the area of law, formal rationalization is the source of a 'subjective freedom' of world-historical importance. Legal formal rationality and the voluntary contract substitutes ascriptive status arrangements of traditional forms of authority for impersonally regulated voluntary contractual associations of legal-rational authority. In the twentieth century, this principle has made inroads into dimensions of social life previously defined as 'private,' such as sexuality, where relations once regulated by customary norms are now increasingly modelled after the pattern of voluntary contracts.

The link between purposive-rational economic conduct and the early modern experience of individual 'liberty' indicates the importance of impersonal, rule-oriented social relations in the legal constitution of modern autonomy. The indifferent objectivity of money transactions epitomizes this type of formally rational social relation. In *The Philosophy of Money*, Georg Simmel argues that money transactions between strangers are paradigmatic of modern social relations.[19] Money transactions require emotional neutrality: typically, they can tolerate neither friendship nor hostility. Money transactions are representative of objectified social relations in the way that expected and actual behaviour of the actors involved in the transaction is guided solely by the impersonal rules of the transaction itself rather than by the subjective qualities brought to the transaction by particular actors.[20] By formalizing social relations, money undermines traditional structures of domination in which power is manifest in terms of overt

interpersonal dependency. Money creates greater interpersonal freedom through impersonal exchange relations. Of course, the dominance
of money transactions makes human life more subject to bureaucratic
regulation and quantitative evaluation; the 'countertendencies' of legal
domination are discussed below.

The formal legal rationality of modern social arrangements promotes the realization of autonomy in terms of the increased scope for
purposive-rational conduct. Legal domination involves the creation of
a 'public sphere' in which norms based on the assumption and discretion of social proximity are replaced with legal code; personal and
spontaneous relations that are resistant to prediction, calculation, and
rational justification are replaced with purposeful and reciprocal relations that are rule-guided, universalizable, and accountable in terms of
means-ends rationality. A general characteristic of modernity is the
wide social and spatial extension of abstract systems of formalized
human interaction, embodied, for example, in the bureaucratic organization and the capitalist market. Formalization is a way of reconstituting elements of the social world with a view to enhancing its
calculability and productivity, through the efficient linking of means
and ends, the lengthening of chains of social interaction, and the
enlargement of scope for purposive-rational conduct.

The modern purposive contract presupposes a formally rational
system of law and the ideal of formal justice. Weber's conception of
formal legal rationality refers to a legal system in which norms are
expressed in general, abstract rules; the legal rules are distinct from
nonlegal norms and ordered in a self-contained and autonomous system. The formal rationality of modern law ensures the generality and
autonomy of legal norms and hence facilitates the calculation of the
legal consequences of individual actions. The formal rationality of the
administration of justice facilitates the prediction of the legal consequences of other individuals' or groups' actions.

According to Weber, this is the meaning behind the legal order's
guarantee of 'freedom': the ability of individuals to control and plan
their own lives is optimized by formal legal rationality. In terms of
the positivization of values and the elimination of ascriptive norms
discussed in the previous section, formal legal rationality opens value-
setting to individual choice. The elimination of ascriptive norms
represents a release of individual conduct from personal forms of domination in the sphere of economic and political conduct, thus disencumbering them from oppressive forms of social proximity found in

the traditional community scenario. Between the self and other there is only distance structured by legal rules of engagement. Individual autonomy is enhanced by the reduction of the power of the community to define the ends of individual conduct.

Formal legal rationality also enhances individual autonomy by increasing the calculability and predictability of the legal consequences of social action. In traditional civilization the particularism of legal norms and the ad hoc quality of their administration makes legal security, as we understand it, impossible. The difficulty of predicting the long-term legal consequences of social action tends to discourage non-stereotypical economic conduct. Legal domination opens opportunities and liberates individual capacities by maximizing the respect and scope for individual choice, which is exemplified by the institution of contractual association. The high degree of legal security that the formal legal rationality of modern social arrangements provides maximizes the ability of individuals to control their lives in a deliberate and planful manner. However, as Weber was well aware, the modern legal guarantee of freedom is riddled with contradictions.

## 4. Formal Legal Rationality versus Individual Autonomy

Weber uses the concept of formal legal rationality as a tool to explicate the ideal-typical character of modern power and authority. But the tightly interwoven connections between this form of rationalism and the conceptions of value and personhood that Weber believes underwrite modern individualism means that his philosophical attachment to the ideal of self-responsible individual autonomy frequently shades into a defence of the sociological expressions of formal legal rationality: capitalism, bureaucracy, and legal formalism.[21] Despite the ambiguity between empirical description and value-judgment in Weber's depiction and evaluation of modernity, his social thought is certainly no panegyric for formal legal rationality.[22] On the contrary, Weber identifies fundamental difficulties with the rationalism of modern social arrangements. As a result, his ultimate judgment of the ethical significance of formal legal rationality for modern individual autonomy is riven with ambivalence.

Weber's conception of formal legal rationality is rooted in liberal suppositions about individualism, intentionality, and the separation of fact and value; formal legal rationality is conceptually congruent with individual autonomy. But as an historically informed sociologist,

Weber also argues that the social instantiation of formal legal rationality has resulted in countertendencies unanticipated in Enlightenment and nineteenth-century liberal identifications of reason with emancipation. Asymmetrical relations of power were supposed to recede over time as 'reason' was progressively institutionalized in modern social arrangements. But Weber points out that, far from automatically promoting emancipation, the rationality of modern structures of power and authority, due to material inequalities which it perpetuates and legitimates, has in its practical effects actually qualitatively and quantitatively *increased* the experience of 'coercion' for a large segment of the population (ES, 731).

The dissonance between formal legal rationality and individual autonomy is reflected in Weber's distinction between formal and substantive rationality,[23] a distinction that itself reflects his more general thesis about the ineradicable tension between the rational calculation of efficacious relations between 'means' and 'ends' and the problem of determining the ends which the powers of calculation are to serve. Formal rationality corresponds to the adequacy of the *internal* relations between means and ends. Accordingly, in social arrangements that exhibit a high degree of formal rationality, all the information required for the selection of means, either efficacious to achievement of a given end or consistent with a given belief, is available within the action-system; here, 'rationality' does not refer to any criteria external to the action system. In contrast, the criteria of substantive rationality are *external* to the action system, that is, they refer to religious, ethical, or political value-postulates.

The more formally rational a system of law becomes, the more it is emancipated from extralegal norms. The distinction between a formal rationality measured in terms of 'internal' consistency and a substantive rationality measured in terms of consistency to 'external' criteria reveals that what is rational from an 'internal' perspective may seem irrational from 'outside.' The internal criteria that formal rationality sets for achieving a predictable and calculable legal result are not necessarily consonant with those external criteria defined by human 'needs.' One of the most important themes in Weber's depiction of modernity – and, as we shall see, perhaps one of the most enduring contributions of his legal theory – is the idea that formal and substantive rationality represent antinomical orientations to the world which have no unitary resolution.[24]

The complex of modern rational social arrangements and the institu-

tional functions designed to embody autonomy for all actually generate factual obstacles to the realization of individual autonomy. Here,
the conflict between formal and substantive rationality is illustrated
by the problems that the formal rationality of contractual association
generates for substantive autonomy. Additionally, the modern social
arrangements designed to facilitate the planful goal-setting of individuals tend in fact to erode the normative import of individual value
choices. In this instance the conflict between formal and substantive
rationality is illustrated by the problems that the formal rationality of
modern domination generates for substantive justification of authority.

### 4.1 Contractual Association and the Problem of Substantive Autonomy

Some of Weber's most trenchant criticism of formal legal rationality is
found in his discussions of the modern institution of purposive contractual association, specifically the wage-labour contract. As we saw
above, the purposive contract is an important legal expression of the
normative power of individual choice and agreement and of the opening of social relations to the planful goal-setting of individuals. Weber
views the growing predominance of legal rationality as a liberating triumph of reason in human affairs, but he also identifies this form of
rationalism as the source of a number of substantive irrationalities that
tend to limit the experience of freedom for a large segment of the population. The institutionalization of purposive contract and increasing
centrality of social relations determined on the basis of 'free' agreement, Weber argues, 'implies a relative reduction of that kind of coercion which results from the threat of mandatory and prohibitory
norms' (ES, 730). But it is not difficult to imagine how this state of
affairs would produce asymmetrical advantages for those who are economically in the position to exploit their legal empowerments. Thus,
Weber argues, a legal order may contain few 'mandatory or prohibitory norms' and ever so many 'freedoms' and 'empowerments' but
'nonetheless in its practical effects facilitate a quantitative and qualitative increase not only of coercion in general but quite specifically of
authoritarian coercion' (ES, 731).

Thus the formal legal rationality of the structure of modern power
and authority provides a formal opportunity for the individual liberation of capacities. But, Weber argues, 'the great variety of permitted
contractual schemata and the formal empowerment to set the content
of contracts in accordance with one's desires and independently of all

official form patterns, in and of itself by no means makes sure that these formal possibilities will in fact be available to all and everyone' (ES, 729). The availability of opportunities to take advantage of the freedoms that formal legal rationality afford is above all else determined by differences in the distribution of property. Weber argues, in a tone reminiscent of Marx, 'the exact extent to which the total amount of "freedom" within a given community is actually increased depends entirely upon the concrete economic order and especially upon the property distribution' (ES, 730).

The archetypical example of the ethical issues raised by the purposive contract and formal legal rationality is the conflict between capital and labour occasioned by contractual relations of employment. The impersonality of modern social arrangements facilitates the purposive, planful conduct of individuals. In the modern employment situation, for example, this means the elimination of forms of vocational ascription based on tradition or kinship. Compared to indentured servitude or entailed apprenticeship, contractual association allows the modern individual to define her economic relationships according to preference, and this choice contributes significantly to the individual capacity to control one's own life in a planful fashion. The problem, of course, is that without the material resources to take advantage of such legal empowerments and to make decisions 'effective,' contractual freedom, particularly in the economic arena of employment contracts, is meaningless. The purposive contract must presuppose a formal equality between contracting parties that is rendered merely nominal by actual differences in wealth and need. For example, an individual with insufficient resources to establish her own business is forced by the 'laws' of the market to sell her time and labour to others who do possess such resources; she must subject herself to the commands of another person. Even under a system of formal legal rationality, 'coercion is exercised to a considerable extent by the private owners of the means of production and acquisition, to whom the law guarantees their property and whose power can thus manifest itself in the competitive struggle of the market' (ES, 730). Weber further argues that the liberty of an economically privileged minority is ultimately purchased at the expense of a qualitative and quantitative increase in the experience of coercion for the majority, who are now subjected to an undiluted rule of the market, a rule of the economically advantaged minority.

The 'free' wage-labour contract, which individuals may or may not enter but which the average person's economic powerlessness forces that person to accept, in combination with the impersonal structure of domination of the economic market, may represent an actual increase in the overall coercion that most individuals experience. Whereas the 'personal' structure of domination behind the traditional employment relationship depended upon 'the personal *wills* of the participants' and thus was more easily 'subjected to ethical requirements and ethically regulated,' the modern employment situation diminishes the degree of personal control that individuals exercise over their employment situation 'in inverse ratio to the degree of rational differentiation of the economic structure' (ES, 585). For instance, Weber writes, 'the rationalization of economic structures of power effectively eliminates any "caritative regulation" in the relationships between stockholders and factory workers, between tobacco importers and foreign plantation workers, or between industrialists and the miners who have dug from the earth the raw materials used in the plants owned by the industrialists' (ibid.). The abolition of direct forms of personal servitude and the expansion of contractual freedom represent an increase in 'real freedom.' However, by eliminating all obligations of brotherliness and all spontaneous human feelings from the impersonal logic of profit calculation, the formal legal rationality of 'labour market transactions' reduces the control held by individuals over their economic existence (ES, 636).

While the authoritarian-hierarchical constraints experienced by the traditional worker were compensated by the ineffaceable affectual elements that inhered to the personal structure of traditional occupational relationships, the authoritarian-hierarchical constraints that persist in the modern bureaucratically disciplined factory or office are that much more exacting. No longer restrained by sentimental attachments, they are governed by the pure calculus of profit, without regard for the needs of particular persons. The loss of control experienced by the majority of individuals transforms the formal freedom of contractual association upon which the capitalist order is based into an 'iron cage' that guarantees the preservation of existing disparities in wealth.

Formal legal rationality vastly extends our capacity to subject human relationships to the impersonal 'laws' of the marketplace, to turn relationships between people into commodities that are bought and sold. In November 1994, British Prime Minister John Major called for 'capitalism with a conscience.' Business and industry leaders, he insisted, must recognize 'wider responsibilities than to make profits for shareholders' by embracing charitable activities and avoiding 'unjustifiable pay rises' that provoke public resentment.[25] But as Weber would have advised him, 'it is impossible to control a universe of instrumentally rational activities by charitable appeals to particular individuals' (ES, 585). For individuals within the economic universe, the only sensible course of action is to look after their own interests in a purposive-rational fashion; 'The functionalized world of capitalism' offers only incidental forms of support for 'charitable orientations.' 'The growing impersonality of the economy on the basis of association in the marketplace follows its own rules, disobedience to which entails economic failure and, in the long run, economic ruin' (ES, 585).

The problems generated by the purposive contract for the realization of substantive individual autonomy are illustrative of the conflict between a formal legal rationality that places a premium on the predictability and calculability of legal processes and a substantive legal rationality based on some conception of good or scheme of distributive justice. From a standpoint that views individual autonomy as the 'purpose' of modern social arrangements, the effective nullification of autonomy through the economic coercion and loss of control experienced by a large segment of the population represents the substantive irrationality of legal domination. This tension between formal and substantive rationality reflects a real social conflict between those groups interested in and benefitting from the formal legal rational provision of legal calculability and efficiency and those interested in and benefitting from the substantive regulation of economic and social life in the name of fraternity and *caritas*.

The conflict between an abstract formalism of legal certainty and the desire to realize substantive goals corresponds with the contradiction between the formal equality presupposed by the purposive contract and the actual inequalities of wealth and need between contracting individuals. Because the modern institution of contractual freedom is tied into the formal rationality of the legal system and a formalist conception of justice, the ethical issues raised by the contradiction between 'formal' and 'effective' contractual freedom have generated political demands for countermeasures embodying substantive legal rationality (ES, 811).

With respect to legal rationality, juridical formalism always appeals 'to those who on ideological grounds' wish to open up 'individual opportunities and liberating capacities' (ES, 813). Economically privileged groups who derive their power from market transactions have a strong interest in maximizing formal rationality: 'capitalist interests will fare best under a rigorously formal system of adjudication which applies in all cases and operates under the adversary system of procedures,' that employs 'a systematized, unambiguous, and specialized formal law' (ES, 814). Formal legal rationality is advantageous to those groups who are in a position 'to make use of their empowerments.' These groups have a strong interest in maximizing formal rationality and its erosion presents the likelihood of arbitrariness and 'subjectivistic instability' (ES, 813).

But economically or symbolically disadvantaged groups have an equally strong interest in subjecting economic life to substantive regulation. From their perspective, the promotion of individual opportunity depends on subjecting economic and social power to substantive regulation, and thus reducing the formal rationality of the structure of domination. As Weber writes, 'in their eyes justice and administration should serve to equalize their economic and social life-opportunities in the face of the propertied classes. Justice and administration can fulfil this function only if they assume a character that is informal because "ethical" with respect to substantive content ...' (ES, 980).

Weber preferred a legal system that exhibits a high degree of formal rationality with maximum calculability and predictability. The universal and fixed norms and rule-bound adjudication of legal formalism greatly increases the possibility of predicting the legal consequences of actions and thus guarantees to individuals optimal conditions for self-determination and a 'relative maximum of freedom' (ES, 811). But the substantive experience of freedom depends upon the location of individuals within the order of property distribution (ES, 730). From the standpoint of nonlegal values, such as the postulates of religious ethics or the political interests of oppressed groups, juridical formalism is substantively irrational because legal consideration of the concrete conditions of social inequality are not only systematically excluded but time and again reinforced by the formal rationality of justice. The tension between formal legal rationality and its substantive irrationality from the standpoint of the values of fraternity and *caritas* is, Weber states, 'one of the most important sources of all modern "social" problems' and an 'unavoidable element of irrationality in economic systems' (ES, 111).

### 4.2 Modern Authority and the Problem of Substantive Justification

Weber's conception of legal-rational authority exposes the modern problem of substantively rational social arrangements. The principle of legitimacy characteristic of modern society, Weber argues, is formally correct enactment: procedural consistency with an existing body of rules. The binding power of legal authority and the significance of procedural consistency and formally correct enactment are linked to the normative force of choice and consent. Formal legal rationality is tied to individual autonomy. Modern social arrangements and institutional functioning are transparent to human reason, open to the value-setting of individuals, and facilitative of the purposive planful action of individuals.

In Weber's positivistic theory of value, values do not inhere in facts and moral evaluations are logically disjunct from cognitive understandings of the world. The differentiation of value-spheres exposed to our awareness by the processes of modernization represents both an opening and an emptying of the human condition. The human condition is 'opened' since, in the absence of objectively valid meanings, individuals must legislate them into existence through an act of decision. The structural concomitant of the disenchantment of God-willed hierarchy is the hypostatization of individual responsibility for value-setting. A pregiven framework of value is either rationally fulfilled or is itself rationalized. Either way, the value-position itself is, at a fundamental level, arbitrary, a product of revelation, convention, or choice. In a post-traditional age, values do not inhere in cognitive understandings; individuals 'must create them, must legislate them into existence' by imposing their will on 'a morally neutral world.'[26]

Despite the loss of moral certitude, the positivization of values contributes to the modern experience of freedom. The idea of 'personal autonomy,' argues Joseph Raz, is the 'vision of people controlling, to some degree, their own destiny, fashioning it through successive decisions throughout all their lives'; the 'ruling idea' is to be 'author' of one's own life.[27] As the earlier discussions of legal-rational authority indicate, the normative force of modern authority is not, for example, based on the imposition of a particular conception of the 'good,' but rather the efficacy of volitionally determined values expressed in the form of choice or consent. Understood as artifacts of human action instead of descriptions of the world or divine commandments, social norms are opened to calculated intervention and deliberate (re)organization. This rationalization unlocks the 'ends' of social action from the constraints of ascriptive norms, thereby enhancing the 'subjective' freedom of individuals. Modernization has transformed 'closed' communities of shared substantive values into 'open' associational societies characterized by value-pluralism and the 'autonomous' personality.

Moral, religious, and aesthetic ideals become redefined as private concerns in modernity because their 'objective' applicability could only be secured by ontological criteria of justification that are no longer philosophically viable: 'the ultimately possible attitudes toward life are irreconcilable' (FMW, 152). This retreat of value into the pianissimo of personal preference is reflected in the purely formal character of the rationality of modern social arrangements. The only real source of value-rationality in the modern world is the individual 'endowed with the capacity and the will to take a deliberate attitude towards the world and lend it *significance*' (MSS, 81). Guided between the antinomical possibilities of the ethics of 'conviction' and 'responsibility,' modern individuals must heroically create weight and direction in life where none exists to begin with (FMW, 122).

With the differentiation of value-spheres and the emergence of a secular culture the modern human condition is also 'emptied.' The traditional conception that normative order to some extent precedes human will endows individual life with weight and direction, just as the traditional conception that social arrangements precede human will endows them with a meaning and weight that is absent in deliberately fabricated arrangements. This sense of weight and direction is difficult to reinvent through self-conscious enactment.[28] While the modern culture of self-realization liberates individuals from sacred and customary restraints, unleashing human capacities and creativities in an unprecedented manner, the primacy of the self-realizing individual, with its emphasis on the volitional source of values, also threatens a peculiar form of senselessness. As Alasdair MacIntyre argues, the price paid for individual liberation from the external authority of sacred and customary norms is the loss of authoritative content in the value-choices of autonomous self-defining individuals.[29]

Weber's conception of modern legal authority, in particular, his conception of legitimacy based on formally correct enactment, on *legality*, provokes endless criticism.[30] As discussed above, the principle of legitimation behind Weber's conception of modern authority appears tautological in character: the legitimacy of a legal rule is based on its formal correctness vis-à-vis its conformity with the existing legal order, and this order is in turn justified by its enactment in accordance with the procedural requirements of the legal order.[31] Habermas complains that Weber elaborates the formal features of law (its 'internal rationality'), by virtue of which it can fulfil the functional imperatives of depersonalized administration and economic commerce (i.e., the 'system rationality' of modern law) but does not explain 'the structural properties in virtue of which it can fulfil these functions.'[32] Weber's account of modern law, Habermas argues, thus fails to provide an adequate treatment of its justificatory dimension, its 'normative rationality.'

I offer here two responses to such critiques. First, formal legal rationality is not altogether devoid of 'value.' On the contrary, it is precisely the moral significance of individual choice and consent in the modern world that finds its structural correlate in the formal and instrumental character of legal authority. The subjective meaning for actors who accept legality as a basis of legitimacy is analogous to the subjective meaning of purposive-rational action – that is, not oriented towards any *particular* values, but rather to the acceptance of a generalized 'means' for the achievement of ends chosen by actors themselves. Legal domination commands allegiance because its impersonal structure, stripped of the restrictions that customary and traditional norms place on individual action, provides a relative maximum scope for purposive-rational, free choice behaviour.

Weber's account of modern law does articulate a 'justificatory dimension.' It is less robust than the desiderata of his critics, but then, given Weber's existential epistemology, he is much more pessimistic about the possibility for value-consensus in modern societies. The formal legal rationality of modern authority, Weber argues, 'enables the legal system to operate like a technically rational machine' that 'guarantees to individuals and groups within the system a relative maximum of freedom' (ES, 811). Formal legal rationality facilitates individual autonomy in terms of enhancing the capacity for purposeful, planful action via the legal security of a predictable and calculable social environment of action. The 'end' towards which formal legal rationality is oriented is not a substantive conception of freedom as embodying a particular content or way of life, but rather freedom in terms of an indiscriminate facilitation of the purposeful pursuit of a variety of substantive ends.

What Weber's critics want to argue is that the 'rationality' of modern law embodies evaluative criteria or a justificatory principle that is nonidentical with procedural form. In some manner they argue for the existence of resources within the rational structure of the modern legal order on the basis of which a 'bad' law, however correctly enacted, can be determinately identified as 'unjust.' However, the way in which

Bills of Rights are constitutionally adjudicated illustrates with painful clarity the nonavailability of such a 'normative rationality' in the actual mechanics of modern authority (see Chapter 6).

Weber's depiction of the formal legal rationality of modern power and authority is not an attractive one, and he had no doubt that political and legal theorists would be reluctant to relinquish the notion of a 'metapositive law above that merely technical positive law which is acknowledged to be subject to change' (ES, 888). Nevertheless, his model remains an apposite sociological characterization of the way in which legal rationality functions in modern societies. Weber's formalistic and positivistic conception of legal-rational authority seeks to highlight that, in the modern age, the legal system, like modern social arrangements in general, is characteristically rational in a purely formal sense. Though its procedures and means may be highly systematized, the potential *content* of modern legislation is radically *open*.

Beyond the jurisdictional and the procedural, the only substantive restraints on the norm-making capacities of legislatures are various quasi-constitutional conventions, such as the universal franchise and the various freedoms over property disposal, belief, association, speech, and so on. The real restraint on legislative powers to alter the substance of such conventions is the accountability of legislators to the electorate. But this process of accountability is itself a rather fragile restraint. Nancy Schwartz, in her critique of Weber's conception of legal-rational authority, argues that 'legislation cannot go in any direction; it must include substantive, natural law preconditions, such as the notion of moral equality.'[33] But in what sense is modern legislation held to account by substantive preconditions built into the rationality of legal order? The United States has had a Bill of Rights since the early nineteenth century. But even a legal order grounded upon one of the clearest and most robust expressions of natural rights doctrine could not, for example, prevent the internment of Americans of Japanese descent during the Second World War and, consequently, the abrogation of their civil liberties.[34] The heuristic value of Weber's conception of legal domination is its cautionary sense of the inherent limitations of legal rationality, and of modern rationalism in general.

This ties into my second response to critiques of the formalism and positivism of Weber's depiction of modern law. The reason why the ideal-typical principle of legitimacy in modernity is so empty of content, so formal, and so circular has to do with the kinds of justice that are possible for autonomous moral agents unconstrained by the externalities of divine law, natural teleology, or hierarchical authority. The rational irreconcilability of value-judgments represents the limits of rationality as an organizing principle for modern social arrangements. According to Weber's positivistic theory of value, only a narrow range of social policy issues, those which involve no conflict over ends or values, have legally determinate or formally rational solutions. What makes critics of Weber's merely formal definition of legitimacy particularly anxious is the implication that, with the principle of the sovereignty of individual choice and consent that ties the competence to make law to democratic will-formation, modern legal-rational authority holds an inextirpable potential for majoritarian tyranny: a validity principle based solely on formal rationality will allow 'bad' laws to be as easily enacted by intolerant majorities as 'good' laws are enacted by enlightened minorities. Weber's model of legal rationality suggests that the legal order can provide only partial protection from tyranny. In other words, we cannot endlessly draw on the notion of legal rationality as a panacea for the ethical problems generated by the powers of modern social arrangements.

Weber's conception of formal legal rationality highlights the power and perils of modernity. For the individual, the instrumentality of the modern legal order represents the opportunity for 'self-realization,' while for the collective it offers greatly enhanced powers of control over the universe of social relations. However, paraphrasing MacIntyre, the price paid for this liberation from the external authority of sacred and customary norms is the loss of authoritative norms valid independently of, and superior to, positive law. The danger inherent in the modern situation is that, in an age in which justification is even less restrained by either a non-human or a supra-individual dimension than it has been in the past, the people who inhabit Weber's 'iron cage' could, in principle, come to justify almost any form of abomination.[35]

## 5. Weber's Disillusioned Affirmation of Formal Legal Rationality

The modern experience of freedom is indebted to the legal reconstitution of modern power and authority. On the one hand, the freedom-guaranteeing capacity of legal rationality is tied into the merely formal and procedural conceptions of legitimate authority. The significance for Weber of the modern legitimation principle of formally correct enactment is that it places individual consent at the heart of the value-setting power of modern authority. Here, modern autonomy is linked to the free choice over the configuration of social arrangements. But the freedom-guaranteeing capacity of legal rationality is also tied into the elimination of traditional social action based on conformance with ascriptive norms and the emergence of social conduct purposive-rationally regulated on the basis of mutual agreement. Weber considers 'purposive'-contractual association the paradigmatic modern social relation. Here, the expanded scope for purposive-rational action is tied into free choice *within* the formal rationality of social, and especially economic, arrangements. But despite the structural congruence of formal legal rationality and individual autonomy, Weber is deeply ambivalent about the legacy of legal domination for the modern experience of freedom. The formal rationality of modern structures of power and authority generates impediments for the realization of substantive forms of individual autonomy; in other words, the freedom-guaranteeing capacity of modern legal rationality is merely formal in scope.

Weber's analysis of the issues of substantive autonomy and substantive justification illustrates the decisive but proximal connection between formal legal rationality and individual autonomy. Modernity means the elimination of customary restraints on individual conduct that follows the disintegration of the authoritarian-hierarchical structure of traditional domination; the growing impersonality of economic and political arrangements; the regulation of social life through abstract, general norms; the growing indispensability of specialized expertise; and the increasingly instrumental, self-interested orientation of social conduct in all spheres of life. All of these features of modern life point in the direction of enhanced means-ends rationality; each contributes in a general way to the 'opening' and 'emptying' of modern conditions of life.

This is the context in which the relationship between individual autonomy and formal legal rationality must be placed. Weber believes that formal legal rationality reflects an underlying philosophical content of individualism, intentionality, and the separation of facts and values. The structure of modern social arrangements is transparent to human reason, open to the goal-setting of individuals, and facilitates purposive planful conduct. While the rationalism of modern social arrangements guarantees individuals 'a relative maximum of freedom,' it also results in the depersonalization and growing salience of calculation in all spheres of life. The distinction between formal and substantive rationality reflects the fact that, far from automatically promoting the project of individual autonomy, the rationalism of modern social arrangements generates factual obstacles to the substantive realization of autonomy which are morally and politically problematic.

In Weber's discussion of modern capitalism, for instance, economic action that exploits money, capital accounting, and 'free' wage labour attains the highest degree of calculability over the entire production process, and thus, according to Weber, exhibits the highest degree of formal rationality. In such an economic system, the freedom of individual economic action is maximal, in that noneconomic constraints on the exploitation and disposal of resources both material and human are minimized, while the scope of various economic options is maximized. But such formally rational economic action, oriented solely towards profit and governed only by the 'laws' of supply and demand on the open exchange market, produces a number of substantively irrational results.

The problematic antinomy between the formal legal-rational guarantee of freedom and the potential for substantive nullification of individual autonomy in the economic sphere is paradigmatic of the countertendencies generated by the rational design of modern social arrangements. The elimination of ascriptive, prohibitory norms and the provision of legal empowerments to freely determine the contents of one's own social obligations represent an historical liberation of individual capacities for self-elaboration and realization. In practice, of course, such a liberation of 'capacities' facilitates the exploitation of economic resources and thus inevitably works to the advantage of the powerful. Lack of property, and lack of economic power in general, generate significant limitations on the ability to exploit legally guaranteed liberties. Although contractual freedom represents a progressive development in the ideal of formal equality and the power of individual choice and consent, because workers are coerced into contracts and subjected to the designs of other, the autonomy of a majority segment of the population is effectively nullified in the sphere of economic relations. As one might summarize, 'all this is seen by socialism as the "domination of people by things", in other words, the domination of the end (the supply of needs) by the means' (ST, 253).

However, the solution to the problem of the substantively irrational consequences of formal legal rationality, Weber argues, cannot be solved simply through the increase of substantive rationality without introducing negative consequences of another kind for the realization of autonomy. The realization of substantive rationality means a sacrifice in the generality of legal norms, the uniformity of adjudication, and the autonomy of the legal order – and hence the reduction of the calculability and predictability of legal processes, and, in effect, the politicization of the legal system. Because there can be no rational solution to the problem of competing ethical standards, the articulation of substantive justice within a modern post-traditional legal system can only be effective when given force by arbitrary political interventions into the administration of justice (ES, 845). Debates in the United States and elsewhere over the issue of affirmative action programs illustrate the conflict between the formal rationality of 'equality before the law' and the substantive rationality of ethical compensation for symbolic and/or economic disadvantage. Attempts to introduce some form of 'ethical compensation' within the machinery of legal order will inevitably be experienced by some individuals and groups as arbitrary, hence political, tampering with the autonomy and generality of the legal order.

Weber's endorsement of the formal legal rational order is tempered by a disillusioned awareness of its inherent limitations as a method for the promotion of individual autonomy.[36] Nevertheless, Weber affirms the formal legal-rational guarantee of individual autonomy, despite the substantively irrational outcomes endemic to its actual functioning. The link between a calculable, predictable legal order and individual autonomy may be indirect but it is highly important. Weber denies the possibility of a value-rational mediation of 'fact' and 'value' precisely to underscore the insoluble problem of substantive justification. The theme of ineradicable conflict between formal and substantive rationality, coupled with Weber's disillusioned affirmation of formal legal rationality, serves to underscore and accentuate the disjunction between 'law as order' and 'law as justice,' between the instrumentalities of modern power and the ethical question of their valid uses, which Weber believes the disenchantment and rationalization of the world irreversibly expose.

Weber's denial of the possibility of a 'normative rationality' also serves to highlight the importance of unending vigilance and resolute will in the maintenance of the conditions for individual autonomy. Weber comes out on the side of formal legal rationality because of a fundamental article of faith: the long-term prospects for individual autonomy in the modern world depend upon *forcing* individuals to be free to choose.[37] For not only is the modern cosmos of rational order structurally incapable of supplying the cardinal references for the guidance of human conduct, it is constitutionally capable of facilitating the rational development of an inhuman plan.[38] As Weber argues in a 1906 article on the prospects for democracy in Russia, there is no 'elective affinity' between the rationalism of modern social arrangements (such as capitalism and a bureaucratically organized state) and 'liberal democracy' (ST, 282). The preservation of the conditions for individual autonomy and democratic government cannot be trusted to formal legal rationality alone; such values must be 'supported by the resolute *will* of a nation not to allow itself to be led like a flock of sheep' (ibid.). In other words, freedom is something that must be *practised* lest we become a collection of ghosts prowling around within the machinery of society. For, as Weber argues, if laws and institutions are capable of being turned around and pointed in a variety of directions, liberty can never be assured by any particular institutions or legal arrangements alone. Weber the 'disillusioned realist' eschews the liberal mythology that identifies freedom with legal reason and the 'rule of law.' Liberty can never be inherent in the structure of things per se. Particular institutional arrangements, however rational or utilitarian in design, cannot promote individual autonomy without also getting in the way of it.

# CHAPTER THREE

# The Developmental History of Modern Law

Interpretation of legal phenomena plays a key role in both Weber's account of the development of the West and his conception of the 'specific and peculiar rationalism' of modern social arrangements: the rationalization of Western law is at the centre of Weber's sociology of law, just as the legalization of modern economic and political structures of power (capitalism and bureaucracy) could be said to form a central theme in his sociology of modernity. The pattern of modern social arrangements and institutional functions evinces a high degree of formal rationality, expressed in terms of transparency to reason, impersonality, and orientation towards control. This formal rationality also presumes a positivistic conception of value and a will-centred conception of personhood. Weber's conception of 'formal legal rationality' is indeed the core of his substantive sociology of modernity.

Yet, few other areas of Weber's work have been the subject of more sustained misrepresentation and stubborn controversy than his account of legal rationalization and conception of formal legal rationality. The past ten to fifteen years have witnessed a renascence in the study of Weber's social and political thought, and his sociology of law has attracted particular attention.[1] But the critical response to Weber's legal thought has remained fairly consistent: his accounts of legal rationalization and the rise of modern legal domination have been found contradictory, while his conception of modern legal rationality has been criticized for divorcing the justification of authority from substantive moral norms.[2]

Nevertheless, Weber's legacy continues to cast a long shadow, and nowhere is this more conspicuous than in Habermas's increasingly law-centred critical social theory.[3] Focusing on Habermas's influential critique of Weber, my aim is to reveal the inner coherence of Weber's often discredited sociology of law with his highly influential sociology of modernity and, in the process, to defend the heuristic value of his legal thought for the interpretation of contemporary legal development undertaken in the following chapters. As we will see, Weber's sociology of law offers a challenge to Habermas's increasing reliance on modern law to enhance democratic possibilities in the West, that is, to gain ethical influence over economic and political organizations through the putative 'normative rationality' of legal reason, and to pursue the project of individual emancipation through the continued legalization of power and authority. The more legal rationalization is tied to the general socio-historical process of rationalization in the West, as Weber insists, the more legal norms and institutions are implicated in the modern social pathologies that Habermas, following Weber, attributes to the unintended consequences of rationalization: the loss of freedom and meaning associated with capitalism and state bureaucracies. Although Habermas criticizes Weber for connecting modern legal rationality to the expansion of those subsystems of purposive rational economic and administrative action that steer a social intercourse largely disconnected from norms and values, he seems forced to agree that this type of rationality does indeed dominate modern culture.

## 1. Legal Rationalization and the Rise of Modern Capitalism

Weber's sociology of law contains two separate but frequently undifferentiated topics of investigation: on one level, a 'sociology of jurisprudence,' which documents the process of increasing rationalization in Western legal thought, specifically the development of 'logically' formal legal rationality as exemplified in the codified civil law of Continental Europe;[4] on another level, a 'sociology of domination' that focuses on the social dimensions of legal development, that is, the relationship between the development of 'extrinsically' formal legal rationality – the calculability and predictability of legal order – and the rise of modern capitalism.[5] The historical origins of modern legal domination and the legal rationalization of modern structures of economic and political power, Weber argues, involved 'a certain conjunction of unique and unrepeatable conditions,' the most important of which were, firstly, 'certain ideal values' and 'distinct religious beliefs' and,

secondly, 'the peculiar economic and social structure of the "early capitalist" epoch in Western Europe' (ST, 282–3). The sociology of jurisprudence is concerned with the narrow type of logically formal legal
thought and the intrajuristic factors behind its creation that function
relatively autonomous of direct economic conditioning; by contrast,
the sociology of domination is concerned with the more general category of 'formal law as such,' or extrinsically formal legal rationality
and its 'elective affinity' with the material interests of an emergent
capitalist order.[6]

Within the 'sociology of jurisprudence' Weber distinguishes between
the 'empirical legal training' of English law and the academic-style
training of the Continent. The English system involves the teaching of
law as a craft: 'apprentices learn from practitioners more or less in the
course of actual legal practice' (ES, 784). The empirical training typi-
fied by the long-standing practices of the English Inns of Courts and
their guild-like monopolization of the legal profession, Weber argues,
tends to impede the logical systematization of the legal order (ES, 787–
8).[7] In contrast to the view of law as 'craft,' 'academic' legal training in
Continental law treats law as a science, and legal thought is oriented
to the elaboration of the legal order in a rigorous systematic fashion
(ES, 789).

Continental legal training had an indelible impact on the direction of
legal rationalization insofar as the 'ideal interest' embodied in the
imperative of logical consistency that it inculcated in juristic practice
competed with, and occasionally prevailed over, the material interests
represented in practical needs. As Weber writes, the consequences of
legal developments in the direction of increasing systematization and
logical formalism 'often bear very irrational or even unforeseen relations to the expectations of the commercial interests' (ES, 855).[8] The
legal theorists trained in this tradition acquired ideal interests in the
rigorous, abstract systematization of legal rules that, on occasion, even
controverted economic interests. Weber argues that the development
of specific intrajuristic contents of modern law has also been only indirectly influenced by economic factors.

Employing this distinction between logically and extrinsically formal law helps to eliminate confusions over the issue of the relationship
between legal and economic rationalization, between ideal and material interests. In some places Weber argues that law is only indirectly
influenced by economic factors; for instance in the development of the
intrajuristic features of law, he claims, 'the prevailing type of legal edu-

cation, i.e., the mode of training of the practitioners of the law, has been more important than any other factor' (ES, 776). In other places, Weber argues that law has a 'strong' influence on economic development (ES, 655). He also argues elsewhere that important features of modern law are a 'reflex' of the market orientation of modern society (ES, 672). If we examine the instances in which Weber argues that law is relatively free of economic conditioning, however, we find that he is always referring to specific intrajuristic features, such as specific legal institutions and doctrines, which vary from country to country. Also, if we examine the instances in which he contends that legal development exerts a 'strong' influence on the development of economic relations, we see that such arguments always relate, first, to his interpretation of the early modern influence of logically formal legal rationality (and/or specific intrajuristic features of law) or, second, to his interpretation of the early modern development of extrinsically formal legal-rational domination, which, as we will see, is a development influenced by ideal factors, such as the belief in a 'higher' law and the search for a post-traditional basis of authority in early modern Europe. Finally, if we examine the instances in which Weber argues that economic factors exert the strongest influence on legal development, we see that such arguments always pertain to the relationship between capitalism in its clearly unfolded economic complexity and modern legal development in its extrinsic formal rationality.

Commentary on Weber's sociology of law frequently seizes upon the so-called English-problem to illustrate what appears to be a serious inconsistency in his explanatory connection of formal legal rationality with the rise of modern capitalism.[9] In a nutshell, the problem is that, historically, England entered into the development of modern capitalism before Continental Europe, and did so with a legal system that was (and still is), according to Weber's typology of legal rationality, less formally rational than Continental legal systems. Consequently, for example, Trubek concludes that Weber's account of the relationship between legal development and the rise of capitalism contradicts the historical record.[10] Having failed to distinguish between extrinsically and logically formal legal rationality, this line of interpretation alleges that Weber argued for the structural congruence of logically formal legal rationality with modern capitalism – that is, Weber allegedly argues that *only* the logically formal rationality of Continental law produces the legal certainty required by modern capitalistic economic activity.[11]

Logically formal rational legal thought systematizes the rules of the legal order in a comprehensive and conceptually transparent fashion; this systematization can lead potentially to a maximum degree of calculability. But what the example of England illustrates is that modern capitalism does not require an environment of maximal legal calculability. The common law of England and the Civil Code of the Continent are simply variants of a larger pattern of extrinsically formal rational legal order. Despite differences in the types of legal training and related structures of domination between England and, say, Germany – in England, casuistic empirical jurisprudence, centralized justice, and rule by notables; in Germany, systematized theoretical jurisprudence and the growth of bureaucratic organization in spite of the absence of political centralization (ES, 977) – both legal systems guaranteed in toto a substantive legal calculability sufficient to facilitate purposive-rational economic conduct. The English judge was strictly bound to precedents and thus to calculable schemes just as the judge in a bureaucratic state like Bismarck's Germany was an 'automaton of paragraphs.' In its own fashion, each system defended the freedom of contract and protected property rights.[12]

From the perspective of the sociology of jurisprudence the fact that 'modern capitalism prospers equally and manifests essentially identical economic traits under legal systems containing rules and institutions which considerably differ from each other' (ES, 890; see also ES, 892) illustrates that capitalism has a very indirect and possibly a weak effect on the *intrajuristic* features of law. Logically formal legal thought, the most systematic and rational expression of law according to Weber's typology of legal rationality, arose in ancient Rome and was later adopted in medieval Catholic countries long before the advent of even early modern capitalism. Intrajuristic factors, such as the imperatives of legal science oriented to the perfection of the juridical form, were behind the development of a pure formal rationality that contributed to an increasing legal calculability and predictability. The early modern invention of formal legal rational modes of thought and legal techniques proved important for laying down the 'tracks' of economic and political development (ES, 687).

From the perspective of the sociology of domination, the extrinsically formal legal rationality of modern legal domination is, despite noneconomically influenced variations in institutions and substantive doctrines between the legal systems of various nation states, covalent with Western capitalism in general. Modern capitalism, based as it is

on continuous rational enterprise and the purposive contractual relations between economic actors, requires the calculable legal environment provided by a rigorously formal system of adjudication and
political administration in accordance with impersonal rules (ES, 814;
ST, 339). As long as substantive 'irrational' elements of law prevailed,
such as the jurisdiction of ecclesiastical courts over land cases, a calculable basis for capitalist investment and production through the exploitation of land was impossible (ES, 823). By placing limitations on
patrimonial discretion and guaranteeing subjective rights to establish
legally binding contractual relations, the extrinsic formal rationality of
the legal order contributed to the predictability of economic and
administrative action, thus facilitating the development of modern
capitalism. In the context of the relationship between legal development and the early modern rise of capitalism, Weber argues that
extrinsically formal legal rationality had a 'strong influence' on economic development: the structure of legal domination can induce the
emergence of certain economic relations (ES, 655, 667). Though capitalism would eventually contribute to the propagation of the formal legal
rationality of social relations, originally, it could not cultivate the rationalism of such relations alone. This relationship between capitalism
and extrinsically formal legal rationality is central to Weber's sociology
of modernity.

*1.1 The Belief in a Theodicy of Higher Law*

While modes of legal education played an important role in the development of modern law, more centrally Weber focuses on the significance of natural law ideals in the rationalization of Western structures
of power and authority. The striking parallels between Weber's sociology of law and his sociology of religion help illustrate the role that he
attributes to natural law in the rise of modern legal domination.[13]
According to his sociology of religion, the 'inner logic' [*Eigengesetzlichkeit*] behind religious rationalization and the 'growing rationality of
conceptions of the world' is located in the problem of theodicy, the
human 'need' to provide an 'ethical interpretation of the "meaning" of
the distribution of fortunes among men' (FMW, 275).[14] All religions,
Weber argues, demand that the organization of the world and the
course of its events be somehow *meaningful* (FMW, 353). This 'need' to
address the apparent 'ethical irrationality of the world' and to create a
comprehensive explanation of the human condition is the driving force

behind the development of ever-improved solutions to the problem of theodicy. In this way the rationalization of religious symbolic forms, Weber argues, contains 'a law of development and a compelling force entirely their own' (PE, 278, fn. 84).

This is the significance of Weber's famous 'switchmen' metaphor: 'not ideas, but material and ideal interests, directly govern men's conduct. Yet very frequently the "world-images" that have been created by "ideas" have, like switchmen, determined the tracks along which action has been pushed by the dynamic of interest' (FMW, 280). Ideas are powerful in orienting actions because the inescapable conditions of human existence cannot be explained, nor can the basic human need that the world be somehow meaningful be fulfilled, through a merely purposive-rational orientation to things. Interests are given their direction by the 'tracks' that 'values' lay. As Tenbruck writes, 'the switchpoint of ideas is, therefore, only the reverse side of the blindness of interests.'[15] For instance, Weber's Protestant ethic thesis argues that material interests alone could not transform the value of worldly activity under premodern mercantilism; it took the pressure of ascetic discipline to break with tradition and promote a new form of economic rationalism (PE, 47–78).

Weber constructed both religious and legal rationalization processes in terms of 'developmental stages' [*Entwicklungsstufen*] differentiated by their degree of disenchantment [*Entzauberung*] and systematization, that is, the differentiation of positive legal norms from revelation and custom and the formalization of norm-making and norm-finding procedures (ES, 882).[16] Although Weber does not explicitly state the analogy, as Hubert Treiber argues, the theodicy problematic, which provides the 'inner logic' in the development of religious world-views, parallels the functional role of 'natural law' in the development of extrinsic formal legal rationality.[17] Just as the Protestant vocational ethic provided a value-rational anchor for the transformation of traditional economic conduct, so natural law doctrines added weight to the inner logic behind the rationalization of power and authority.[18]

But if the natural law ideal supplied an inner logic to legal development, why development in the direction of increasing formal legal rationality – increasing calculability and predictability of normative power? In Weber's definition, 'natural law' refers to 'the sum total of all those norms which are valid independently of, and superior to, any positive law' (ES, 867). As Roberto Unger argues, the value-oriented striving to perform 'justice' according to the natural law idea placed a premium on the generality and autonomy of legal norms.[19] Legal norm setting and application were consequently released from the arbitrary dictates of executive convenience and the particularistic standards organically forged in daily life, thereby increasing the extrinsic formal legal rationality of social arrangements.

The notion of a higher law also influenced the development of legal autonomy, another crucial factor behind formal rationalization and a central characteristic of extrinsic formal legal rationality. As Unger again explains, because the higher law 'cuts across space and time,' the more perfect positive law becomes by approaching the meta-model, the more it should be independent of the particular practices of specific times and places. Specialized institutions, occupational groups, and modes of legal discourse slowly developed to ensure that the making and administration of legal norms acquired a measure of critical independence from politics and religion.[20]

From the seventeenth century onwards the Western legal order achieved a certain measure of autonomy from religion and from the political will of kings and princes, its norms becoming increasingly abstract and universal. The generality and autonomy of the legal order provides the basis for the 'rule of law,' the *Rechtsstaat*. The paradox of this process is that, like the relationship that Weber posits between the Protestant ethic and the rise of capitalism, the natural law axioms that contribute to this legal development are eventually nullified by the very process of systematization and disenchantment of legal norms (ES, 873–5). Of course, this is Weber's controversial interpretation, to which I return later.

Weber's account of legal development would be wide open to charges of idealism if the 'inner logic' of natural law ideals and the 'intellectual needs' of jurists mentioned above were alone responsible for formal legal rationalization. However, the value-oriented striving to perform 'justice' was 'carried' and ultimately reinforced by emergent material interests in the generality and autonomy of legal norms, specifically the calculability and predictability of the legal consequences of social action, supplied by 'formal law as such.'

*1.2 Legal Domination and the Societalization of Power*

While Weber's sociology of law traces the significance of 'certain ideal values' in the development of modern legal domination (the 'intellectual needs' of jurists and the belief in a 'higher' universal law), one must rely more on his later sociological work in order to reconstruct the specific features of European society that precipitated and carried this process along. It seems in Weber's view that the increasing functional differentiation of religion, economy, and rulership in early modern society, along with growing division between a variety of social groups, each claiming a right to rule while none possessed the power to effectuate its claim, created a crisis of order and legitimacy for the authoritarian-hierarchical structure of traditional domination. Although Weber does not expressly outline the role of legal rationalization in the transition from traditional to legal-rational domination in the West, legal rationalization appears related to the social complexification created by functional differentiation and growing division of labour. In other words, early modern problems of social integration and legitimation were resolved by the kind of 'societalization of power' that the legal rationalization of power and authority promotes (cf. FMW, 228).

According to Weber's developmental history of the West, as rationalization and disenchantment proceeded from the High Middle Ages onwards, the early modern societies of Europe grew larger and more functionally complex. Weber refers to this process as a differentiation of life-orders [*Lebensordnungen*] and value-spheres [*Wertsphären*], involving a growing causal and normative autonomy of distinct societal domains (FMW, 328).[21] For the purpose of explicating the factors behind the formal rationalization of law and the emergence of what Weber terms legal-rational domination, one can interpolate from his account that the differentiation of life-orders and value-spheres created a growing disordination and pluralization of social powers. For example, the rationalization of religion, economy, and law do not proceed in a unified and parallel fashion, but rather according to their own 'inner logics' [*Eigengesetzlichkeit*]. These distinct processes of rationalization not only differentiate societal domains but also push in directions of development that are in increasing tension with one another.[22] Thus, for instance, with the rise of the modern economic system a growing conflict emerges between the impersonal formal rationality of the market and the person-oriented values and substantive rationality of religious ethics (ES, 578–9). Similarly, the formal rationalization of law involves a growing differentiation of and tension between abstract, positive legal rules and norms derived from religion and custom (ES, 810).

The differentiation of life-orders and values-spheres created a growing disordination and pluralization of social powers. As the organic and homogeneous social order of medieval society fragmented the question of legitimate social authority became ever more acute. Disjunctions emerged between the purposes and ends generated by various social organizations and the purposes and ends of individual and group conduct; the monarchy, the aristocracy, the churches, and the emergent middle classes formed separate groups, each unable to occupy a permanently dominant social position or to claim exclusive right to govern (ES, 846–8). The validation of authority on the grounds of custom or religion became decreasingly plausible as hierarchical structures of traditional authority were increasingly exposed as adventitious privilege.

According to Weber's complex typologies of rationality, just as the formal rationality of modern economic and political structures of power (capitalism and bureaucracy) relates to the degree that means and ends of economic and administrative action become susceptible to calculation, and to which knowledge of 'facts' become differentiated from judgments of 'value,' so the formal rationality of modern law refers to the systematization of law-making and law-finding and the differentiation of legal from non-legal norms.[23] Weber famously stresses the important affinities between the formal rationalization of law, with its orientation to abstract, formal and universal rules, and the development of capitalism, with its impersonal means-ends lawfulness of the market. According to him, the formal, general, and positive characteristics of modern law maximize the predictability and calculability of the legal consequences of social action, thereby facilitating the individual exercise of planful and purposive conduct.

What is the significance of the economic and social structure of the 'early capitalist' epoch in Western Europe for the emergence of modern legal-rational domination? Weber seems to imply that the problems of social integration and legitimation created by the differentiation of life-orders and value-spheres provided a significant inducement to the kind of formal rationalization of law that constitutes legal domination. The problem of order and legitimacy placed a premium on those qualities of legal generality and autonomy that formal legal rationality furnishes.[24]

Formal, abstract, and general norms allow power to be distributed in a way that can be justified or at least tolerated by the widest range of group interests. By replacing traditional forms of domination with the 'rule of law,' the creation and administration of power-backed norms could be autonomous (at least in principle) vis-à-vis concrete economic and political interests and applied with predictable generality to all individuals. The formal rationalization of modern legal domination, Weber argues, created 'an unambiguous and clear system ... free of irrational administrative arbitrariness as well as of irrational disturbance by concrete privileges' (ES, 847). As Unger explains, by canalizing power through general and autonomous rules, formally rational law could function as a 'balance wheel of social organization,' making possible relations between strangers who do not have shared values or common traditions.[25]

Also, the formal legal rationality of modern domination provides the solution to problems of legitimate authority. Under legal-rational domination the state is absolved from orientation towards any particular religion or conception of the 'good' and becomes defined in more instrumental terms as the means of the legal exercise of bureaucratically organized authority. The person is reconstituted as a 'rights-bearing' strategic actor, free within 'civil society' to engage in the pursuit of personally chosen aims by rational, instrumentally effective means. This is the early sociological embodiment of the modern experience of 'freedom': the purposes and ends of individual conduct were released from social ascription and rendered the subject of planful individual choice. In early modern times, those social relations involving economic conduct were first transformed in this sense, legal-rational domination providing a calculable and predictable basis for the free disposition through market transactions of property and working power (ES, 811–14). But as Weber observes, rationalization and the rise of modernity have, inter alia, involved the inexorable expansion of the social applicability of such planful and purposive conduct and the legal-rational infra-structure that undergirds it (ES, 30).

## 1.3 The Demise of the Metaphysical Dignity of Law

In early modern Europe, both the ideal interests embodied in the aspiration for 'law as justice' (the belief in a metapositive law) and the material requirements for 'law as order' placed a premium on the generality and autonomy of legal norms, thereby pressing the development of law in the direction of increased formal rationality. One could say that the contribution of legal rationalization to the creation of modern society involves a 'formalization' of social relations and a 'positivization' of social norms. These two main characteristics of modern legal development have contributed immensely to the differentiation, change, and social integration of industrial market societies. The formalization of social relations represents an emancipation of individuals from the kind of social considerations imposed under the personal structures of traditional domination. The positivization of values refers to the basis of modern norms in deliberate enactments, or posits, rather than 'found' or 'revealed' aspects of the world.

The positivism in Weber's characterization of modern legal rationalism is a prominent source of controversy. In Weber's view, the normative order of modern legal domination becomes divorced from its value-rational roots in natural law by a combination of intrajuristic and sociological factors: the intellectual scepticism of jurists; the growing secularity and individualism of a pluralistic market society. In contrast to substantive conceptions of legitimacy based on the belief in the teleological or the immanent qualities of law, the validity of modern legal norms is 'ideal-typically' based on formal consistency vis-à-vis existing law (ES, 37). Weber acknowledges that this radically desubstantive model of authority is not a robust basis of legitimacy. But it does reflect the fact that, with disenchantment and the disordination of social powers, questions about the 'ends' of human life, or the content of the 'good life,' are no longer readily resolved by recourse to conceptions of common good or collective purpose. As Weber contends, 'precisely the ultimate and most sublime values have retreated from public life either into the transcendental realm of mystic life or into the brotherliness of direct and personal human relations' (FMW, 155). Hence, to paraphrase Rogers Brubaker, the 'ends' towards which the social arrangements created by legal domination are oriented are not really 'ends' at all, but rather *generalized means,'* indiscriminately facilitative of the purposeful pursuit of a wide range of *individually* defined substantive ends.[26] This abstract formulation fails to mention that the most powerful and influential sectors of society will be best placed to exploit these generalized means. The more formal rationality increases in the economic and legal spheres of the market society, the more powerful the role that private property and capital accumulation play in defining the 'substantive ends' of social relations (ES, 730–1).

Weber takes great care in emphasizing the affinities between formal legal rationalization and the rise of capitalism, but it is important to remember that, in his account, the relationship is not straightforward. On the one hand, the rise of capitalism relies on a pre-existing degree of legal-rational domination. In Weber's famous thesis, the Protestant vocational ethic provided a 'moral instrumentality' that ruptured traditional patterns of economic action and helped lay the 'tracks' for economic rationalization. Analogously, through the influence of 'ideal factors,' such as the 'intrinsic intellectual needs' of Continental jurists and the belief in a 'higher law' effectuated by the natural law tradition, Western law seems to have provided the 'legal instrumentality' for the development of a market society. Modern capitalism, based as it is on continuous rational enterprise and purposive contractual relations between economic actors, depends on a calculable and predictable legal foundation for market transactions (ES, 814). According to Weber, the essential elements of this foundation of extrinsically formal legal rational authority were already in place prior to the rise of capitalism (ES, 687–8).[27]

On the other hand, Weber stresses that capitalist society in its clearly unfolded complexity exerts a very strong influence upon legal development. Recalling his 'switchmen' metaphor, it is important to avoid overemphasizing the autonomy of the 'inner logic' of legal rationalization. Weber insists that, regardless of their intrinsic merit, ideas and values spread through a culture and become the motor of significant socio-cultural development only when they are 'carried' by a well-rooted strata.[28] For example, in a traditional economy where self-sufficiency prevails and exchange is lacking, Weber argues, the legal order 'will mainly define and delimit a person's noneconomic relations and privileges with regard to other persons in accordance, not with economic considerations, but with the person's origin, education, or social status' (ES, 668). But in a growing capitalist society, 'those who have market interests constitute the most important group. Their influence predominates in determining which legal transactions the law should regulate by means of power-granting norms' (ES, 669). The centrality of contractual association in modern allocative and authoritative practices represents the 'legal reflex' of a capitalist society (ES, 672).

Thus, Weber seems to suggest that, in contrast to the importance of 'ideal interests' in the precapitalist era, when the mode of legal education and, especially, natural law beliefs were a strong influence behind legal rationalization, once capitalism and its carrier class have become sufficiently rooted, the process of legal rationalization is strongly conditioned by the functional requirements of market transactions and capital accumulation (ES, 334). For the solutions that modern law provided to problems of social integration and authority – the objectification and depersonalization of social relations and the emancipation of individual choice through the positivization of normative power – also provided the channels for the 'disembedding' of economic relations and the sociological embodiment of 'freedom' in the guise of purposive-rational behaviour in the market. The formalism and positivism of modern law allow for the abstraction of social relations from those which are integrated by tradition and commonly shared values. The disembedding of economic relations creates a morally neutralized sphere of action in which individuals can exercise decision-making powers free from moral considerations for tradition or community. In fact, the market-centred society depends on a high degree of legal formalism and positivism for its social integration and legitimation needs precisely because it relies so heavily on the decentralized decisions of self-interested individuals in morally neutralized spheres of action.

Indeed, Weber's account of legal rationalization and his ideal-typification of legal rationalism are designed to accentuate the formalism of modern social relations and the positivism of modern norms. But, in his judgment, these features of modern society are so developmentally axial and sociologically consequential that it is difficult to overstate their significance.

## 2. The 'Thorn' of Weber: Habermas and the Problem of Modern Authority

Weber's account of legal rationalization has been the subject of much debate and criticism – with good reason. Weber manages to tie the development of modern legal authority so closely to the socio-historical process of rationalization in the West that legal rationalization itself becomes identified with modernity's countertendencies. In Weber's account, the rise of legal domination disembeds economic and administrative action (capitalism and the bureaucratic state) from traditional orientations to use-value and moral norms and reconstitutes them as formally organized action domains. Thus, in Weber's account, legal rationalization lies behind the organization of complex market societies around impersonal principles of abstract calculation, technical efficiency, and profit, which generate the modern pathologies of alienation, reification, normalization, and surveillance – in short, the famous 'iron cage.' Moreover, the problem of how to view the legitimacy of these modern instrumental structures of power and authority simply reflects the larger problem of post-traditional legal authority in general, under which legitimacy, in Weber's diagnosis, is based more on procedural consistency than on fidelity with substantive ethical postulates. This is the 'thorn' that Weber creates for Habermas's critical project: how can modern law be a force for enhancing individual freedom when hypertrophic legalization of power and authority has created the freedom-threatening 'iron cage' in the first place?

A good way of addressing these issues and evaluating Weber's account of the relations between legal rationalization and modernity is provided by Habermas's comprehensive and influential critique of Weber's sociology of modern law.[29] One strategy employed by Habermas to discredit Weber's account of the rise of legal domination is to argue that Weber neglects the 'ideal' factors that historically provided the justifications for purposive rational action orientations and institutional orders associated with the modern experience of freedom.[30] But is this a fair interpretation of Weber's account of the rise of legal domination?

The significant correlations between Weber's accounts of legal rationalization and the rationalization of religious world-views discussed above provide one avenue for addressing this issue. Just as the 'intellectual need' for consistent and comprehensive solutions to the problem of theodicy provided an 'inner logic' to the development of religious world-views in the direction of increasing systematization and disenchantment, so the belief in a 'higher law' – and, in the special case of 'logical' formal legal rationality, the importance of the 'intrinsic intellectual needs' of legal academics for logical consistency – supplied an inner logic to the rationalization of law in the direction of increasing generality and autonomy of norms, thus in the direction of increasing extrinsic formal legal rationality.

However, in Weber's view, these patterns of religious and legal rationalization are in a sense eventually subverted, both by their own inner logics and by the dynamic of interests that they institute. The Protestant ethic created a disciplined, work-oriented personality and a will to control things through practical knowledge which turned out, by a great irony of history, to be superbly functional for the take-off of a fundamentally profane market society.[31] Western religious rationalization paradoxically culminates in a Protestant logic of secularization; likewise the value-rational axioms of natural law are eventually undermined by the very rationalization of legal norms they encouraged, in Weber's view, a process of systematization and disenchantment that exposes a fundamental tension between legality and legitimacy, between 'law as order' and 'law as justice' (ES, 873–5).

Although capitalism originated in part through the moral value given to worldly economic activity by the Protestant vocational ethic, the process of economic rationalization eventually becomes self-perpetuating, capable of educating and selecting through the 'economic survival of the fittest' the subjective attitudes and dispositions requisite to its reproduction (ES, 731). Just as economic rationalization is no longer driven by the 'moral instrumentality' once provided by Protestant religious beliefs, so also the rationalization of the general structure of legal domination need no longer be driven by the philosophical elaboration of 'higher' law. Modern legal systems – for example, English common law and Continental civil law – may differ in terms of their non-economically conditioned intrajuristic contents, which are continually evolving in response to contextual issues. But from a comparative historical perspective, they all exhibit the degree of extrinsic formal legal rationality requisite to the functional needs of capitalism in particular and modern social arrangements in general. The structural parallels between religious and legal rationalization illustrated here suggest that, in Weber's view, modern legal development is conditioned by the mutually reinforcing factors of secularization and value-pluralism on the one hand, and the dynamic of interests generated by the market society on the other.

To be fair to Habermas, Weber may place too great an emphasis on natural law ideas of 'reason' and 'nature' as the basis of modern authority. Weber argues that such natural law ideals have become discredited through secularization and growing intellectual scepticism, and thus he concludes that procedural consistency becomes the only basis for legitimating modern legal authority. But even if such ideals are no longer available, a nonfoundationalist theory of contractualism, a 'normative rationality' based on the idea of consensual agreement through uncoerced communication, might as Habermas argues remain latent in modern conceptions of authority.[32] However, Weber's account of rationalization poses thornier problems for Habermas. What if the loss of 'those norms which are valid independently of, and superior to, any positive law' is not simply a consequence of the 'disintegration and relativization' of meta-juristic axioms, but rather is tied into structural features of modernity itself, such as secularization and the functional differentiation of societal domains, which confine the legitimation of modern economic and political institutions to formally correct procedure at the expense of broader norms of consensus formation?

## 2.1 Legal Rationalization and the Juridification of Power and Authority

Habermas's account of legal rationalization in the rise of modern capitalist society is deeply Weberian in derivation, though important analytical refinements are added in an effort to rescue modern law from its fated instrumentalization and divorce from ethical development in Weber's hands. To begin with, Habermas makes a key distinction between 'lifeworld' and 'system,' lifeworld referring to the taken-for-granted stream of everyday routines and interactions in the private sphere of life connected with family and neighbourhood, which contrasts with the formally organized subsystems of the economy and bureaucratic state administration. With legal rationalization, the organic social relations of the lifeworld are reconstituted by modern law into formally organized domains of action which then function independently of the lifeworld.[33]

According to Habermas, modern legal domination develops through four waves of 'juridification' [*Verrechtslichung*], each involving both a quantitative expansion of law into previously unregulated social relations and an increased density of law and complexification of social organization.[34] The first two waves of juridification involved the seventeenth-century institutionalization of rule by formal rational law and the eighteenth-century institutionalization of civil rights. Juridification thus involved the constitutionalization of political authority. The formation of the liberal constitutional state 'tamed' government executive authority through the 'rule of law.' Although this legal rationalization did not originally include the democratic participation of 'citizens' in the selection of office holders, it did secure actionable rights against arbitrary use of political power. But juridification guaranteed the free-choice behaviour of the property-owning citizen within the economic sphere of civil life, thereby opening the economic sphere to the rule of purposive-rational conduct. From the seventeenth century onwards, the liberty and rights originally connected with bourgeois market activity were slowly extended to other spheres of civil life. With the third wave of juridification, involving the nineteenth-century institutionalization of political rights, executive political authority was further constitutionalized through the formation of the democratic liberal state and the establishment of the right of citizens to participate in the political decision-making process.

Though more systematic in exposition and specific in historical periodization, Habermas's account of legal rationalization is substantively congruent with Weber's. In Weber's account, as I illustrated above, the development of modern legal domination involved the 'societalization of power,' that is, the legal rationalization of economic and political structures of power and the expansion of purposive-rational free-choice behaviour. In Habermas's version, the juridification of economic and political structures of power reconstitutes the organic social relations of the lifeworld into formally organized domains of action, which in effect become autonomous institutional orders or 'subsystems,' disembedded or 'uncoupled' from the lifeworld: 'the social relations we call "formally organized" are those that are first constituted in forms of modern law.'[35]

Habermas's account does serve to clarify an element of legal domination imprecisely conveyed by Weber's ideal-typification of formal legal rationality but nevertheless expressed through his substantive explications of legal rationality: the process of legal rationalization behind the formation of modern legal domination involves a remapping of social relations in terms of both legal rules and rights. The development of legal domination creates subjective legal rights through the positivization of normative encumbrances on individuals in a newly defined civil society and objective legal rules through the formalization of social relations, their disembedding from customary social intercourse. For example, just as the formal rationality of economic structures of power disembedded the economic sphere from the web of traditional domination, creating a functionally differentiated subsystem that operates according to its own inner logic, so the opening of a sphere of economic relations to the rule of purposive-rational conduct provided the social embodiment of 'freedom' in the guise of the reason-guided, self-realizing individual and bearer of 'rights.'[36] The link between legal rules and legal rights implied by Weber's conception of legal rationalization is paradigmatic of subsequent legal development, where the functional differentiation of life-orders (the legal rationalization of economic and political structures of power) runs in tandem with the deepening application of individual free-choice behaviour.

Of course, Weber was deeply ambivalent about the consequences of these developments. Legal rationalization contributes to the functional differentiation of society and thereby the modern experience of freedom. At the same time, these formally organized subsystems of economy and state, as Habermas puts it, 'steer a social intercourse that has been largely disconnected from norms and values, above all in those subsystems of purposive rational economic and administrative action that, on Weber's diagnosis, have become independent of their moral-political foundations.'[37] With the uncoupling of the material reproduction of society from the cultural reproduction of the lifeworld, the legal rationalization of modern structures of power and authority is ambiguously freedom-enhancing. The countertendencies of legal rationalization are expressed by Habermas in terms of his 'colonization thesis': areas of social life integrated on the basis of norms and consensus formation fall prey to the systemic imperatives of economic and administrative subsystems, which operate according to their own logics.

## 2.2 Recovering the Normative Rationality of Modern Law

To this point in Habermas's account, it would appear that legal rationalization remains as much the culprit behind the social pathologies of modernity as it is in Weber's sociology. But Habermas's long-term revamping of critical social theory has aimed to dissociate legal rationalization from the socio-historical development of capitalism and to save 'rationality' from a purely formal and instrumental fate. Habermas attempts to accomplish this aim by distinguishing between the 'systemic' and 'normative' rationalities of modern law, between law as 'medium' and law as 'institution,' that is, legitimation via formally correct procedures versus legitimation via the substantive norms of consensus formation. This distinction parallels the one between 'system' and 'lifeworld.' On the one hand, law takes on the role of a 'steering medium,' a means for organizing functionally differentiated subsystems independent of the background norms in the lifeworld. Habermas concurs with Weber that this 'system' dimension of law is legitimated through formally correct procedure alone. On the other hand, Habermas maintains that law is also an expression of the lifeworld's moral and ethical development. Legal norms 'stand in a continuum with moral norms' in the lifeworld.[38] Departing from Weber's account, Habermas argues that modern legal rationality remains connected to the moral structures of society from which it draws its legitimation.

Although the distinction between law as medium and law as institution has been replaced in Habermas's recent work by 'facticity' versus 'validity,' his conception of modern law remains substantively the same.[39] Habermas's recent work gives equal conceptual weight to the systemic and normative dimensions of modern legal rationality, viewing law as a hinge between system and lifeworld.[40] Habermas's central claim is that modern law not only institutionalizes subsystems, it also translates messages from the lifeworld into the special codes of power and money that steer political and economic systems.

In Habermas's version of the iron cage, the centrality of institutions and performances where instrumental and purposive rationalities are crucial to profit and control creates a disequilibrium of rationalities in the modern world. If, to paraphrase Georg Simmel, this 'preponderance of the objective' is the source of modern social pathologies, then the key political question for Habermas becomes how to gain greater lifeworld influence over the system. If the instrumental and formal rationalities of modern economic and political organization are by definition resistant to internal democratic transformation – direct democracy and workplace citizenship having been consigned to the dustbin of history, perhaps prematurely – then ethical influence over these subsystems must be derived externally, namely, from the lifeworld. Since law is the only hinge between system and lifeworld, Habermas's critical social theory must entrust law with the sizable task of ethically 'taming' modern social arrangements and mediating value-conflict in general.

There are several problems for this undertaking. First, Weber clearly links legal rationalization not only with its freedom-enhancing effects but also with the social pathologies that are freedom-threatening. Habermas illustrates this problem in the context of the fourth and most recent wave of juridification, which institutionalizes a wide range of social welfare benefits but also 'colonizes the lifeworld.' According to Habermas, the institutionalization of social rights tames the economic power of private enterprise and thus has 'from the perspective of their beneficiaries as well as from democratic law givers, a freedom-guaranteeing character.'[41] However, in a reprise of Weberian ambivalence, Habermas recognizes that the extension of social benefits through provision of legal entitlements also draws systems rationality into previously informally regulated areas of the lifeworld: 'the situation to be regulated is embedded in the context of a life-history and of a concrete way of life; it has to be subjected to violent abstraction not merely because it has to be subsumed under the law but in order that it can be handled administratively.'[42]

Habermas's optative account of juridification attempts to confine the countertendencies of legal rationalization – loss of freedom and loss of meaning – to the fourth wave of juridification. Yet, as Tweedy and Hunt point out, each wave of juridification, with its institutionalization of political and civil rights, has entailed analogous countertendencies: 'like social rights, these rights also clearly exhibit negative side-effects which are directly associated with their systemic dimensions.' They argue that 'it is important to remain conscious of the complex interpenetration of regulatory knowledge, surveillance, and the creation of disciplinary techniques associated with all forms of institutionalized rights.'[43]

As Weber's sociology of law cautions, juridification is always ambiguously freedom-enhancing precisely because the modern experience of freedom is so closely allied with purposive-rational economic action and the bureaucratization of administrative action. The institutionalization of freedom may invoke the normative dimension of modern law, but it also entails the system dimension of legal rationality. Of course, the problem of law being ambiguously freedom-enhancing is not simply an issue of conceptual tension between its normative and systemic dimensions. For though Habermas insists on the equal conceptual weight of the normative and system dimensions of modern law, it remains unclear how this equilibrium between rationalities, and also between lifeworld and system, is to be achieved. After all, as Habermas acknowledges, money and power in modern society are firmly behind the system dimension of law and hence the colonization of lifeworld.

## 3. The Heuristic Value of Weber's Disillusioned Realism

At the heart of Habermas's critique of Weber's sociology of law is his rejection of the latter's characterization of legal development as a process of increasing formal rationality of legal processes and positivity of legal norms. To the extent that modern law functions as a channel of support for formally organized domains of action (the means-ends rationalism of capitalism and bureaucracy), its rationalism, Weber argues, is purely formal and instrumental, its validity tied to principles of positive enactment. According to Habermas, this model of formal legal rationality neglects the ethical dimension of postmetaphysical law, namely, its internal connection with principles of justification.[44]

What the reconstruction provided above illustrates, however, is that Weber's larger sociology of modernity does indeed provide an account of the 'normative properties' of formal legal rationality by virtue of which it can fulfil the functional requirements of individual autonomy. According to Weber, formal legal rationality contributes to the experience of freedom through institutionalization of purposive-rational action, particularly in the economic and political arenas of public life. Historically, this was achieved through the depersonalization and objectification of power and authority and the devolution of value-setting to individual responsibility. The impersonal and objectified qualities of modern structures of economic and political power provide a secure and predictable environment for individuals to effectuate their self-regarding aims. The scope individuals possess for defining the ends of their social conduct, and the environment of legal security they require to realize the planful determination of these ends, are supplied through the formal legal rationality of modern social arrangements and the positivity of values.

Weber was well aware that the legal guarantee of individual autonomy is a rather narrow and perhaps culturally desiccated one. Although the legal reconstitution of economic and political arrangements that transformed the authoritarian-hierarchical structures of traditional domination into a liberal market society was freedom-enhancing, the formal guarantee of freedom and concomitant reduction of legitimacy claims to issues of legal form and process as such generates substantive deficiencies for the realization of individual autonomy and justification of authority in modern society (ES, 729–31). Habermas may be correct to argue that this conception of legitimacy unfortunately divorces the basis of legal validity from broader substantive principles of rational justification. But there is no point in blaming Weber's sociology for this deficiency of modern law: because of the relativization of values on the one hand and the functional requirements for the exploitation of economic power on the other, the operative theory of justice in the market society *is* structurally predisposed to devolve questions of validity into issues of legal form and process, allowing only 'asymmetrical solutions' to the problem of rational ·authority and, as a consequence, a truncated form of democracy.

Habermas criticizes Weber for identifying legal rationality with formal rationality divorced from substantive norms: 'the particular accomplishment of the positivization of the legal order consists in *displacing* problems of justification, that is, in relieving the technical administration of the law of such problems over broad expanses – but not in doing away with them.'[45] Yet he is forced to agree that this type of legal rationality does dominate modern culture: 'modern legal subjects content themselves in actual practice with legitimation through procedure, for in many cases substantive justification is not only not possible, but is also, from the viewpoint of the lifeworld, meaning-less.'[46]

Habermas also criticizes Weber for implicating legal rationalization with the expansion of institutional subsystems and the growing scope of purposive-rational action. But again he is forced to agree that contemporary legal rationalization, as Weber might have predicted, is driven in some significant degree by the systems dimension of modernity, especially the ever-expanding capitalist market:

> the trend toward juridification of informally regulated spheres of lifeworld is gaining ground along a broad front – the more leisure, culture, recreation, and tourism recognizably come into the grip of the laws of the commodity economy and the definitions of mass consumption, the more structures of the bourgeois family manifestly become adapted to the imperatives of the employment system, the more the school palpably takes over the functions of assigning jobs and life prospects, and so forth.[47]

Weber recognizes the contribution of legal rationalization to the modern experience of freedom and the enormous enhancement of human powers. But he also reflects on its countertendencies: the alienation of structured but meaningless realms of instrumental action; the reification of brute economic 'laws' that render the market the final arbiter of social priority. This is the paradox of modern society and the 'Weberian thorn' in the side of efforts to recapture control over social priorities via the influence of law: the very institutions and social arrangements that promote modern autonomy also trivialize it.[48] Though Weber may overemphasize the detachment of modern law from normative justification, Habermas cannot rectify this deficiency by conceptually legislating a more significant role to the normative dimension of modern legal rationality, especially when the dynamic of contemporary economic and political interests is so firmly behind its systemic dimension. At the least, Weber's account of legal rationalization remains a salutary call for prudence in relying on *law* to ethically influence the formal and instrumental rationalisms of modern social arrangements, especially when it is the ethical influence of law – namely its objectification of power and positivization of authority – that constitutes this particular 'societalization of power' in the first place.

One measure of evidence supporting Weber's concern that modern legal development is perhaps, to employ Habermas's terminology, more about 'steering mechanisms' for power and money than a 'channel' of influence for the 'lifeworld' on 'formally organized domains of action' is provided by the rise of the rights-oriented polity. Weber's critics frequently assume that constitutional adjudication of Bills of Rights represents an empirical rebuttal to his unpopular claim about the 'irresistible advance of legal positivism' and concomitant 'disappearance of natural law conceptions.'[49] But, as research on American and Canadian constitutional adjudication indicates, rights litigation reveals a resolute pursuit of formal legal rationality.[50]

According to Weber's account, one of the hallmarks of the formal rationalization of law is the increasing emphasis on formal criteria of 'reason' in principles of justification at the expense of substantive, extrajuristic criteria (ES, 868–71). The substantive version conceives of rights as entitlements to definite substantive goods, such as the 'right to a minimum standard of living' (ES, 872). By contrast, in the formal version, a conception of fixed and universal rules is tied to a system of individual rights the cornerstone of which is the right to an almost unlimited freedom to engage in property acquisition through purposive contractual arrangements. In this formal conception of right, an economistic theory of power prevails in which social relations are construed as contractual exchanges between formally autonomous agents.

An Economic Bill of Rights that guarantees minimum standards of housing, education, and employment, such as the one proposed in the United States by Franklin Roosevelt in 1944 but never implemented, would be representative of a substantive version of legal right.[51] But nowhere in the West, and least of all in the so-called rights-oriented polities of North America, have such substantive rights been realized. With few exceptions, the tension between formal and substantive definitions of 'right' historically has been resolved, as Weber predicted, in favour of the formal conception (ES, 874).

Why this particular pattern of legal development? Again, the Weberian hermeneutic of suspicion would point out that formal definitions of 'right' maximize the capacity of law to institute purposive economic action and to function as a steering mechanism of power and money. The more law is allowed to become, in Habermas's words, a 'channel of influence' for the 'lifeworld,' the more power is granted to extraeconomic criteria of value, for example, conceptions of the 'good' or schemes of distributive justice. Such criteria, however, interfere with the means-ends efficiencies of the market and render the consequences of economic action less calculable and predictable (ES, 811–14). Economically privileged groups who derive their power from market transactions strenuously resist such substantive regulation as an arbitrary, politically motivated infringement upon their free disposition over private property and 'working power.'

Whatever contributions the rights-oriented polity has made to strengthening due process protections in criminal law or enhancing antidiscrimination provisions in the name of formal equality, it has also and with much less fanfare served to further entrench the power-granting norms protecting market transactions. Given the relationship of affinity between economic and formal legal rationalization and the structural links between modern law and capitalism that Weber's sociology elucidates, perhaps it is not just a coincidence that the rights-oriented polity has emerged in the West while, at the same time, the post-Keynesian round of economic rationalization has sought to uncouple market transactions from 'excessive' regulatory intervention and to renew an entrepreneurial culture based on the 'enterprising self.'[52] However one wishes to evaluate the increasing scope of formal rationality in these particular societal domains, the fact of its growing importance should be acknowledged.

# The 'Dynamic' of Legal Rationalization: An Interpretation of Recent Trends in Legal Development

Modern social arrangements and institutional functionings evince a high degree of formal rationality, expressed in terms of their transparency to reason, their impersonality, and their orientation to control. The formal rationality of modern law, and of modern social arrangements in general, presumes a positivistic conception of values and a will-centred conception of personhood. According to Weber, formal legal rationality contributes to the modern experience of 'freedom' through the institutionalization of purposive-rational action, particularly in the economic and political arenas of public life. Historically, this institutionalization was achieved through the objectification and depersonalization of social arrangements and the subjectification of normative power. The impersonal and objectified quality of modern structures of economic and political power provide a secure and predictable environment for the individual pursuit of self-regarding aims.

Although the legal reconstitution of economic and political arrangements that transformed the authoritarian-hierarchical structures of traditional domination into a capitalist market society was, one might say, 'unambiguously' freedom-enhancing, the formal legal-rational guarantee of freedom generates problems for the substantive realization of individual autonomy and the substantive justification of authority. As I argue below, the constitutionalization of economic and social processes through a legal administrative-regulatory structure attempts to address the problems of substantive autonomy paradigmatically exposed by the purposive contract in the area of economic relations between workers and employers. Similarly, the constitutionalization of individual legal rights and the rise of rights-litigation attempt to address the modern problem of substantive authority.

However, in view of Weber's theory of legal rationalization, do not these strategies ironically enhance and extend the formalization of social arrangements and the positivization of normative power that lie behind the original sense of lack of freedom and meaninglessness? Perhaps they actually *deepen* the countertendencies that arise out of the relationship between formal legal rationality and individual autonomy. Building on Weber's depiction of the axial dimensions of modernity (i.e., rationalization and intellectualization and the unfolding differentiation of life-orders and value-spheres), I will outline the dynamic of legal development in contemporary structures of power and authority, which lies behind the contemporary unabated growth of objective legal rules and subjective legal rights.

## 1. The Developmental Directions of Legal Rationalization

The rise of modern legal domination transformed feudal society into a capitalist market society.[1] With the depersonalization and objectification of economic and political structures of power, economic action orientations were uncoupled from the normative web of traditional relations of power, allowing economic action to be directed by purely economic considerations. This development involves not only the formalization of economic relations but also the positivization of norms pertaining to the sphere of economic activity, that is, the opening of the economic sphere to the unchallenged rule of purposive-rational conduct. Formal legal rational order constitutes the property-owning legal subject as the bearer of economic 'rights.' In a sense, the rationalization of the economic sphere created a 'training ground' for the practice of individual autonomy, a sphere in which individuals could formulate the ends of their actions free from the constraining considerations of custom and morality. From the eighteenth century onwards, the liberty and rights originally connected with the economy and the ownership of wealth were slowly extended to other spheres of social life and eventually deepened to inhere in the very core of modern conceptions of selfhood.

Subsequent stages in the history of the social permeation of formal legal rationality involved the constitutionalization of political structures of power. The formation of the liberal constitutional state 'tamed' governmental executive authority through the 'rule of law.' Although

the rule of law did not initially allow citizens to participate in a democratic formation of the sovereign's will, it did secure actionable rights
against the arbitrary use of political power, thereby increasing the calculability and predictability of the legal environment of economic and
political conduct. With the formation of the democratic constitutional
liberal state, executive political power was further constitutionalized
through the establishment of the right of citizens to participate in the
political decision-making process.

Where the nineteenth-century development of formal legal-rational
social arrangements involved the liberal constitutionalization of political arrangements – that is, the mitigation of authoritarian structures of
political authority – twentiethth-century developments have involved
the taming of the economic order with the formation of the modern
'interventionist' welfare-regulatory state. The shortening of working
hours, freedom to organize unions, and social security are examples of
the extension of legal regulation and actionable rights into the world of
work previously subordinate to the unrestrained power of the private
owners of the means of production. Just as the liberal constitutional
state emerged through efforts to rationalize the structure of political
power, the interventionist state emerges as a result of the attempt to
moderate the economic system, in particular to cushion the social
repercussions of the substantive irrationalities generated by the
market.

The modern pattern of objectified social arrangements and subjecti-
fied value-orientations corresponds with the two polar dimensions of
formal legal rationality: the constitutive capacity of modern law to
remap social relations in terms of both 'rules' and 'rights.' The development of legal domination implicates formal legal rationality in
subjective legal rights, through the positivization of normative encumbrances on individuals, and in objective legal rules, through the
formalization of social arrangements. The formal legal rationality of
economic structures of power 'disembedded' the economic sphere
from the web of traditional domination, creating an autonomous economic order propelled by its own dynamics; similarly, the opening of a
sphere of economic relations to the rule of purposive-rational conduct
provided the first significant sociological embodiment of the individual as a bearer of 'rights.' In other words, the inner core of formal legal
rationality involves the nexus of mastery and control with the idea of
the reason-guided, self-realizing individual.

The link between the legal rules and legal rights contained in the concept of formal legal rationality is paradigmatic of subsequent legal development, where the functional differentiation of life-orders in terms of the legal rationalization (constitutionalization) of economic and political structures of power is concomitant with the deepening application of individual free-choice behaviour, eventually securing it a justification independent of any particular social status, supposedly inhering in human subjectivity per se. Corresponding to the objective and subjective moments within the concept of formal legal rationality – the formalization of modern social arrangements and the positivization of normative power – the salient features of contemporary legal domination are the regulatory-administrative state and the rights-oriented polity.

## 1.1 The Formalization of Social Arrangements

A general characteristic of modernity is the wide time-space extension of abstract systems of formalized human interaction typical, for example, of the bureaucratic structures of the state and the world capitalist market. Formalization is a way of reconstituting elements of the social world with a view to enhancing its calculability and productivity through the efficient linking of means and ends and the lengthening of chains of functionally differentiated social interaction. The relationship of formalization to the modern experience of freedom is linked to the capacity of formally rational legal rules to release individuals from the restrictions and obligations characteristic of the premodern community.

Legal domination releases individuals from personal ties and thus disencumbers them from certain moral responsibilities to the community. Between the self and the other there is distance structured solely by legal rules. The formulation of the purposes of individual conduct is freed from terms of collectively defined common ends, thereby enhancing the autonomy of individual conduct. The modern structure of legal domination epitomized in social arrangements like the bureaucratic organization and the capitalist exchange market may be described, in the words of Zygmunt Bauman, as 'machines for keeping moral responsibility afloat.' By allowing individuals to define their own ends without the pressure of social obligations and considerations, individual moral responsibility is, in a sense, 'floated.'[2]

With the bureaucratic organization and the capitalist division of labour, the autonomy of individual action occurs in separately organized spheres of interaction. The resultant lengthening chain of social interaction increases the managerial and productive power of humans immensely. It also segments and differentiates the responsibility held by any particular individual for the outcome of any particular institutional or economic activity. Modern legal domination creates a 'public sphere' in which morality is replaced by legality; the moral proximity of the neighbourhood is replaced with the reason-mediated distance of the urban 'strangehood.' The ideal of the modern legal order is to discourage human inclinations resistant to prediction and rational justification and to facilitate impersonal, purposeful, reciprocal, and contractual associations. Modern social relations are rendered paradigmatically calculable, rule-guided, and universalizable via the systematic detachment of individuals from one another and the floatation of their moral responsibilities to their communities.

In this view, the impersonality of modern social relations must be construed not as an unfortunate side effect of the disencumbering of individuals, but, on the contrary, as its method of implementation. The functioning of all the representative institutions of modern society depends on the continuous maintenance of social distance between individuals. In turn, individual autonomy is construed as purposive-rational, free-choice behaviour; a predictable and calculable public environment amenable to means-ends calculus is maintained by the formalization of social arrangements through legal rules in order to facilitate the effectuation of this form of autonomy.

The formalization of social arrangements, however, also generates countertendencies for the realization of autonomy. As the earlier discussion of Simmel's characterization of money transactions illustrated, formalization decreases our dependence on the vicissitudes of individual personalities and, more specifically, their manifestations of virtue in personal relationships. Yet, paradoxically, the lengthening chain of interdependence instituted by formalization increases enormously our dependence on the conduct of a multitude of people we will never meet.

Simmel pointed out that money transactions can be regarded as a paradigmatically modern objectified or formalized social relation. From the standpoint of the goal of individual autonomy, the formalization of social relations contains both positive 'enabling' and negative 'constraining' moments. The historical transition from simple barter to an abstract monetary system corresponds to the transition from premodern to modern society. The dominance of money transactions between strangers in the modern world is a reflection of the prominence of impersonal, abstract social relations. By formalizing social relations, money undermines the traditional world in which power was manifest in terms of overt interpersonal dependency. Money creates greater interpersonal freedom through impersonal exchange relations; money makes exchange at a distance possible. At the same time, the dominance of money transactions makes human life more subject to bureaucratic regulation and quantitative evaluation. As Simmel writes,

> the dependency of human beings upon each other has not yet become wholly objectified, and personal elements have not yet become completely excluded. The general tendency, however, undoubtedly moves in the direction of making the individual more and more dependent upon the achievement of people, but less and less dependent on the personalities that lie behind them. Both phenomena have the same root and form the opposing sides of one and the same process: the modern division of labour permits the number of dependencies to increase just as it causes personalities to disappear behind their functions.[3]

Money transactions are paradigmatic of the relationship between the formal legal rationality of social arrangements and the modern experience of freedom: although money liberates people from personal dependencies, it also makes them more functionally interdependent.

The problems generated by the functional interdependence of strangers for the legal guarantee of freedom are at the heart of the modern regulatory-administrative structure of legal domination. A well-known face of modern legal domination is the enormous expansion in the scope and pervasiveness of regulatory laws. Theodore Lowi has studied the manner in which responsibilities for 'injuries' has been allocated in American society since the 1840s.[4] His study charts the development from emphasis on individual responsibility to what he terms 'distributional balance.'

Until the 1840s, Lowi argues, communities met the fundamental problem of how to allocate responsibility for injuries with the relatively simple question of who's action was to blame. This way of allocating responsibility was highly individualistic: the passive party had the stronger right, and responsibility for injuries was borne by the party who set the action in motion. It corresponded to a more agrarian community, in which actions that cause injury could be linked with their agent more easily. Not surprisingly, this form of tort litigation was conservative, antidevelopment, and anticapitalist. In a sleepy agrarian community, the construction of a new factory on farmland will probably cause various 'injuries' not only to the people who work in increasingly dangerous mechanical workplaces but also to the surrounding environment, which may become polluted with the by-products of the manufacturing process. If the party who sets action in motion is to be blamed for unforeseen consequences, the financial penalties incurred by innovative economic activity are practicably incalculable. The maintenance of conservative conceptions of obligation and individualistic methods of allocating responsibility for injuries would have prevented entrepreneurship and economic growth.

Commercial and industrial activity in the United States increased greatly through the 1840s and 1850s and as formal contractual relations between strangers displaced informal arrangements among neighbours one can observe a corresponding increase in tort cases. But a number of changes in American legal doctrine in the mid-nineteenth century greatly reduced the 'costs' of commercial and industrial activity carried by the entrepreneur. Legal devices were invented for separating people from the consequences of their economic actions by spreading the moral responsibility for the consequences of economic conduct.[5] New legal doctrines, Lowi writes, 'helped adjust tort law to the requirements of economic development and mechanization wherein the innovator could either avoid or spread responsibility.'[6] These doctrinal developments helped to shift a greater portion of the costs of industrialization onto its victims.

Informal norms are sufficient for regulating the relationships between families and neighbours in small community settings; legal norms with individualistic methods of allocating responsibilities for action are sufficient for small towns and cities with a slightly more developed economic system and division of labour. But by the beginning of the twentieth century, the capitalist economic order had become complex enough to render the presumption of individual responsibility for injuries problematic. If a particular manufacturing process in a large industry involved hazardous labour conditions, who was responsible for workplace injuries: the company, the worker, or 'society'? If economic boom was followed by bust, who was responsible for taking care of those impoverished by loss of work or a collapse in investments: the workers and investors themselves, or 'society'? When hazards are detected in modern societies, although we know they are the outcome of some particular social action, the complex functional differentiation of modern society makes it nigh impossible to attach responsibility to any particular individual or group of individuals. Almost every undertaking involves a long chain of people, each one of whom performs but a small part of the overall task. The number of people involved is so great, and the actual input of particular individuals is so fragmentary in relation to larger aims and functions of organizations, that no one particular individual can be reasonably charged with the 'authorship' of the end results.

As Lowi argues, with the growing sophistication of the economic order and the division of labour in particular, the presumption of individual authorship of action was slowly displaced by a conception of system in which strangers are interdependent. The system perspective represents a shift from individual to collective indemnification; a shift from concrete actions of particular individuals to abstract 'system tendencies' calculated in terms of 'probable' outcomes. Economic organization in effect emancipates itself from the constraints imposed by moral considerations to 'community': 'injuries can be permitted to happen by indemnifying the victim. The cost is spread to the whole society, and the injuries can be combined in a universe large enough to deal with it statistically (collectively, publicly).'[7]

Thus, paradoxically, increasing individualism occurs in tandem with functional interdependency and regulation, for the emancipation of individual action from considerations to community and tradition is purchased through the socialization of responsibility in the larger society. Lowi's concern is that, once responsibility has been socialized, practically everyone has an incentive to compete over the allocation of costs. States are obliged to respond to, moreover to anticipate, any and every argument putting forward some particular action and some consequence seeming to flow from it. Once all injuries and dependencies, regardless of source or cause, become 'social costs' the state must reduce the incidence of injury as a way of containing costs. But just as the costs of injuries can no longer be billed to individuals blamed for setting the injurious action in motion, the incidence of injury can no longer be reduced by appealing to individual caution and caretaking. Injury can only be reduced by regulation.

Lowi's research illustrates Weber's account of the relationship between the role of formal legal rationality in the early modern development of capitalism and the modern experience of freedom in terms of the capacity for purposive-rational orientation of conduct. As long as 'personal' elements predominated in the dependency of people on one another social relationships were more or less immune to calculation and prediction. What this means from the standpoint of an individual who wishes to set up a new factory is that his or her responsibility to the community for the social repercussions incurred by the inevitably disruptive introduction of the new pattern of action are incalculable. As Lowi's discussion indicates, modern capitalism could only emerge with the implementation of legal devices for limiting the liability of such novel forms of economic conduct. As Weber argues, capitalism must be able to function 'according to *calculable rules* and "without regard for particular persons"' (FMW, 215). The disembedding of economic conduct from traditional norms evident in the example of the transformation of American tort law involved a redefinition through legal rules of the moral responsibility owed by economic actors to their communities for the negative consequences of their action. In this sense, modern social organization emancipates individuals from the constraints imposed by the moral impulses of more personal, face-to-face forms of interaction.

The explosive growth of a formal legal-rational complex of state regulation and administration in the twentieth century is a reflex of the functional interdependence of strangers. As Lawrence Friedman argues,

> *strangers* are in charge of important parts of our lives – people we do not know, and cannot control ... The people whose hands and machines create the conditions of life we depend on are totally invisible to us. We never see in person the people who make and repair automobiles, buses, trains, and airplanes. We never see in person the people who make sure the water we drink is pure and safe. But if these people are careless in their work, their mistakes can kill us. We cannot control the processes *personally*, cannot influence the outcomes. Yet the process *can* be controlled. Hence we demand norms from the state, from the collectivity, to guarantee the work of those strangers whose work is vital to our lives, which we cannot guarantee by ourselves.[8]

In this view, the regulatory-administrative framework of the modern welfare state is part of the structure of capitalist democracy. The neoconservative policies of the 1980s that sought to shrink government and reduce regulation inevitably ran up against these insuperable limits: the economically privileged are as unwilling to trust the market to get rid of poisoned foods, to keep airplanes well-maintained and drinking water clean, as anyone else. Ironically, the very economic exchange market championed by the deregulators is, in terms of the development of the legal dimension of modernity, the (perhaps primary) historical vehicle of the growth in regulation that they deplored.

The socialization of risk has contributed to the contemporary expectation of what Friedman calls 'total justice.' Before the twentieth century, the state played a much more limited role in people's lives. This owed in part to cultural values about the primacy of individual responsibility and was in part a result of significant technological limits in the capacity of the state to master uncertainties. Chance and fate – the existential uncertainties of disease and health and economic uncertainties – governed peoples' lives. Technological developments in medicine, transportation, communications, and so forth, dramatically increased human control over natural and social processes. These developments, combined with the development of public controls necessitated by the burgeoning capitalist market, led to a great revolution in expectations: 'first, a general expectation that the state will guarantee total justice, and second ..., a general expectation that the state will protect us from catastrophe.'[9]

The two expectations are intimately linked. If a house slips down into a ravine, the owners expect that the state will compensate them for the destruction of their home. It is a matter of justice, since the state regulates housing construction through a building code. If the house was ill-sited or improperly constructed, a building inspector should have spotted those problems. The home owner should not be made to suffer as a result of an unforeseeable catastrophe. Catastrophe is no longer attributed to bad luck, fate, or the hand of God, but to a process under human control, more specifically a process for which some state-enforced legal regulation is in place to prevent.

The constraining dimension of legal domination embodied in the impersonal bureaucratic regulatory-administrative complex of the modern state is thus linked to the enabling dimension of formal legal rationality itself. Modernity emancipates individuals from the stultifying social proximity of traditional domination, but this emancipation is purchased through the floatation of responsibility and socialization of risk that necessitates large-scale structures of bureaucratic regulation and administration. Old forms of personal domination are replaced by new, impersonal ones lacking the consolations of belonging and direction once imparted to individual life by the community. Individuals are disencumbered of ascriptive customs and restrictive social consid-erations for others, but they are increasingly entangled in a web of impersonal, formally regulated interdependencies.

## 1.2 The Positivization of Value-Orientations

Another general characteristic of modernity is the development among individuals of a calculating orientation to the selection of the 'ends' of social conduct, ends that were previously beyond the rule of free-choice behaviour, tied into a God-willed, teleological, nonequivocal normative order. The disembedding of economic relations and the resultant opening of a sphere of social relations to the rule of purpo-sive-rational conduct provided the first significant sociological embod-iment of the imaginary signification of rational mastery in the principle of the sovereignty of individual choice. The constitutionalization of structures of political power provided a sociological embodiment of the imaginary signification of autonomy in the principle that individu-als shall be bound only by those social arrangements to which they have chosen or given consent.

These developments represented a 'positivization' of value in the sense that, on the one hand, the ends of particular forms of social action were detached from ascriptive determinations and opened to the rule of individual means-ends calculation and, on the other hand, the legitimacy of set norms referred no longer to the 'objective' author-ity of tradition or revelation but ultimately to the binding power of individual choice. Historically, the sovereignty of choice was at first confined to the sphere of economic conduct. Subsequent extensions of the social permeation of formal legal rationality extend not only the functional differentiation of life-orders in terms of the rationalization of economic and political structures of power but also the social per-meation of individual free-choice behaviour, and they secure it an increasingly generalized justificatory basis.

If the modern identity of the individual is defined in terms of the capacity for autonomous generation of purposes, and if in the modern world the orientation of conduct to individually defined ends has only subjective validity, what kind of 'authority' can these value-prefer-ences possess? In the social scenario in which modern individual iden-tity is formed the authority of external forms of defining individual purposes (formerly teleological-theistic) is loosened, thus opening immense opportunities for individual self-elaboration by releasing purposes as the subject matter of individual choice. But the value-postulates according to which such individual identity is articulated no longer carry the authority formerly attributed to the perception of external authority as objective.

With the liberation of the individual from the external authority of prescribed purposes some sort of device is now required that will provide a secular justification for the moral autonomy of the individual, a device that will also bestow authority upon the value-postulates chosen by the autonomous individual. In modern legal domination this device is provided by the idea of individual legal rights. Modern legal rights purport to supply a foundation for a particular set of subjectively defined value-postulates. For instance, some contemporary efforts to protect the environment propose assigning 'rights' to animals and natural objects.[10] Whether or not animals, trees, or mountains eventually acquire such protections, these tactics reveal the centrality of rights conceptions in contemporary moral vocabulary.

The relationship between the positivity of values and the will-centred structure of selfhood illustrates the importance of efficacy and autonomy to modern identity. The autonomy of the modern individual involves following an internally generated purpose and owing allegiance only to those social arrangements that enjoy our consent; the efficacy of the modern individual involves the aspiration of mastery over self and nature in order to effectuate one's purposes. Legal rights facilitate individual autonomy by providing the moral authority for individuals to take a variety of value-oriented stances that would otherwise suffer from a deficit of authority. The role of legal rights in the facilitation of individual 'efficacy' can be understood as follows: if pursuing one's life in a properly human way means exercising control to effectuate one's purposes, if being a rational, autonomous moral agent means influencing and altering the world around us according to our own ends, how do we protect ourselves from being manipulated as the means to someone else's end?

This concern is crystallized in the problematic relationship between the autonomous individual and the purposes and ends generated by various social organizations. The bureaucratic rationality of social organizations, a rationality of matching means to ends with economy and efficiency, represents a specifically manipulative mode of power involving the limitation of someone's rights in the name of someone else's utility. With the opening of the purposes and ends of social conduct to planful manipulation some sort of device is required to prevent human life from being subsumed within a calculus of mastery that would vitiate the modern identity of moral autonomy. The notion of legal rights provides a safeguard for autonomy through the formulation of immunities due to people in terms of legal rights that anchor individual autonomy as an 'end' in itself.

Weber's interpretation of the meaning of modernity in terms of the disenchantment of metaphysical-theistic world-views and the thesis about the resultant positivization of values that can be derived from his social thought would seem to provide a narrow shelf for the conceptualization of legal rights in contemporary structures of legal power and authority. But Weber observed modernity from an early twentieth-century German vantage. As Maxwell Cohen wrote in 1968, no one before the end of the Second World War could have predicted the power or the consequences of legal rights discourse, 'its absorption into the wider arena of political debate in this generation, and the ease with which it has become part of the political dialogue, part of the debating experience of peoples in all parts of the world.'[11] Weber may have been prescient on a number of counts, but he was not clairvoyant.

Historical context, however, is obviously not the only reason for lacunae in Weber's sociology of modern law. In his interpretation of the objective structure of modernity in terms of the process of rationalization – that is, the formalization of social relations, the functional differentiation of life-orders, and the constitution of modern forms of authority – the role of formally rational legal rules features conspicuously. Not surprisingly, the Weberian interpretation of modernity in terms of irreversible bureaucratization and the concentration of power forms a percipient companion, if at times only in the background, to current efforts to understand the heteronomy of modern legal domination, particularly in discussions concerning the contemporary hypertrophy of the legal regulatory-administrative complex.

By contrast, Weber's emphasis on the emergence of large-scale organization and the application of formalized rules in the historical development of the structure of modern legal domination seems to have much less to add to current discussions of the 'explosion' of legal rights. Weber appears to have failed to anticipate that, in modern democratic capitalist societies, the notion of subjective legal rights would become an increasingly powerful term in the articulation of the identity and the social claims of modern individual autonomy. More to the point, he seems to have overemphasized the impact of the disenchantment of natural law doctrines of classical liberal theory on the social durability of notions of legal rights.

Weber's discussion of the role of individual rights in the structure of modern legal domination occurs primarily in the context of his contention that modern law becomes detached from 'natural law,' its original legitimatory basis, and rationalized in accordance with the instrumental logic of proceduralism. With the disenchantment of enlightenment 'reason,' the metajuristic implications of the modern legal order – the natural law doctrines of classical liberal philosophy – supposedly expire *in toto* (ES, 874–5). Despite such prognoses however, Weber never imagined that the sociological relevance of the liberal notion of rights would disappear altogether, unless the ideal of individual autonomy itself was somehow superseded. As he remarked, 'it is a gross self-deception to believe that without the achievements of the age of the Rights of Man any one of us, including the most conservative, can go on living his life' (ES, 1403).

More significantly, although Weber insisted that the desubstantivization and positivization of norms renders the classical liberal philosophy of natural rights doctrine incapable of supplying a philosophical foundation for modern law, his critique does not preclude the possibility that the social diffusion and institutionalization of legal rights might eventually draw from other justificatory significations. In fact, the contemporary identification of individual autonomy with the capacity for rights-assertion and the concomitant rise of the rights-oriented polity, with its regulation of value-conflict through adjudication, are anticipated by Weber's interpretation of the relationship between formal legal rationality and the modern experience of freedom and by his depiction of modernity in terms of rationalization and intellectualization.

According to Weber's rational-individualist theory of 'personality' discussed earlier, individuals become fully realized moderns to the extent that they are capable of organizing their lives through teleological action, a process involving the maintenance of a certain degree of inner distance vis-à-vis one's inner nature, external nature, and other people. Translated as a program, the rational-individualist theory of the self involves the liberation of people from subjection to nature and unchosen ties to others. Through the disengagement of the telos of individual conduct from social determinants in key areas of modern life, and the elimination of social proximity to extended others, legal domination enables individuals to fulfil this modern program of rebellion against fate and ascription. Whereas premodern individuals derived their identity from the fulfilment of purposes specified by external authorities such as divine law, natural teleology, and, more generally, moral custom and hierarchical authority, modern individuals follow and effectuate internally generated purposes.

A recurring theme in Weber's sociological depiction of modern society is the continual growth of value-conflict that results from the disintegration of community and the weakening of moral custom. Value-orientations are generated by an individual's 'constant and intrinsic relation to certain ultimate "values" and "meanings" of life, "values" and "meanings" which are forged into purposes and thereby translated into rational-teleological action' (RK, 192). In other words, value-orientations are subjectively generated out of the inner properties of individuals, their beliefs, attitudes, and value-commitments.

Given the basis of value-orientations in the inner, subjective properties of individuals, the conflict between divergent orientations is a universal historical phenomenon describable in terms of Weber's concept of charisma. But there are two important aspects of modern society that sharpen the conflict of value-orientations. First, with the diminishing determinacy of custom and revelation in the creation of value and purposes, the modern situation underscores the issue of existential meaning as an individual's problem, thereby increasing the functional importance of subjective preference based on the inner properties of individuals in the formation of their identities. The inescapable question faced by any self-aware modern individual is 'which of the warring gods should we serve'? (FMW, 153). Moreover, the importance of subjective preference in relation to the requirements of existential meaning ceases to be a concern of the virtuosi few, a marginal phenomenon of the rare charismatic individual. Rather, modern subjectivity per se, that is, the modern self in its most general and ordinary forms, is based on the charisma of self-expression.

A second aspect of modern society that sharpens the conflict of value-orientations is illustrated in an important point made by Brubaker: as Weber's use of the concept of charisma indicates, throughout history the charisma of individual value-creation has not only divided communities with a creative disruption of tradition but has also 'swept through the great communities like a firebrand, welding them together' (FMW, 155). In the past the charisma of individual value-creation has thus been both disruptive and integrative, divisive and binding. In the modern world, however, rationalization and disenchantment increase the divisive potentiality of charisma. While the disenchanted character of modern culture enlarges the moral significance of individual value-creation for the formation of 'personality,' the rational character of modern social arrangements diminishes the causal significance of individual acts of value-creation in the forging of community. As a result, Brubaker argues, 'individual value-creators lose their power to bind communities together ... But value-creation by individuals retains its significance as a great *divider* of communities. The struggle between ultimate value-orientations in the modern world is not, as formerly, a struggle of entire solidary communities against one another: it is *increasingly* a struggle of *small sects*, and *ultimately* a struggle of *individuals*.'[12]

The redefinition of modern normative power as individual choice and consent means that all the 'moral givens' of tradition are called into question. Moreover, as modern societies define the duties and obligations that follow from social roles in increasingly abstract, formal, and impersonal rules, the attitude of moral rebellion and questioning that was once the privilege and virtue of heroes, prophets, and moral sages increasingly becomes part of the everyday structure of life. The corollary of the normative power of individual choice is the assertion of individual efficacy and autonomy in terms of legal rights. The notion of legal rights facilitates individual efficacy by bestowing authority upon the subjective preferences behind the formulation of individual purposes; it also protects individual autonomy from the interference of other individuals' subjective preferences.

An expansion of the importance of subjective legal rights in the articulation of social claims and the interpretation of individuals' public identity as citizens can be discerned with varying degrees of conspicuousness in the Western capitalist democracies.[13] A recent study conducted by David Engel of the attitudes held by individuals in a rural county of Illinois towards the assertion of individual efficacy through the litigation of legal rights clearly plots a transformation of conceptions about the relationship between individuals and the larger community, expressed in the changing form of legal subjectivity.[14] Engel discovered that the older generation in this county were much more averse to suing for damages than the younger generation. He sees 'individualism' as a core value in American culture but distinguishes between two distinct types: individualism emphasizing 'self-sufficiency and personal responsibility' predominated among the older generation of the community while a 'rights-oriented individualism' was common among the younger generation. The older form of individualism, despite its emphasis on self-sufficiency, retained values from 'an earlier face-to-face community.' In particular, it retained a concept of 'personal responsibility' that functioned to situate the self vis-à-vis the community according to the notion of a 'general welfare' that provided an outer limit to the expression of self-interest of particular individuals. By contrast, the newer form of individualism places the goal of realizing one's own person as paramount to the purposes and ends defined by the community. This form of individualism does not hesitate to seek remedies for whatever damage to self-interest the individual suffers.[15]

The contrast between the older and newer forms of individualism drawn by Engel parallels the contrast between the 'situated self' and the 'unencumbered self' (to borrow MacIntyre's felicitous terminology) that features in the debate between communitarians and liberal rights theorists. These competing conceptions of selfhood and their attendant forms of legal subjectivity are summarized in a compact manner by Michael Sandel. The liberal conception of unencumbered personhood, he argues, is linked with a rights-based ethic that 'begins with the claim that we are separate, individual persons, each with our own aims, interests, and conceptions of the good, and seeks a framework of rights that will enable us to realize our capacity as free moral agents, consistent with a similar liberty for others.'[16] By contrast, according to the communitarian conception of situated personhood we are defined by the communities we inhabit and thereby implicated in the purposes and ends characteristic of those communities.

The Kantian liberal rights, communitarian debate in all of its vicissitudes cannot be pursued here. It is worthwhile to note, however, that even commentators sympathetic to the communitarian critique of the Kantian liberal hypostatization of individual rights concede that a number of features of modern social arrangements – such as the division of labour and the partitioning of modern life into a variety of segments, each with its own norms and modes of behaviour – represent structural handicaps to the possibility of conceiving of society in the inclusive, unified fashion required by the communitarian project.

What emerges as an underlying agreement in the debate is the observation that, notwithstanding how one wishes to assess this development, the conception of personhood socially manifest in the capitalist democracies is increasingly correspondent with the liberal rights version of the unencumbered self. As MacIntyre laments, whether or not this liberal unencumbered self is 'true,' it is increasingly ascendent over earlier, more 'situated' conceptions of personhood. Thus the optimal notion of personhood that prevails in the West is one of atomic, apolitical individuals maximizing their self-interest.

The institutional corollary of rights-asserting individualism is the rights-oriented polity. If the conception of personhood ascendent in the West is one of the unencumbered self, then individuals' self-understanding of their public identity increasingly involves the assertion of rights against, and the diminution of responsibility to, the larger community. Charles Taylor draws a contrast between the rights-oriented society of unencumbered selves and the 'participatory' society that situates and implicates individuals in the purposes and ends of the community. As Taylor argues, 'virtually every polity today claims to be a rights society, and all liberal democratic ones effectively are,' but 'a rights model society is very likely one where broad social goals are pursued through the courts' and the self-understanding of citizens' public identity 'resides crucially in the ability to secure one's rights, even against the political will of the majority.'[17]

The transition from a 'participatory' to a rights-oriented polity and the eclipse of the notion of the 'common good' by the fundamentalism of rights is reflected in the greater emphasis on the defence of rights through court action as a substitute for the sense of having a say in collective decision-making processes such as the democratic forum. As Sandel argues, liberty in the participatory republic 'was defined, not in opposition to democracy, as an individual's guarantee against what the majority might will, but as a function of democracy, of democratic institutions'; 'civil liberty referred not to a set of personal rights, in the sense of immunities, as in the modern "right to privacy", but, in Hamilton's words, "to a share in the government".'[18] By contrast, liberty in the rights-oriented polity 'is defined, not as a function of democracy but in opposition to democracy, as an individual's guarantee against what the majority might will. I am free insofar as I am the bearer of rights, where rights are trumps.'[19]

The rights-oriented polity and the rights-asserting conceptions of unencumbered selfhood mean a greater penetration of formal legal rationality into areas of social life previously informally regulated. Lawrence Friedman illustrates this development with the example of the importation of notions of 'due process' into the administration of North American institutions such as universities. The extension of formal legal rationality into social milieux previously dominated by the informal discretionary power of status-based hierarchy and privilege represents the spread of courtlike procedures into areas of social conduct that were once only indirectly regulated by law. Until well into the twentieth century, the discretionary power of universities to fire staff and discipline students was nearly unlimited because such institutions enjoyed both practical and legal immunity. Today, however, professors and students have the 'right' to some sort of formal review within the university over a wide range of issues bearing on their relationship to the organization. As Friedman writes, 'the organization is expected to do justice, to live up to the standards of justice. And it should do so both in terms of the *procedures* it follows, and in terms of the rules and norms it applies.'[20] The spread of formally rational courtlike procedures to the environs of institutions like the modern university is only one example of a more general legalization of political structures of power and authority under way in the advanced capitalist democracies today.

## 2. The Developmental 'Dynamic' of Legal Rationalization: The Entanglement of Detached Selves and the Detachment of Entangled Individuals

The formalization of social arrangements and the positivization of value-orientations illustrate the general character of modern legal domination. Weber's conception of formal legal rationality anticipates the unfolding of the broader sociological processes that underlie the legal developments pertaining to the emergence of the regulatory-administrative state and the rights-oriented polity. In this final section, I wish to illustrate the interconnection between these two salient dimensions of contemporary legal domination. The crux of my argument is that rights-oriented conceptions of the relation between self and other and the expanding regulatory-administrative structure of the modern state, the ideal of individual emancipation and the project of rational mastery, have the same root in the structure of legal-rational domination and form the opposing sides of one and the same process of legal rationalization.

In Weber's account of the developmental history of Western law, the corollary to the functional differentiation of the subsystems of economy and state is the constitution of the property-owning legal subject as bearer of economic rights. The formal legal-rational constitutionalization of economic and political structures of power has extended the application of legal rights from their original link with property relations. The extension of individual rights and the formal legal rational guarantee of individual autonomy and the normative power to effectuate volitionally assigned purposes has occurred, paradoxically, through the rationalization of economic and political structures of power that tend to dictate the channels through which individual purposes can be effectuated. Thus, alongside the rise of modern capitalism and bureaucracy, the cosmos of formally rational social arrangements, one can observe an expansion of the forms and applications of individual rights that extends far beyond the classical political and property rights of the eighteenth and nineteenth centuries. The modern conception of the individual as an autonomous generator of purposes is tied increasingly to the legal rights concept.

To illustrate the dynamic of legal rationalization behind these developments I will turn to Anthony Giddens's discussion of the 'transformation of intimacy' and the emergence of 'pure relationships' in contemporary 'love forms.'[21] The transformation of intimacy that Giddens observes in contemporary society is a telling example of the dynamic of legal rationalization precisely because the realm of intimate, interpersonal relations is a social context in which one would least expect to find legal processes at work. It is important to bear in mind, however, that formal legal rationality is as much bound up in modern conceptions of selfhood as it is implicated in more obviously 'legal' manifestations of social organization. In a sense, law is never absent from the face of modern social relations, even in those 'private' domains where voluntarism and intimacy rule. It is through the legal rationalization of modern social arrangements that such zones of personal discretion are constituted in the first place.[22]

As Lawrence Stone argues, the institution of the lifelong irreversible marriage of the past was founded upon the inequality and subordination of women.[23] In a sense, the transformation of intimacy reflects a final emancipation of love relationships from the social functions they were once meant to serve. But, not surprisingly, the form of this emancipation bears a family resemblance to the liberal conceptions of autonomy that originally emerged in the sphere of economic activity, where autonomy represented freedom from the social obligations of community and, apropos of pure relationships, moral responsibilities to the other. Pure relationships are assumed *not* to be 'till death do us part'; rather, they are lived through as episodic, meaning that the togetherness of the partners is 'until further notice.' As Bauman argues, the conveniences and flexibilities of modern intimacy derive from its elimination of 'all reference to moral duties and obligations,' in other words, its 'floatation' of moral responsibility.[24]

Weber's distinction between 'status' and 'purposive contracts' is highly apposite to this transformation in modern love forms. Premodern status contracts, which 'involve a change in what may be called the total legal situation (the universal position) and the social status of the persons involved' (ES, 672), correspond with the traditional love form of the monogamous, 'till death do us part' marriage. In contrast to the status contract that transforms the 'universal position' of the legal subject, the purposive contract, which presupposes the idea of the individual as possessing an identity that exists independently of the particular attributes that may be added or subtracted as a result of contractual agreement, corresponds with the modern 'pure relationship.' In contrast to the unlimited, exceptionless responsibility entailed in the traditional status-contract pattern of lifelong monogamous marriage, a pattern of 'pure relationships' reminiscent of the purposive contract is emerging in which, as Giddens writes, the relationship 'is continued only in so far as it is thought by both parties to deliver enough satisfactions for each individual to stay with it.'[25]

The construction of pure relationships exemplifies a process in which the traditional norms governing a particular social practice have been desubstantivized of their sense of naturalness and inevitability and positivized such that a calculating orientation may attach itself to the figuration of 'ends' formerly considered beyond the application of free-choice behaviour. One of the most important aspects of the process of 'rationalization' of action, Weber argues, is the displacement of 'unthinking acquiescence in customary ways as well as of devotion to norms consciously accepted as absolute values' by the 'deliberate adaptation to situations in terms of self-interest' (ES, 30).

Just as the costs of purposive economic conduct had to be distributed and contained through a network of legal regulations, the freedom to arrange love relationships more fully in accordance with the logic of personal choice has been given statutory embodiment in a complex of legal domination that formalizes the social practices and positivizes the norms involving intimate relations. By eliminating moral proximity legal domination increases the predictability and calculability of human relations, thus facilitating individual autonomy.

At first sight, these legal instruments (such as 'no-fault divorce,' family courts for dealing with child support and custody, etc.) appear to break up domination structures within the old-style patriarchal household. Marriages are no longer cast in immutable form but can be reversed by choice. But choice is most telling to the ears of the strong. Although pure relationships float moral responsibility between the partners, the problem is that love relationships are frequently consequential, producing new and growing responsibilities that may not be symmetrically borne by the participants. Child-rearing is just one example. The practical consequences of the emergence of pure relationships may bring advantages for individual family members, but also, for example, greater state involvement in the allocation of custody of and/or care for children's welfare. The legal recipes on offer for managing the inevitable fallout of failed pure relationships differ from the traditional care of children in the way the latest tariff of welfare handouts differs from sharing a meal. Thus on closer inspection 'emancipation' may prove to be a vehicle of another form of domination. The arena of individual choice is enlarged but the bureaucratic-regulatory structure of the state increases the density of formally organized action pertaining to the family. As legal articulation of the relevant action systems is the official sponsor behind this floatation of responsibility, emancipation from the constraints imposed by customary norms is exchanged for the heteronomy of regulatory-administrative organizations supervised by state agencies.

An important part of the feasibility of modern pure relationships involves the development of legal enabling devices like the 'no-fault' divorce and legal privileges such as those attached to non-marital forms of cohabitation. The right to divorce was first asserted against religious authority by King Henry VIII in 1528 but divorce remained a privilege of wealthy men well into the twentieth century; the full social diffusion of divorce as a universal right was not achieved until the late 1960s. It may seem odd to consider divorce a legal right; after all, in the West, divorce provisions are technically statutes rather than codified articles of any constitution. However, since the late 1960s uncomplicated access to divorce along with non-marital patterns of cohabitation have become part of the paraphernalia of individual freedom. If today an American or Canadian government attempted a statutory proscription of divorce, the legislation would certainly strike many people as an infringement upon their freedom of association and their right to fashion their private lives according to personal preference.

This advance of legal rights cannot occur without a fuller social permeation of the concept of the atomic individual, separate from the community context and oriented to the maximization of self-interest. The disencumbering of the self from the constraints of social considerations is accompanied by a positivization of norms (in the sense that the community is reduced to nothing but an aggregation of private interests) and a formalization of the now increasingly impersonal relations between strangers. To disengage individuals from the constraints of the locale, however, requires a floatation of the kind of moral responsibility to community that face-to-face interactions between family and neighbours demand. This is achieved through the extension of social relations in time and space by modern institutions such as the capitalist market.

However, the greater the number of people that are freed from social ties to community, the more complex and extended structures of social organization must become to sustain their disengagement. With the sophisticated division of labour of modern capitalism and the ever-extending chains of interaction laid by modern institutions, people become more functionally interdependent at the same time as they become more estranged from one another. An environment combining delocalized impersonality with functional interdependence makes bureaucratic regulation and adminstration indispensable. The wide extension of social relations in time and space created by modern institutions, though freeing individuals from the constraints of the locale, also exposes them in an unprecedented fashion to the unintended consequences of economic and political activities conducted far and near, for which no one particular individual or group can be realistically assigned responsibility. In a sense, the moral requirements of modern society are raised far beyond the level demanded by the face-to-face interactions of the premodern community. At the same time, however, the likelihood of obtaining such an enhanced moral 'responsivity' in the arena of social action is diminished not only by the structural features of modernity – such as the 'thinning' of social relations due to the disintegration of community and the functional differentiation of society – but also from the loss of universally accepted foundational criteria for grounding moral standards that results from the process of disenchantment and intellectualization.

In this cultural scenario, when disengaged individuals feel caught up in a threatening tangle of incomprehensible dependencies, an immediate response is to seek to reinforce autonomy through an augmentation of legally protected rights and immunities. If modern society is heading towards irreversible bureaucratization and concentrations of power, and if this process is accompanied by an increasing atomization of individuals, then, as Charles Taylor suggests, the most obvious device at our disposal to rescue and give expression to the dignity of free agents is perhaps a greater emphasis on the defence of rights through court action.[26]

Of course, the more rights-oriented conceptions of modern selfhood become, the more individual dignity is identified with the assertion of legal rights against the 'community.' The more individuals are disengaged from collectively defined entities such as 'community,' the less they can rely on informal norms of assumption, and social interaction becomes increasingly dependent on deliberately enacted legal norms to provide the 'traffic rules' of engagement. But given the absence of a sense of connection with common purposes, the rules are experienced by detached selves as unwanted entanglements. Entangled individuals struggle to reinforce their detachment through legal rights and the circle turns onwards. This is the sense in which the relationship between individual autonomy and formal legal rationality means 'the greatest possible freedom through the greatest possible domination.'[27] As this paradoxical formulation suggests, it is the ambivalent nature of modernity (at least in its historically instantiated, formal legal-rational version) that the movement and aspiration to subjective freedom seem quixotically bound up with new forms of objective domination.

The threat of a kind of 'self-cancellation' of modernity via its own practices is a prominent element in the pathos of Weber's prognosis of the future of the West: as the imaginary significations of modernity (individual autonomy and rational mastery) are socially diffused and actualized, they themselves may undermine the realizability of modernity as an historical project. It is difficult to assess whether or not the problem here lies with the imaginary significations themselves, or with their specific historical instantiation. But Weber's account of the developmental history of legal rationalization places a strong emphasis on the import of the autonomous logic of capitalist economic rationalization on the shape and direction of legal development. Not surprisingly, some recent studies have pointed out the striking homology between models of individual freedom as choice and patterns of consumption that have emerged since the Second World War.[28] By drawing on the resources of money and markets individuals can rely less on social resources and need not prudentially maintain social ties on grounds of required support. This expression of 'freedom' augments the functional interdependence of people within the capitalist economy.

The early modern constitutionalization of economic and political structures of power and authority facilitated a qualitative and quantitative growth in the capacity for the individual exercise of autonomy, expressed in terms of the possibility for purposive-rational conduct within a wide sphere of private discretion. This legal rationalization also produced substantively irrational consequences, such as the proletarianization of labour resulting from the uneven effects of the purposive contractual schema of association. Thus, the relationship between formal legal rationality and individual freedom has been proximal, limited in its development by social and economic inequalities. But unlike earlier stages of legal development, it seems almost as if the countertendencies produced by the contemporary dynamic of legal development result from the character of formal legal rationality itself. To paraphrase Habermas's assessment of the current predicament of law: it is now the very means of guaranteeing freedom which has come to endanger freedom.[29]

It is a striking feature of modern societies that they offer a powerful promise of individual autonomy at the same time as they implicate individuals in a formidable array of dependencies and expectations that they did not choose and which they increasingly reject. A central theme in Weber's interpretation of modernity is that, while the rationality of modern social arrangements captures individuals within an iron cage of structured but impersonal realms of purposive-rational conduct, a concomitant dissolution of 'community,' or 'privatization of ideals,' increasingly dissolves the ties between them. These developments leave individuals, in Sandel's words, more *entangled* but less *attached* than ever before, 'entangled in a network of obligations and involvements unassociated with any act of will, and yet unmediated by those common identifications or expansive self-definitions that could make them tolerable.'[30]

# The Constitutionalization of Individual Rights in Canada: A Case Study in the 'Dynamic' of Legal Rationalization

One of the signal characteristics of contemporary social experience in the advanced capitalist democracies is the pervasive legalization of social relationships. The salient features of our contemporary structure of legal domination are the regulatory-administrative state *and* the rights-oriented polity. Both features of contemporary legal domination can be explicated within the framework of Weber's conception of formal legal rationality and by extrapolating Weber's account of legal rationalization. The interpretation of the regulatory-administrative dimension of modern societies in terms of formal legal rationality and purposive-rational action need not be laboured here. Even Weber's critics more or less accept the applicability of these concepts to the instrumental, regulated dimensions of modern society, such as the capitalist market and the bureaucratic organization.[1]

Nevertheless, many commentators argue that Weber's concept of formal legal rationality is no longer apposite to important aspects of contemporary legal development, particularly the rise of the rights-oriented polity. Kettler and Meja, for example, state that 'few disagree that adjudication ever more visibly depends on reasonings which Weber considered substantive,' as the rise of the rights-oriented polity brings 'broad purposive principles and diversified adjudicative methods into prominence greater than the systematized norms and technical legal procedures of Weber's formal rationality model.'[2] For many commentators, legal development today in general reflects a pattern of 'deformalization' – that is, a substantive rationalization of the structure of legal domination – which Weber's account of legal rationalization failed to anticipate.[3] Identification of the institutional reality of legal

rights with a more general process of legal rationalization is unortho-
dox and warrants some form of empirical substantiation.[4] This chapter
will examine the impact of constitutional adjudication of individual
rights on Canadian political culture.

According to Charles Taylor, a rights-*oriented* society must be understood as a polity 'where broad social goals are pursued through the
courts' and the self-understanding of citizens' political activity 'resides
crucially in the ability to secure one's rights, even against the political
will of the majority.'[5] Other polities – the United States, for example –
might seem a more obvious empirical referent for this kind of study.
However, Canada provides an ideal context for an investigation of this
type. The new Constitution Act and the Charter of Rights and Freedoms were formally enacted in Ottawa on 17 April 1982. Although the
constitutional adjudication of individual rights in Canada is thus comparatively recent, the Canadian modification of the British legacy of
parliamentary supremacy by an empowerment of the judiciary to
review legislation in the name of promoting and protecting individual
autonomy, and the Canadian movement from a participatory to a
rights-oriented polity, provides a perspicuous example of the dynamic
of legal rationalization and its countertendencies for individual autonomy. This developmental dynamic can be detected more generally, but
less obviously, in most advanced capitalist democracies of the West.

The first section of this chapter will illustrate that the legitimacy of
judicial review in Canada is rooted in the idea that judicial reason is
impartial and non-ideological; it draws its legitimacy from the putative
formal legal rationality of its decision-making processes (ES, 656–7).
The record of constitutional adjudication, however, reveals the problematic relationship between the rationality of the judicial decision-
making process and the subjective preferences and values of judges. In
Weber's view, it is precisely this fundamental difference between facts
and values that provides the unifying principle linking the economic
and political arrangements of modern society with their legal integument. Thus, like all other modern rationalisms, the rationality of the
judicial decision-making process pertains only to the efficient linking
of 'means' with 'ends,' in this case, the determination of whether or not
a law is formally 'correct' in terms of its consistency with procedures of
enactment and with existing laws (ES, 37). In other words, the rationality of judicial decision-making does not extend to the setting of ends,
that is, it cannot determine 'whether there should be law and whether
one should establish just these rules' (FMW, 144).

But the setting of ends is precisely the task into which judicial powers of review are inevitably drawn. As we will see, Charter adjudication in Canada reveals a pattern of incoherent interpretive approaches to the constitution. This pattern is symptomatic of the contradiction between the 'square' of a formally rational judicial decision-making process and the 'circle' of determining the legal meaning of various individual 'rights' and 'freedoms': squaring the circle in this case would involve finding rational, legally correct solutions to issues of social and economic policy without reference to extrajuristic values. As Weber's model of modern legal rationality would suggest, the task is impossible precisely because solutions to problems of competing ethical standards must be posited: they are inherently political. The rise of judicial forms of power in Canada represents the 'inappropriate' legalization of the value-setting function of the political, legislative arm of the state by judicial forms of decision making, and hence a depoliticization of political processes by legal rationalization.

The second section of this chapter argues that, despite the incoherence and inconsistency of Charter adjudication in its interpretation of the constitution, the record of rights adjudication in Canada reveals a substantive pattern behind the ways in which individual autonomy has been given legal protection and promotion. Whenever courts interpret rights and freedoms they enact into law a particular vision of society. The record of Charter adjudication reveals an emphasis on formal individualistic rights, an anticollective bias in attitudes towards state regulation and labour interests, and the treatment of private property as sacrosanct. It is the combination of the way in which the Charter defines the substance of individual autonomy and the way in which it then depoliticizes this value-setting as the only legally correct vision of freedom available that makes the overall functioning of Charter adjudication in Canada representative of a larger process of formal legal rationalization. The impact of the Charter on Canadian society displays the tell-tale pattern of the dynamic of legal rationalization described in the previous chapter, that is, the formalization of social arrangements and the positivization of value-orientations.

## 1. The Rise of Judicial Forms of Political Power in the Rights-Oriented Polity

Until the 1982 enactment of the Constitution Act and the Charter of Rights and Freedoms, the British convention of parliamentary supremacy governed the relationship between the judiciary and representative institutions in Canada. Legislatures were responsible for making positive law while the judiciary was confined to applying it (cf. FMW, 219). The setting of values involves the imposition of preference and is thus a political activity reserved for legislators who are democratically accountable; once so determined, values can be applied by judges in a technically rational fashion. Thus, in the Canadian state before 1982, the institutions with ultimate responsibility for deciding the degree to which the rights and freedoms of individuals could be tolerably constrained were the legislatures, which could impose any rule they liked, provided the subject matter was within their jurisdiction, and established procedures for rule making were followed. Under this arrangement the judiciary was empowered to determine whether or not a legislature had violated these restraints. The courts, however, could only adjudicate the procedural and jurisdictional correctness of legislatively enacted rules; they could not pronounce on the contents of those rules. The interpretive nature of judicial inquiry gave the courts some content-regulating powers, but they had always to justify such activity by resorting to the claim they were merely engaging in jurisdictional and procedural review.[6]

In addition to procedural and jurisdictional restraints supervised by the judiciary, legislatures were also restrained by political conventions that were non-legally binding, yet quasi-constitutional in character. For example, conventions such as the universal franchise and the various freedoms that individuals possess to dispose of their property as they like, to believe what they wish, to hold preferences in religious belief, to associate with others of their own choosing, to speak freely about any matter, to assemble for peaceful purposes, and so on, could not be altered by the legislature without threatening the election prospects of the government. The real restraint on legislative powers to alter such conventions was the accountability of legislators to the electorate.

With the 1982 advent of the Charter, the judicial power to review legislative activity has become the linchpin of the new institutional framework of the Canadian state. As Glasbeek writes, 'the courts are, by definition, no longer bound to accept an otherwise properly enacted law as a legitimate exercise in democracy.'[7] The rights and freedoms expressed in the Charter are not new to Canadian society; in fact, they have long served as the background norms for a relatively open and tolerant parliamentary democracy. It was generally accepted long before the Charter that Canadians possess certain fundamental rights and freedoms. What the Charter does is, first, clearly identify and explicitly codify what those rights and freedoms are and, in theory, provide redress through the courts should they be denied or infringed by any of the federal or provincial governments. More significantly, as we will see, the constitutional entrenchment of rights and freedoms means that, whereas parliament and elected legislators once supplied the content of these fundamental rights, under the Charter, the courts and non-elected judges have now been given content-determining powers.

A central theme in arguments in favour of the constitutional entrenchment of rights and the empowerment of the judiciary to review legislation in accordance with the protection of these rights was that fundamental rights and freedoms are too important to Canadian political culture to be left as nonlegally binding political conventions. The governments formed from temporary majorities of elected legislators should not have the power to limit the scope of fundamental entitlements. Thus, this argument continues, fundamental rights and freedoms should be entrenched in a Charter and the judiciary empowered to scrutinize and invalidate legislative actions that run contrary to its provisions.

Note that the central premise of this argument is that, while decision making in the legislative arena and any other participatory political process is influenced by passion and opinion, judicial decision making is structured by reason and neutrality: judges can tackle difficult issues in 'a principled, disciplined fashion.'[8] Already, there is cause for concern with this argument. If Weber's conception of legal rationality is accurate, then the discipline and neutrality of judicial reason holds only within narrow formalist parameters, which the demands of judicial review, involving the assessment of the substantive *content* of legislatively enacted norms, would inevitably exceed.

The legitimacy of judicial review in a democratic state depends on the claim that judicial decision making is uniquely disciplined by its legal rationality. If decision making about the rights and freedoms which are said to be at the centre of the Canadian political system is transferred from the legislatures, which can be held accountable through the electoral process, to the courts, which are unelected and unaccountable, judicial reasoning must be distinguished from and disciplined by mechanisms absent in the political arena. But does the actual performance of the Canadian judiciary support these claims?

*1.1 Formal Legal Rationality and the Problem of Value-Setting*

From the record of Canadian constitutional adjudication one can discern three ideal-typical strategies that have been employed by jurists to legitimate judicial review powers.[9] Corresponding to Weber's conception of the ideal-typical basis of legitimacy in legal-rational authority, the first strategy appeals to 'restraint.' Here, it is argued that discretion and personal choice are involved in the resolution of value-conflicts, but judicial decision making can be disciplined and thus 'rationalized' to the extent that judicial review is formally confined to procedural and jurisdictional analyses of statutes. The judiciary must minimize its activism and defer on substantive or policy issues to the discretion of the legislature. The pre-Charter institutional role of the judiciary in the Canadian state corresponds with this approach to the legitimacy of judicial activity.

With the 1982 Constitution Act, the jurisdictional and procedural correctness of legislative action are no longer sufficient grounds for the courts to uphold the constitutional validity of an enacted statute; the judiciary has been handed a specific mandate to assess the constitutional validity of government action. The problem is that the Supreme Court has failed to formulate a consistent response to the issue of judicial review. The record of Charter adjudication reveals an arbitrary pattern of restraint in some cases, activism in others. The Supreme Court–argued labour relations (*Alberta Labour Reference*), provincial Sunday closing legislation (*Big M Drug Mart* and *Edwards Books and Art*), and language rights (*Société des Acadiens*) were issues of policy, that is, political matters, in which the court chose to defer to the judgment of the legislatures.[10] Yet anti-combines legislation (*Hunter v. Southam*), abortion (*Morgentaler*), and the testing of cruise missiles (*Operation Dismantle*) were within the mandate of judicial intervention.[11] Note that there is no uncontroversial way to draw the line between these cases. Surely the very question of whether or not a case is 'political,' and therefore requires judicial restraint, is itself a political issue that cannot be neutrally decided. A selective use of judicial restraint is as bad as no restraint, for it gives the courts tremendous discretion to shape government policy under the guise of assessing the constitutional viability of legislation. This discretionary power has never been coherently justified by the Supreme Court.

A second 'intermediate' strategy for legitimating judicial review appeals to 'trust.' Acknowledging that some discretion and personal choice is involved in all judicial decision making, it is argued that we can trust the judiciary more than the legislatures to balance competing issues impartially and reasonably. Trust-based legitimation arguments accept that judicial policy making is not only necessary but a desirable aspect of constitutional adjudication. Accordingly, judges solve cases through a form of arbitrated interest-balancing. Judges must articulate the competing interests involved in a dispute, then impartially and reasonably evaluate the merits of each and the consequences of allowing one set of interests to prevail over another. For example, in *Dolphin Delivery*, the court ruled that freedom of expression did not imply the Charter protection of secondary picketing.[12] The court weighed the interest of unions in free expression versus the public's interest in avoiding the adverse consequences of union picketing, and concluded that the latter interest 'reasonably' outweighed the former.

The problem with a trust-based legitimation argument is that it depends on a conception of the judge as neutral, disembodied, and disinterested. Interest-balancing is an expedient device for giving legal decision making the appearance of technical calculation: the metaphor of 'weighing' interests suggests impartial quantitative evaluation of issues. But it does not actually eliminate the subjectivism of judicial choice. First, interests must be defined. Judges portray the process of defining interests as if it were self-evident and uncontroversial, but it is not. The manner in which an interest is characterized has enormous implications for the perceived importance of the interest. The courts can define an interest as universal or specific, as a matter of principle or of contingent political bargaining. Interests can be made to look more or less important in relation to one another, depending on how the courts define them. Second, even if one could arrive at an uncontroversial definition of the interests involved in a particular case, the balancing of those interests is itself controversial and highly susceptible to the influence of the subjective preferences of judges.

Judges are aware of the problem of the partiality of the judicial perspective and very keen to nurture an image of ideological neutrality.[13] The problem is that the judiciary *does* represent particular social interests and judges *are* embodied members of society who cannot be presumed impartial. Judges operate near the centres of economic and political power in society, and within an institutional framework committed to preserving and perpetuating the economic and political order as it exists.[14] The nub of the problem with trust-based legitimation arguments is that they beg the question of why we ought to trust judges to articulate interests objectively, balance them neutrally, and to find just solutions to controversial political issues when the viewpoints they bring to their judicial interpretive activity are so manifestly partial.

Finally, corresponding to Weber's conception of value-rational forms of legitimation, a third strategy for legitimating judicial review activities appeals to 'constraint.' This approach argues that judges do not substitute their preferences for those of elected officials, for they are constrained by the 'truth' of the constitutional text, or by the unique modes of interpretation they are trained to employ for ascertaining the legal meaning of the text. The central difficulty constraint-based theories of legitimacy face is that constitutional texts are so open-textured. The Charter contains phrases like 'freedom of conscience,' 'freedom of expression,' 'freedom of association,' 'the right to liberty,' 'principles of fundamental justice,' 'the right to equal benefit of the law without discrimination,' and so on. Supreme Court Justice Wilson wrote that 'the protected rights are enumerated in a brief written document and they are couched in broad and contestable terms such as "liberty", "security" and "equality". These are concepts upon which libraries have been written, kings have been beheaded and revolutions have been waged. It would therefore be a considerable understatement to say that fundamental human rights are "open-textured".'[15] Justice McIntyre complained in *Morgentaler* that 'the courts must confine themselves to such democratic values as are clearly expressed in the *Charter* and refrain from imposing or creating rights with no identifiable base in the *Charter*.'[16] But as Russell argues, cutting constitutional rights out of vague generalities is exactly what the court must and has been doing: 'I think of these phrases as limp balloons which the constitution-makers have handed to the judiciary; the judges must now decide how much air to blow into them.'[17]

It is obviously quite implausible to argue that judicial decision making is constrained by its fidelity to the 'truths' of the text, for the text of the Charter, like any other text, is open to interpretation. Thus constraint-based legitimation arguments are forced to devise auxiliary models of interpretation to discipline the process of rendering determinate meanings from the constitutional text. One such model for squaring the circle of Charter adjudication is the idea of purposive interpretation, which argues that judicial reasoning is allegedly constrained by the principles that underlie the constitution, or the purposes served by its provisions.

The question of what sources should be used to determine purposes is itself difficult to resolve. Since Charter provisions are general, an interpretation of their meanings must rely on supplementary references to extrajuristic sources, such as history, traditions, or 'fundamental values.' This approach to the textual indeterminacy of the constitution fails to eliminate the problem of subjective preference. For just as legal experts will disagree about, for example, whether or not the Charter guarantee of 'freedom of association' includes a right to strike, appealing to historical understandings of the role of 'freedom of association' in the development of the Canadian polity will deliver no less controversial answers.

The criteria for selecting defensible purposive readings are difficult to devise. Judges have frequently appealed to extrajudicial values in defending their purposive readings of Charter provisions. The principle identified by the court as the purpose of a particular constitutional provision is allegedly grounded in an extrajudicial consensus about 'history,' the 'fundamental values of society,' or the conventions of constitutional doctrine. If the purposive elaboration of the constitution is guided by societal norms, then adjudication is more plausibly independent of the personal preferences of judges.

In *Alberta Labour Reference*, the court appealed to an alleged extralegal consensus about the historical value of the freedom of association to defend its interpretation of the purpose of this freedom. There is however no societal consensus about the meanings of rights and freedoms. As John H. Ely argues, consensus about such broad political principles does not exist. Canada is a society structured by difference and domination. The fact that, from the perspective of a particular group, such as the members of the court, a consensus might appear to exist, 'is likely to reflect only the domination of some groups by others.'[18]

There is a marked lack of consensus in Canada about the meaning of the various rights and freedoms codified by the Charter in a vague terminology. As J. Skelly Wright argues, 'we are wary of the non-elected judiciary making value choices precisely because they are so contested in our society. We want judges to decide cases without reference to values because we acknowledge that individuals disagree about them. Thus it makes little sense for judges to refer to some purported agreement on fundamental issues when it is existing disagreement about them that impels the search for a neutral referent.'[19]

One final example of the difficulties faced by the Supreme Court in disciplining its decision making, given the legislative review tasks it has been delegated, is provided by the problem of adjudicating s. 1 of

the Charter, which states, 'the Canadian Charter of Rights and Freedoms guarantees the rights and freedoms set out in it subject only to
such *reasonable* limits prescribed by law as can be *demonstrably justified*
in a free and democratic society.'[20] While s. 1 is like the funnel through
which all adjudication of the Charter must flow, its provisions are
indeterminate. Whether or not a government action is 'reasonable' and
'demonstrably justified in a free and democratic society' seems more of
a political than a legal question. The Supreme Court was left to determine for itself what constitutes a reasonable limit to a particular right
or freedom.

In *R. v. Oakes* the court established a set of criteria (the Oakes test) to
structure s. 1 inquiry in all Charter cases.[21] The Oakes test involves a
four-step legal test: government action will be upheld under s. 1 only if
i) the purpose of the impugned action is 'sufficiently important to war-
rant overriding a constitutionally protected right or freedom'; ii) the
measures adopted are 'fair and not arbitrary, carefully designed to
achieve the objective in question and rationally connected to that
objective'; iii) the measures, even if rationally connected to the objective in the first sense, 'impair the right in question as little as possible';
and iv) there is a proportionality between the effects of the limiting
measure and the objective – the more severe the deleterious effects of a
measure, the more important the objective must be.[22]

But why do these four criteria constitute a uniquely correct interpretation of s. 1? Even constitutional experts were mystified by the court's
ability to 'discover' previously unknown doctrines that allowed them
to fill in the gaps of the constitutional text. The court provided no rationale for this particular articulation of s. 1, as if the four criteria were
legally self-evident. Criteria one and four are very vague while two
and three are slightly more specific. The court has tended to avoid criteria one and four as a justification for any action for or against government legislation. However, criteria two and three have played a central
role in the Supreme Court's review of legislation. As Bakan argues,
because the second and third criteria involve a means/ends proportionality test, they appear more formally rational and hence 'technical'
and 'objective' than criteria one and four. Thus, criteria two and three
are more able to sustain the appearance that judicial review is rationally constrained than are the first and fourth criteria.[23]

However, the *Oakes* test only appears to constrain judicial reasoning. For despite the technical appearance of criteria two and three, the
court must first define the purpose or 'objective' of the legislation to

be tested. As discussed above, the definition of a purpose requires subjective interpretation and cannot be obtained merely by application of a piece of legal rule. Bakan's analysis illustrates, for example, that the court can manipulate the characterization of a piece of legislation's purpose such that there is a perfect fit between the current scheme and the purpose of the scheme. In *Edwards Books and Art*, a case involving the constitutionality of Sunday-closing legislation, the court characterized the purpose of the legislation most generally as 'providing uniform holidays to retail workers' and most specifically and ultimately as to enforce a uniform day of rest for retail employees and firms with fewer than eight employees and fewer than 5000 sq. ft. of floor space.[24] Here the purpose of the legislation is defined as equivalent to its terms; any alternative scheme would be ruled out because it did not do what the current scheme did. The purpose is defined as tautologically equivalent to the legislative provision and thus no other provision would be capable of achieving the 'purpose' as well as the current provision. Conversely, the court could have characterized the purpose of the legislation in a manner that forced it to fail the *Oakes* test. That test does not eliminate or constrain discretion because there is no legally determinate source for identifying the 'true' purpose of a legislative provision.

### 1.2 Judicial Review and the Depoliticization of Value-Setting

The foregoing analysis of Canadian constitutional adjudication of individual rights and freedoms reveals a variety of interpretive approaches in the resolution of contentious social issues. As former Justice Wilson acknowledged, by preferring one interpretive approach over another, judges can obtain different results on the same set of facts.[25] Constitutional adjudication inevitably involves choice according to social and economic preferences. The internal structure of judicial reasoning does perhaps distinguish it from the less disciplined decision making processes of the legislatures, but not enough to legitimate the special institutional powers of review given to the judiciary under the Charter. The problem that Charter proponents face is how to justify an elite means of decision making when claims for its special coherence and disinterestedness begin to wear thin.

The whole debate over the issue of the legitimacy of judicial review powers is shaped by the same implicit but fundamental distinction between 'facts' and 'values' that underlies the rationalism of modern social arrangements in general. Weber contends, 'it is one thing to state facts, to determine mathematical or logical relations or the internal structure of cultural values, while it is another thing to answer questions of ... how one should act in the cultural community and in political associations' (FMW, 146). Formally rational judicial decision making, he argues, 'establishes what is valid according to the rules of juristic thought, which is partly bound by logically compelling and partly by conventionally given schemata. Juridical thought holds when certain legal rules and certain methods of interpretations are recognized as binding. Whether there should be law and whether one should establish just these rules – such questions jurisprudence does not answer' (FMW, 144–5). The administration of justice can be rational and objective only to the extent that discretion is eliminated from the process of judicial decision making. The rational and objective administration of justice implies 'a conception of the modern judge as an automaton into which the files and the costs are thrown in order that it may spill forth the verdict at the bottom along with the reasons, read mechanically from codified paragraphs' (FMW, 219).

This depiction of judicial activity is of course a polemical exaggeration. There is always room for some degree of interpretive creativity in court procedure and in law-making and law-finding, particularly within the common law tradition. Nonetheless, Weber argues, this 'freely creative' activity has nothing in common with the 'freedom' of arbitrary action, of mercy, and of *personally* motivated favour and valuation (FMW, 220). The rule of law and the demand for legal guarantees against arbitrariness necessitate a formal and rational objectivity of judicature, as opposed to the personally free discretion flowing from the 'grace of the old patrimonial domination. As former Supreme Court Justice Wilson argues, in a formally rational legal order there is 'no plausible justification for us to substitute *our* personal values and *our* moral choices for those of the elected legislature.'[26]

The coherence and disinterestedness of judicial decision making is directly proportional to the extent that adjudication remains straightforward 'mechanical interpretation' of a pre-existing legal code, that is, to the extent that judicial activity corresponds with the restraint model of legitimation. In other words, judicial decision making is most coherent and disinterested when it involves no more than the adjudication of pre-existing norms, that is, norms which have been legislatively enacted in the political arena. But the Charter adjudication of economic and social policy issues inevitably draws judges into evaluations of competing ethical standards that cannot be resolved by merely linking 'means' in a consistent or instrumental fashion with predetermined 'ends'; thus Charter adjudication inevitably draws judges into discretionary interpretations and extrajuristic evaluations.

The popularity of the Charter in Canada lies in the common acceptance of the formal rationality of modern law, the belief that, while decision making in the legislative arena and any other participatory political process is influenced by passion and opinion and is to some extent arbitrary, judicial decision making is rational and neutral: judges are trained to tackle difficult issues in a reasoned, non-ideological fashion. The problem is that this conception of formal rationality only holds for a specific kind of rule-application and 'mechanical interpretation' and not for legislating social policy.

From lifestyle options to economic policy, value choices are highly contested in our society. The resolution of value-conflict is an interminable, highly taxing process. Despite the demise of traditional conventions and standards, there is an ongoing search (and, perhaps, a deep need) for neutral referents to govern the solution of our disagreements. Perhaps the Charter in particular and the notion of rights adjudication in general has wide appeal because it appears to provide an objective referent for the resolution of social conflict. Constitutional adjudication of fundamental rights and freedoms allows a post-traditional, pluralistic society like Canada to maintain the fantasy of 'objective value,' the promise of grounding values in reason, or, more specifically, resolving disputes surrounding the question of 'what shall we do and how shall we live' via appeal to the 'truth' of a constitutional text.

But the record of Charter adjudication in Canada reveals that, as Weber would have predicted, the judicial decision making process is unable to resolve social issues that entail competing normative standards of value without a supplementary element of choice and discretion. Because the Charter forces judges to spell out the contents of vaguely articulated individual rights and the specifics of how they apply to concrete situations, Charter adjudication inevitably demands 'creative' interpretation from the judiciary. As Weber's typology of legal thought suggests, the more judicial decision making departs from mechanical interpretation of explicitly coded law, the more problems of adventitious discretion are introduced into the process of judicial decision making (FMW, 219–20).

In a post-traditional society the creation of norms and the setting of values is a political activity par excellence. This is the meaning of Weber's insistence that the most pressing issues of social life, relating to general cultural values, must be objects of *debate* whose solutions must be *posited* (MSS, 56). But when the Supreme Court becomes involved in deciding whether or not stores have a constitutional right to open on Sundays – as if such questions have an objective legally determinate answer that can be unproblematically extracted by judges from the text of the constitution – judicial processes neutralize the political import of value-setting. For the questions that arise in constitutional argument involve normative standards of evaluation and the legal materials relied upon to answer them are indeterminate; thus, interpreters of the constitution, whether judges or anyone else, must make choices and exercise discretion. But the formal legal rationality of the logic of judicial decision making is such that issues of choice and discretion are obscured and marginalized.

The depoliticization of value-setting is further extended by the diversion of political problems from legislators to judges. If social issues can be unloaded onto the courts and resolved in a supposedly neutral, reasoned fashion, then legislators can avoid making difficult value decisions. In this manner, social conflict can be institutionally structured in a format that appears to approximate rational management. But courts make surreptitious value-choices and constitutional adjudication under the Charter functions as a disguised form of politics. As I argue in Chapter 6, Weber sought to politicize the problem of value-setting in the 'iron cage' precisely because, in a post-traditional society, the 'thin' reason of modern social arrangements reifies values, which tends to depoliticize structures of power and authority, particularly economic ones.

## 2. The Underlying Substantive Coherence of Charter Adjudication

Despite the incoherence of Charter adjudication arising from the divergent interpretive approaches which the courts have assumed in various cases, an underlying pattern of interpretation emerges from the record. Whenever courts interpret rights and freedoms they enact into law a particular vision of society. The record of Charter adjudication, I argue, reveals an emphasis on formal individualistic rights, an anticollective bias in attitudes towards state regulation and labour interests, and the treatment of private property as sacrosanct.

Charter adjudication increases the predictability and calculability of the legal environment for capitalist enterprise. In terms of Weber's conception of legal rationalization, the Charter facilitates an increased formalization of social arrangements and positivization of normative power: while social arrangements become more depersonalized and open to the logic of purposive-rational action, community links between individuals based on the neighbourhood or regional identity are increasingly eroded by the atomizing logic of the rights-oriented conception of political identity. In some instances, undoubtedly, the Charter has augmented the legal protections individuals possess against external compulsion.[27] But, as I argue below, the kind of 'external compulsions' from which individuals are protected are nearly always of the non-economic type, despite the fact that, as Weber argues, it is the cosmos of economic relations that today determines the lives of individuals with irresistible force. Similarly, the conception of empowerment the Charter offers to individuals is modelled primarily after the archetypical economic actor engaged in purposive-rational contractual relations with others.

## 2.1 The Selective Protection and Promotion of Individual Autonomy

The link between legal and economic rationalization discussed in Weber's developmental history of modern law in Chapter 3 suggests that, as one aspect of contemporary legal development, the rise of the rights-oriented polity is perhaps connected with a larger process of economic rationalization. If this is the case, then the pattern of constitutional adjudication of the value-conflicts that arise between workers and employers might provide some support for this hypothesis.

*Dolphin Delivery* was the first Canadian Supreme Court case that dealt directly with the issue of what labour rights, if any, were protected under the Charter. This case has been immensely controversial.[28] For although *Dolphin Delivery* involved the issue of whether or not secondary picketing is a protected activity under the guarantee of freedom of expression, of even greater general relevance, the case raised the issue of the Charter's applicability to private litigation and the common law. The Supreme Court ruled unanimously that the granting of the injunction and the common law on which it was based were beyond the scope of Charter action, that judge-made common law may not be challenged by the Charter in cases involving the application of common law to private litigation. The majority did hold that picketing was a form of expression protected by the Charter. However, the common law restriction in *Dolphin Delivery*, even if it had fallen under Charter scrutiny, would have constituted a 'reasonable limit' under s. 1 of the Charter.

The Supreme Court concluded that the Charter can only apply to common law where some additional governmental (statutory) presence exists. It argued that the powers of judicial review under the Charter apply to legislation regulating private relationships, but not to the common law that regulates private relationships. Thus legal relationships within the 'private' sphere of civil society, or the 'private' ordering of society, are beyond reach of the Charter.

What presumptions underlay this judgment? The 'common law' referred to by the court in *Dolphin Delivery* is *judge-made* common law as opposed to *statute* law enacted by Parliament and the provincial legislatures. The first important legal presumption of the judgment in *Dolphin Delivery* was that when judges make laws they merely articulate pre-existing, found norms; thus the body of rules that constitutes common law is like a 'natural' object. As the influential seventeenth-century jurist Sir Edward Coke wrote, common law is 'nothing but reason.'[29] In *Dolphin Delivery*, the court presumed that when judges have been called upon in the course of dispute resolution to elaborate or introduce some new element to this body of the common law, they have done so in a reasoned, objective fashion. Common law norms elaborated by judges inhabit a private sphere governing the prepolitical relations of civil society. In contrast, the state inhabits a public realm of positive, politically enacted norms. Thus the court conceptualized state-enacted statutes as discretionary impositions arising from transitory political decisions that intersect with a pre- or apolitical social order of which the common law is a reflection.

The conception of common law employed by the court is a legal fiction: judge-made common law is just as 'positive' as the body of statutes enacted by the various legislatures.[30] In *Dolphin Delivery*, the legal fiction of common law as 'found' law was especially troublesome for the judges to maintain. For the particular law at issue in *Dolphin Delivery* was quite obviously unrelated to ancient customs or admirable maxims: the industrial tort of inducing breach is a doctrinal device invented by English and American courts during the mid-nineteenth century to deal with increasingly militant labour organizations.

This is where the sophistical pirouetting began, for although the court had to acknowledge that the common law at issue in this particular case is the creation of courts and thus possesses a positive – that is, political – origin, they had also to preserve at all cost the idea that such judge-made laws were and continue to be qualitatively distinct from the statutes positively enacted by legislatures and thus, unlike statutes, exempt from Charter scrutiny. The question of where the private and public spheres separate is philosophically complex, to say the least.[31] But in *Dolphin Delivery*, the court presumed that private and public spheres divided uncontroversially along the boundaries between the private world of individuals engaged in the market exchange of property and the public world of government and politics.

The political consequences of the *Dolphin Delivery* judgment are profound. Take, for example, the Supreme Court's adjudication of labour cases versus its treatment of corporations or business interests. Since *Dolphin Delivery* established the non-application of the Charter to common law governing so-called private relationships, whether an organization is treated as a 'public' or a 'private' entity by the courts carries enormous implications. Defining an organization as private gives it greater latitude of action outside the moral imperatives of the Charter; at the same time, an organization identified as private obtains the status of a personlike entity and thus is more likely to be accorded Charter rights as a weapon against government regulation, popular scrutiny, and accountability. It comes as no surprise, then, that the court has proceeded to define labour unions as public entities, while corporations have been defined as private actors.

In *Hunter v. Southam*, the court merely assumed that the corporation in question was a private entity and, employing a rather generous purposive reading of s. 8, held that a privacy right could be conferred upon it. Again, in *Big M Drug Mart*, a corporation was permitted to invoke the right to freedom of religion to challenge a closing law deleterious to its economic interests. The courts have also displayed a propensity for interpreting the fundamental rights of s. 2 as applicable to the protection of market activity. For example, in *Irwin Toy*, the court restricted the manner in which television advertisement of toys could be directed at children. The court argued that commercial speech (advertising) is protected by the Charter under the freedom of expression.[32] The court's tendency to protect market activity is reflected more generally in its antistate, antiregulation bias, the assumption being that the courts play a more 'neutral' role by striking down rather than repairing legislation.

The contrast between the court's treatment of business corporations and labour unions could not be more stark. In a series of labour cases, the Supreme Court employed a strict formalist mode of interpreting the Charter in refusing to extend freedom of association to essential union activities.[33] Justice Le Dain, writing for the majority decision, refused to grant Charter protection to collective bargaining and strike action, reasoning that unions are 'the creation of legislation, involving a balance of competing interests in a field which has been recognized by the courts as requiring specialized expertise.'[34] Le Dain pressed home the conceptual boundary that allegedly separates the political/collective from the prepolitical natural realm of private individual relations. His decision effectively treated labour as just another interest group in the arena of pluralistic politics, which represents a remarkable disregard for the historical fact, alluded to by Chief Justice Dickson, that the concessions to labour that were required in the twentieth century to make capitalism politically tenable represent essential structural features of the post–Second World War welfare state status quo rather than just momentary bargains traded between individuals.[35]

As several commentators have argued, labour has not fared well under the Charter.[36] Where small successes have been obtained, the court has merely upheld existing protections, such as laws restricting the hours when large retail employers can open for business.[37] The perception that union powers are public makes them more vulnerable than corporations to Charter challenges. Thus, while the courts would dismiss out of hand a Charter challenge against the power of corporations to employ shareholder's money for political purposes, the courts in *Lavigne* agonized over whether the Charter limits the power of unions to use workers' dues in precisely the same way.[38]

In a remarkable passage from the landmark 1989 *Andrews* case, Justice McIntyre described how discrimination developed in Canada:

> discrimination as referred to in s. 15 of the *Charter* must be understood in the context of pre-*Charter* history ... With the steady increase in population from the earliest days of European emigration into Canada and with the consequential growth of industry, agriculture and commerce and the vast increase in national wealth which followed, many social problems developed. The contact of the European immigrant with the indigenous population, the steady increase in immigration bringing those of neither French nor British background, and in more recent years the greatly expanded role of women in all forms of industrial, commercial and professional activity led to much inequality and many forms of discrimination.[39]

Justice McIntyre clearly identified the world of *private* ordering outside the realm of explicit government action as the cause of systemic inequalities and discrimination. Yet, following *Dolphin Delivery* regarding the non-application of the Charter to common law and civil society, the court went on to rule that 'the mere fact of systemic discrimination is not, *a priori*, a basis for s. 15 action: the state must have exacerbated it or caused it.' In other words, although the court identified the private ordering system of the capitalist economy as one of the most significant sources of inequality in society, it argued simultaneously that such a system must be left alone for the same reasons that common law lay outside the sphere of Charter scrutiny in *Dolphin Delivery*.

The court has treated the current distribution of power and wealth as a prepolitical norm not subject to Charter scrutiny; of course, this economic 'norm' is thereby all the more validated and entrenched. Because the power of judicial review under the Charter applies to legislation that regulates private relationships, but not to common law that regulates private relationships, the 'private' ordering system relating to the exploitation of economic power has been protected from public controls. In other words, under the doctrine of the Charter's nonapplication to the sphere of common law activities established in *Dolphin Delivery*, private power can be deployed in a largely unchecked and democratically unaccountable fashion. The Charter helps narrow the basis on which public controls over private power can be established, for it tends to treat government action as the great threat to individual liberty, while the operations of big business are removed from Charter scrutiny.

## 2.2 The 'Dynamic' of Legal Rationalization

One of the most common arguments for the legitimacy of the Charter in Canada is that the power of judicial review protects individuals from coercive majoritarian politics exercised through the representative institutions of the legislatures or the oppression of arbitrary, overreaching actions of the government. In either scenario, the Charter protects the autonomy of individual self-determination from the external interference of the state. Charter proponents boast that individuals are now protected by the judiciary from threats to individual liberty emanating from arbitrary government intervention. But, ironically, Charter cases that are supposed to represent victories for workers and women are ones in which the courts have simply preserved existing legislative benefits: *Edwards Books and Art* upheld a statutory common pause day for retail workers; *Canadian Newspapers* upheld a provision of the Criminal Code allowing complainants in sexual assault cases to request a bar on the publication of their names; and *Lavigne* upheld the power of trade unions to spend compulsory union fees on political causes.[40]

What liberal Charter proponents fail to address is that, in the advanced capitalist nations of the West today, the single largest threat to individual autonomy is far more likely to stem from the vicissitudes of the business cycle and the functional imperatives of the market economy than from oppressive government action. As Weber notes, 'the exact extent to which the total amount of "freedom" within a given legal community is actually increased depends entirely upon the concrete economic order and especially upon the property distribution' (ES, 730). The market confers enormous power upon those who possess property to enhance their liberty at the expense of others (the vast majority) who must yield to their rights of ownership. The richest 10 per cent of Canadians own 57 per cent of Canada's total personal wealth, while the poorest 40 per cent of Canadians own only 1 per cent.[41] From the point of view of the majority who have little say in the market, a sense of control over one's life is more likely to be advanced, rather than curtailed, by mobilizing the regulatory and redistributive functions of the state through the democratic electoral process.

The presumption underlying the public/private dichotomy and the nonapplication of the Charter to the latter category is that existing distributions of wealth and power are the product of private individual initiative. But the accumulation of wealth always depends on state-supported laws and institutions for its maintenance and legitimacy. Because existing distributions of wealth and power lie outside Charter scrutiny, such distributions will form a natural base line on which Charter rights are grounded and the constitutionality of state action is judged. By limiting Charter application to the public realm and government activities, the major source of inequality and individual powerlessness in Canadian society – the distribution of wealth and the lack of accountability for how wealth is made and deployed – is excluded from Charter scrutiny. As a result, the judiciary ignores primary causes of social injustice in its determination to restrain the arm of the state best equipped to redress those causes: the democratic limb represented by the legislature and the executive.

Since the early twentieth century, certainly since the late 1930s, the capitalistic economic system would not have been politically viable nor would the continued accumulation of wealth be possible without massive state involvement in the steering of the economy and non-market forms of wealth distribution. These measures represent limits placed by a democratically empowered majority on the exercise of private economic power. In the legislative arena, power depends on numbers – the one respect in which the average citizen has an advantage in political terms over the economically powerful. Not surprisingly, most of the social welfare reforms of the past half-century were enacted by legislatures in the face of stiff opposition from the judiciary. The victories that have been won in this century on behalf of workers, the unemployed, women, and other socially and economically disadvantaged persons have been achieved, for the most part, through the democratic mobilization of the state.[42] The powers of judicial review under the Charter diminish the capacity of governments to place such public controls over the private disposal of wealth.

According to the political theory that underwrites the Charter, enemies of freedom are forms of state power. The Charter is not only blind to the use and abuse of unchecked private power, it is blind to the role of government as a promoter of liberty. Judicial review under the Charter has been used to chip away at the regulatory framework of the state: under the freedom of association, governments have been prohibited from interfering with the formation of business partnerships by the Alberta Court of Appeal;[43] legislation granting government powers to search corporate records for evidence of anticompetitive behaviour has been struck down by the Supreme Court as infringing a corporation's right to privacy;[44] the Nova Scotia Court of Appeal has invoked mobility rights to strike down legislation requiring door-to-door sellers to be permanent residents of the province in which they do business;[45] the B.C. Court of Appeal has interpreted the right to liberty as prohibiting governments from regulating the number and location of doctors who practice medicine in the province;[46] and the Supreme Court of Canada has concluded that freedom of expression protects commercial signs from government regulation.[47]

Another common argument made in favour of the Charter is that the constitutional entrenchment of codified rights and freedoms empowers individuals to claim directly the benefits accorded to them by the fundamental values of the political system. Instead of having to rely on cumbersome mass political processes, such as the electoral system for delegating representatives in the legislatures, under the Charter individuals are given the means, via judicial appeal, to enforce and/or obtain what is due to them as citizens. The Charter empowers individuals by creating a greater awareness of what rights can properly be claimed in a democracy and by ensuring that individuals' views and interests, which might be lost in the 'cruder' world of mass electoral politics, are strengthened and heard.

One feature of the judicial system that makes it a less amenable arena for advancing the interests of the average individual – and particularly the disadvantaged – than the exercise of democratic action through the legislatures is the cost of employing the judicial system. With variation between provinces, legal aid is generally available only for criminal cases. In the 1989 *Lavigne* cases, the National Citizens Coalition, a right-wing lobby group, spent $400,000 on their challenge against the use of union dues for political causes.[48]

One effect of this high cost is that scarce political resources are siphoned from the democratic to the judicial arena. Women's groups have raised many thousands of dollars to engage in Charter litigation; a considerable portion of this war chest is used solely to defend already existing legislation of benefit to women. For example, the Women's Legal Education and Action Fund (LEAF) intervened in *Shechuk and Richard* to argue that child support benefits ought to be extended to men rather than taken away from women, in *Seaboyer* to defend a provision of the Criminal Code that limits the ability of defence counsel in sexual assault cases to cross-examine complainants on their sexual histories, in *Canadian Newspapers* to defend a provision of the Criminal Code allowing complainants in sexual assault cases to request a ban on publication of their names, in *Schachter* to argue that maternity benefits provided to women under Canada's unemployment insurance scheme do not violate the equality rights of men, and in *Andrews* to argue that treating unequally advantaged complainants equally only perpetuates inequality.[49]

The high cost of litigation also influences the judicial interpretation of Charter guarantees. The rights set out in the Charter are expressed in vague, general terms. The scope and content of each Charter provision must be developed by the judiciary on a case-by-case basis in response to the particular facts and interests brought before the courts. Because of the cost of asserting one's rights through litigation, the issues raised in non-criminal Charter cases tend to represent the interests of those with economic resources. As a result, Petter argues, the interpretation of Charter rights will inevitably respond to and, over time, reflect those same interests; 'it is not necessary that judges consciously seek to benefit such interests. The disproportionate attention that they command will, of its own accord, shape the court's perception of the nature and scope of rights, thereby influencing their interpretation.'[50]

One explanation for the increasing importance of judicial power, advanced by communitarian political theorists, argues that the increasing emphasis on courts as instruments of political leverage relates to our relative lack of control over the priorities of social organization, particularly in the sphere of the capitalist economy. This loss of control represents a challenge to the identity of the modern individual as self-determining, controlling rather than being controlled by things. As Charles Taylor argues, in these circumstances, 'the sense of the dignity of the free agent has been identified more with the bearer of rights than with the citizen participator.'[51] The constitutionalization of abstract individual rights affirms an unencumbered individualism in sharp contrast to the tangled network of unwilled social obligations.

Yet, the growth of legal rights contributes in a counterintuitive manner to the overall structure of legal domination. We are accustomed to viewing the legal phenomenon of individual rights as the Dr Jekyll of the regulatory-administrative structure's Mr Hyde. We tend to assume a kind of zero-sum relationship between legal rights and legal rules, that a strengthening or extension of the legal protection of individual rights somehow tips the balance wheel of social organization for the individual in the direction of less unwanted entanglement. But as the earlier interpretation of Weber's model of legal domination suggests, the constitutionalization of rights-oriented conceptions of citizenship and the concomitant shift of political power from legislative arenas to the judiciary is integral to a larger pattern of rationalization of economic and political structures of power.

The way in which legal rights are institutionalized in the rights-oriented polity contributes to the pervasive legalization of social relationships, the experience of which prompted the search for ways to protect and promote individual autonomy in the first place. That the constitutionalization of individual rights contributes to the formalization of social arrangements described previously is evidenced in the impact of Charter adjudication. Despite the general popularity of the Charter, in areas of social and economic policy it represents an instrument for increasing the formal rationality of economic relations. By diminishing the political control over private wealth that, in pre-Charter days, the majority exercised through representative institutions of the state, the Charter increases the legal predictability and calculability of economic transactions and liberates possibilities for the exploitation of economic power. In other words, the structural concomitant of the constitutionalization of individual rights is the deconstitutionalization of mechanisms for collective political control.

The Charter protects and promotes individual autonomy in highly selective ways. The legal interpretation of autonomy emphasizes individual rights of the universal, abstract variety, and an anticollective bias against public forms of regulation. The operative vision behind this conception of rights corresponds with the relevance of purposive contractual relations between monadic individuals as the paradigmatic modern social relation. The rise of judicial forms of political power is accompanied by a highly politicized fragmentation of individuals who compete with one another for available material and symbolic resources. Individuals are empowered in ways that actually increase their dependence on money and markets.

The judicial forms of political power that accompany the rise of the rights-oriented polity function to depoliticize the normative questions involved in setting the ends to which social and economic power are to be directed. Weber confined judicatory activities within the formalist parameters of 'mechanical interpretation' and application of pre-existing law precisely because the formal rationality of modern law is incapable of supplying reason-dictated solutions to the competing ethical standards that various social and economic policies entail. In a post-traditional society, value-setting is an inherently political, contestational activity (MSS, 57). The extension of judicial powers beyond the minimal 'restraint-based' model envisioned by Weber depoliticizes value-setting. The powers of judicial review under the Charter represent a mode of value-setting which, under the guise of the ideological neutrality of adjudication, systematically obscures the fact that any value-setting is occurring at all.

Given the clearly unfolded rational complexity of present-day structures of economic and political power, individual autonomy is far more likely to be protected and promoted by strengthening democratic institutions than by allowing a small group of jurists sweeping powers to administer vague entitlements such as 'liberty' and 'equality,' the contents of which they are themselves responsible for defining. Although the formal legal rationality of modern social arrangements has contributed enormously to the modern experience of freedom, the countertendencies of legal rationalization today call out for alternatives to the endless legalization of social relationships. Weber's political thought was motivated by an anticipation of the countertendencies of pervasive rationalization *cum* legalization, which he defined in terms of the loss of control over the ends to which political and economic power are directed, a routinization of material interests that narrows the scope of political imagination, and more generally, an inexorable concentration of economic power within larger and larger corporate organizations. In a specific sense, Weber's political thought represents an attempt to formulate the limits appropriate to the empire of modern law, in view of its merely formal rationality and the rational indeterminacy of values in the modern world.

# The Limits of Formal Legal Rationality: An Interpretation of Weber's Theory of Modern Politics

The promotion and protection of individual autonomy through the litigation of individual rights and the concomitant rise of judicial powers of review may have the counterintuitive consequence of actually expanding the legal-rational web of functional interdependencies that contributes to the individual's experience of being dominated by unwilled forces. Although the earlier historical stages of the formal legal-rational reconstitution of social arrangements in the West may have been 'unambiguously' freedom-enhancing, the countertendencies generated by subsequent stages of legal development signify the extent to which formal legal rationality itself has come to impede meaningful individual autonomy.

According to Weber's interpretation of the countertendencies of modernity, the pervasive legal rationalization of social arrangements threatens a form of cultural devitalization ('loss of meaning') and political servitude ('loss of freedom').[1] Weber argues that values are external to the purely formal rationality of bureaucracy, and, for that matter, to the rationality of modern social arrangements in general. Nonetheless, formal rationality tends to exert an influence upon modern cultural values and the formation of individual 'personality,' contributing to the routinization of thin forms of reason and the ascendance of the type of 'shallow-willing' personality epitomized by the techno-managerial specialist – the Fachmensch. Given the purely formal rationality of modern law and its incapacity for rationally determining values (which the example of Charter adjudication manifestly illustrated), one can say that, paralleling Weber's premonitory account of the bureaucratization of politics, legal rationalization is dysfunctional to the extent that it inappropriately subverts the relationship between rationality and values by exerting an influence over the setting of the latter and contributes to the erosion of democracy through its facilitation of the accumulation of economic power within ever larger organizations. The countertendencies of rationalization tie into Weber's theory of modern politics: his proposal for a 'plebiscitarian leadership-democracy' represents a specific political formula for resisting the influence of the thin reason of means-ends rationality on the articulation of the ends to which the power of social instrumentalities are directed.

Weber's specific political formula is objectionable: he believed that only a charismatic leader could subordinate the powerful instrumentalities of modern institutions to responsible political control. As critics have pointed out, oligarchy is a peculiar remedy for resisting the social forces that threaten individual autonomy. The heuristic value of Weber's political thought lies in its identification of the problematic relationship between formal legal rationality and individual autonomy in terms of the former's tendency to subvert the value-setting capacity of the latter. The political task of modernity in this interpretation of Weber is to prevent the processes of rationalization from bridging the fundamental tension between means-ends rationality and the judgment of values that inheres within the liberal cultural system, a tension that cannot be bridged without reifying the 'kingdom of ends' or reducing modern politics to a form of technical administration. The inner significance of Weber's theory of politics is its recommendation for the maintenance of a strong division between the rule orientation of legal rationality and the conflict orientation of politics, between social conduct involving conformity with impersonal rules and social conduct requiring participation in the practical judgment of the political ends to which the powers of rational social arrangements are to be directed.

## 1. The Countertendencies of Rationalization

Returning briefly to Weber's theory of bureaucracy, he advances four key propositions: first, bureaucratic rationality involves the technically efficient linking of administrative and organizational resources to pre-given goals or ends; second, although bureaucracy is an efficient (and for modernity indispensable) instrument of administration and organization, it is dependent upon an external form of end-setting; and third, bureaucracy possesses an inherent tendency to exceed its 'proper' function. The form of the bureaucratic 'means' begins to exert a value-setting influence over the 'ends' of bureaucratic action. Finally, such rational organizations possess an inherent tendency to both internally complexify and expand their field of social application. In Weber's words, the efficient political organization of resources and provision of services and, in the economic sphere, the productive accumulation of wealth, increasingly determine the way in which political affairs are managed and increasingly define social priorities and goals in general (ES, 1403).

Bureaucratic organization exemplifies formal legal rationality. Just as modern law denotes for Weber a framework of formal-rational rules rather than an informal fabric of norms, so the hallmark of bureaucratic organization is the formalistic impersonality of its abstract rule-governance. In epistemological terms, bureaucracy is a technically efficient instrument for linking means to pregiven ends. In fulfilling this project, bureaucratic rationality involves more than just adherence to impersonal, abstract, and formal rules; it also involves the application of social scientific knowledge and expertise. Geared towards efficiency of performance and outcomes, bureaucratic organization adjusts means to pregiven ends following the dictates of purposive-technical or instrumental calculations of benefit. The important point is that values are external to the formal legal rationality of bureaucratic organization and administration. Bureaucratic organization is dependent upon end-setting external to its rule-machinery. By emphasizing the technical instrumentality of bureaucracy Weber highlights a fundamental limitation in its particular kind of rationality. Bureaucratic rationality is efficient at linking means to pregiven ends, but it cannot determine those ends itself, for the determination of ends involves the exercise of value-preference, which Weber argues is fundamentally an individual issue of choice and consent. Weber emphasizes the 'precise, soulless and machine-like' quality of the bureaucratic apparatus not so much to highlight its technical efficiency but rather to undercut the 'romantic' conception that bureaucratic rationality embodies any superior wisdom for practical political judgment. He contends that bureaucracy is a social liability precisely because its rule machinery is incapable of supplying goals for political action.

Despite these limitations, in Weber's view, bureaucratic organization, like the market economy in general, is indispensable to modernity. Bureaucracy is an inescapable feature of modern social arrangements, due to the functional needs of both mass democracy and capitalism (ES, 1094–5). Modern institutions presuppose the formal equality of all persons and thus depend on the nondiscretionary, impersonal performance of tasks characteristic of bureaucratic rationality. The social and economic bases of modern life place a premium on the reliable, knowledgeable administration of resources and require a high degree of calculability and predictability of social processes (ES, 223). The formal legal rationality of modern social arrangements increases our collective capacity to administer resources, to calculate and achieve precise goals through the routinized application of specialized concepts and expert knowledge. What worried Weber was that, in his view, bureaucracy possessed an inherent propensity for overstepping its 'proper' function of matching means to pregiven ends in an instrumentally rational fashion. By exceeding its proper function bureaucracy subverts the relationship between means and ends, thereby inappropriately influencing the ends to which power is directed.

These propositions about bureaucracy – its merely formal rationality, its indispensability to modernity, and its propensity to exert an influence over the politics of value-setting – are obvious enough. But within the context of Weber's political thought alone, it is difficult to understand the reasons for the depth of his concern over the cultural impact of bureaucratization. The significance of the theme of bureaucracy's influence over value-setting must be interpreted within the wider context of Weber's conception of the role of ideal-interests and value-rational conduct in historical innovation and the deleterious impact which he believed modern rationalism in general exerted upon these ideal factors. The problematic relationship between formal legal rationality and individual autonomy and the dynamic of legal rationalization must be situated within the larger cultural dynamics of 'charisma' and 'routinization,' which Weber believed lay behind social and historical processes of change.

### 1.1 The Dynamic of Charisma and Routinization: The Role of Value-Oriented Conduct in Cultural Innovation

The distinction Weber draws between traditional and legal-rational domination and charismatic domination is based on a contrast between the 'everyday' and the 'exceptional,' between the orientation to existing material interests and a disruptive striving towards non-everyday or other-worldly ideals. The contrast between the forces of routinization and charisma most famously appears in the guise of the conflict between rationalization and the creative impulses of the charismatically gifted leader. One of the most important characteristics of bureaucracy, Weber argues, is 'continuity.' Bureaucracy is rooted in the 'structures of everyday life,' 'rooted in the need to meet ongoing, routine demands.' Bureaucracy is a 'permanent structure,' a 'system of rational rules, oriented toward the satisfaction of calculable needs with ordinary, everyday means' (ES, 1111). The social locus of bureaucracy is in the sphere of material interests'; its paradigmatic form of social action is purposive-rational. By contrast, Weber writes, 'all *extra-ordinary* needs, i.e., those which *transcend* the sphere of everyday economic routines, have always been satisfied in an entirely heterogeneous manner: on a *charismatic* basis' (ibid.). Thus the phenomenon of charisma is evinced by the example of persons in history who by force of personality, rather than inherited right or promotion within an established institution alone, gain power and are treated as 'legitimate' rulers. The force of individual personality as political power is most evident in times of disorder and distress. In such times people are more apt to invest someone with the aura of superhuman power so that a leader may appear who possesses the authority to deal with extra-ordinary situations others cannot handle.

The charismatic qualities that people perceive in a particular individual lie in what is thought to be this individual's connection with, or possession of, some very central feature of human existence. This perceived link with what Edward A. Shils calls 'centrality,' coupled with its intensity of expression in a given individual, is the kernel of the 'extraordinary.'[2] The connection perceived between a charismatic individual and the 'centre' of life is the source of that individual's formative power in initiating, creating, governing, transforming, or maintaining what is thought to be vital to human life. The power of charisma to move people so forcefully, Weber believes, lies in the 'ethical irrationality of the world,' the deep need for meaningful existence and the desire to conceive of the world as a meaningful cosmos.

The concept of charisma emerges in Weber's social thought as a structural constant of all social life. Charisma is not only evidenced in phenomena like new religious movements but also in dramatic expressions of human creativity, such as political, economic, and scientific ideas; artistic expression; confident reality-transforming activity; and so forth (FMW, 136). The contrast between charisma and routinization can thus be cast more generally in the terms of value-rational versus purposive-rational conduct, and ideal and other-worldly interests versus material interests. Charisma operates as the value-oriented striving of individuals for ideal and other-worldly interests of a non-everyday nature; rationalization operates as purposive-rational adaptation to pre-existing values, that is, material interests. Rationalization channels action into the reinforcement of the existing constellation of interests, while the charismatic value-oriented action of individuals, because it aims at exceptional rather than everyday goals, can bring such pressures to bear on social reality that the course of everyday life is given a new direction.

The impact of the two types of social action upon the social order is thus very different. While purposive-rational action favours adaptation to given social conditions and the progressive realization of its immanent principles via routinization and rationalization, value-rational action oriented by non-everyday or other-worldly values is less constrained by considerations of exterior factors and thus amounts to a challenge to the given social order.

Over the course of history, routinization and rationalization have been predominant, and the material concerns of the 'everyday,' however they may happen to be defined at a given time, largely shape the pattern of social intercourse.[3] Despite this disposition of human life to routine and stability, as Weber's Protestant ethic thesis illustrates, value-oriented conduct can play a revolutionary role in the transformation of material interests. As Benjamin Nelson writes, 'the roads to modernity are paved with "charismatic" breakthroughs of traditional structures.'[4]

What worried Weber was that, in his view, the developmental history of the West is marked by the increasing pre-eminence of rationalization and routinization as forces of cultural change. Modern times are characterized by the assault of routine against charisma, rules against spontaneity. The quotidian quality of the legal-rational order of domination and capitalist economic relations, the general social environment amenable to the rational calculation of gains and losses, result in relative repetitiousness, monotony of events, predictability and regularity. 'Modern life,' Simmel writes, 'is overburdened with objective content and material demands.'[5]

Weber does not argue that charisma will disappear from modern culture altogether.[6] As his comments about the durability of religion indicate, people will always seek solutions to the problem of the 'ethical irrationality' of human existence, as evidenced today in the undiminished importance of supramundane aesthetic, erotic or religious 'experiences' (FMW, 155). His concern is that the predominance of routine and rationality in modern economic and political arrangements diminishes the opportunities for, and the relevance of, forms of conduct oriented towards non-everyday ideals in modern 'public life.' The eighteenth-century separation of religious belief from public life that formal legal rationality instituted in the spheres of political and economic conduct originally represented an unambiguous enhancement of individual opportunities for self-determination. But with the emergence of large-scale capitalist organization and rational structures of mass democracy, the elimination of religious intolerance from public life has been transformed into a marginalization of value-oriented human striving. Directed inwards to the 'smallest and most intimate circles of life' (e.g., the private embellishment of individual 'lifestyles'), value-oriented conduct not only has less impact on society at large, but actually tends to reinforce the existing constellation of material interests, that is, the pattern of consumer consumption.[7]

What fuelled Weber's anxiety in particular was that, not only are the rational orders of modern institutions far more comprehensive and resistant to paradigm-threatening change than any previous historical formation, but the resultant degree of routinization of social life makes the material demands of everyday existence that much more irresistible and total. If we take into account the importance Weber assigns to value-oriented conduct for cultural innovation and for the development of the highest qualities in individuals, such as their capacity for individual responsibility and their drive towards 'higher things,' it becomes immediately apparent why the increasing domination of people by their material needs would provoke the greatest concern for Weber. The following sections examine the countertendencies generated by the forces of rationalization and routinization.

## 1.2 *Cultural Devitalization and the Reification of Values*

A recurring theme in Weber's sociological thought, Wilhelm Hennis argues, is the question of what kind of individual qualities, or particular character types, are produced by various institutional settings and social arrangements.[8] Weber contends, 'every type of social order, without exception, must, if one wishes to *evaluate* it, be examined with reference to the opportunities which it affords to *certain types of persons* to rise to positions of superiority through the operation of the various

objective and subjective selective factors' (MSS, 27). Given that historically specific social arrangements form particular types of personalities, Weber asks, 'what happens "characterologically" ... to those
people who are put into those legal and actual conditions of existence
which we are concerned with today' (GASS, 399).[9]

Weber believes that the rationalization of economic and political
structures of power threatens the kind of individualism he valorizes.
As the increasing size of organizations took them beyond the range of
individual or family ownership and control, and as the individual was
everywhere separated from the means of production and administration, the scope for independent self-financed entrepreneurial activity
in all spheres of life was narrowed. The individual entrepreneur
became a manager within a large capitalist organization; the independent parliamentarian a member in a party machine; the individual
scholar intellectually proletarianized within the large-scale organization of the university, and so forth. Today, the vast majority of people
must sell their time and labour as subordinates within huge, hierarchically structured organizations. Weber argues that, as the satisfaction of
political and economic needs is increasingly rationalized, discipline in
the factory and the office inexorably takes over, restricting the importance of charisma and individually differentiated conduct (ES, 1156).

Why was Weber so concerned about the impact of rationalization
and routinization on the formation of modern personhood? Bureaucra-
tized domination exercises a considerable influence on culture and
upon the selection and development of particular character types.
Bureaucracy, Weber argues, strongly furthers the development of
'rational matter of factness'; it fosters the cultivation of 'men of calling
and professional expertise' and, in general, it induces an ethic of
adjustment, of adaptation to a narrowly defined conception of the
'possible' (cf. MSS, 24). In tracing the link between bureaucracy and the
growth of higher education, Weber argues that the rationalization of
economic and political structures of power promotes the growth of
techno-managerial forms of knowledge in the universities and the
prestige of certifications of applied education. He laments that the
typical values of such Diplom-menschentum were status, security, and
order: 'men who cling to some minor position and strive only for a
bigger one' (GASS, 414).[10]

Here we arrive at the main crux of Weber's contention with bureaucracy in particular and rationalization in general. In contrast to an egalitarian tradition of liberal thought which views modern 'freedom' as

inherently valuable for the scope it provides for self-determination, because of the central place Weber assigns to the value of creative individualism, the value of 'freedom' for him must be measured by the quality of the human characteristics it allows to flourish.[11] Borrowing a distinction that Joan Tronto makes between 'shallow' and 'deep-willing' forms of personhood, in the modern world of state and economy the kind of character modern rational social arrangements 'select' and 'develop' is of the 'shallow-willing' variety.[12] In Weber's constant juxtaposition of bureaucratic officials and leaders of politics and economic entrepreneurship, and in his anxiety over the loss of value-oriented conduct, can be detected a concern for defining people in terms of their capacity to develop intelligent willfulness.

The importance of 'willing' appears time and again in Weber's existentialist epistemology and, obviously, in his conception of modern 'will-centred' personhood. According to his positivistic theory of values to select values people are ultimately guided by will rather than intellect; according to his conception of modern personhood, individual 'will' lies at the heart of the formation of autonomous moral responsibility. Weber values deep-willing persons more than shallow ones. People who committed themselves to deeply held values, such as the original Protestant saints, were portrayed by Weber as heroes (PE, 98–129). The early Protestants were driven to make the world conform to their deeply held beliefs; their value-rational action interpreted and shaped events to make them conform to their world-view. Modern social arrangements and conceptions of personhood did not originate from the gratification of material interests alone, but rather from the discipline and the motivation of non-everyday ideals.

Weber fears that the deliberate elimination of individual initiative and the premium placed on subordination to impersonal rule observance and organizational discipline within the authoritarian-hierarchical organizations of the office and the factory cultivate shallow-willing individuals and the repression of the kind of responsible behaviour that contributes to the formation of autonomous moral 'personalities.' The rationality of bureaucratic organization and capitalist markets fosters rule observance and profit calculation, that is, formalism and instrumentalism, without regard for persons. In other words, the rational political and economic structures of the modern world foster superficiality and discourage the cultivation of deep-willing personalities.

For Weber, only a self-monitored 'constancy' in relation to certain ultimate values lifts individuals out of an undifferentiated quasi-vegetative existence, or an unquestioning habituation to the present. In particular, a single-minded orientation to values that transcend the existing constellation of material interests can have the most far-reaching effects in the formation of individual 'personality' (RK, 192). The forces of rationalization and routinization in the modern world, however, insidiously transform individuals 'from without' by determining the conditions of adaption and the means and the ends of social action (ES, 1116–17). The conduct governed by immediate practical concerns, the 'shallowness of our routinized daily existence,' triumphs over and eventually substitutes for the pursuit of supramundane ideals. The form of personhood that corresponds with the formal legal-rational structures of bureaucracy is that of the technomanagerial official, the Fachmensch, whose conduct is constrained by immediate practical tasks and whose moral responsibility for the consequences of action is 'floating.' This process of rationalization and routinization is parallelled by the bureaucratization of the administration of law. As discussed in the previous chapter in the context of Charter adjudication in Canada, eventually not only the application but also the creation of legal norms is systematized to some extent: norm creation is expropriated from the legislative arena of 'dilettantes' (legislators) and given to the judicial forum of expert 'officials' (jurists).

### 1.3 Political Servitude and the Depoliticization of Value-Setting

Just as a distinction can be drawn between 'deep-willing' personalities such as the Protestant saints and the 'shallow-willing' personalities characteristic of modern Fachmenschen, borrowing from Mark E. Warren, we can also distinguish between 'broad' and 'thin' conceptions of reason.[13] Although Weber does not make such distinctions explicit, they correspond with evaluative assumptions embedded in the thinking behind his typology of rationality. Thin conceptions of reason are characterized by consistency and instrumentalism (cf. FMW, 293). In terms of their expression as action orientations, both consistency and instrumentalism involve purposive-rational action. In contrast to these two thin forms of reason, in 'Politics as a Vocation' Weber sketches a 'broad' form which he labels an 'ethic of responsibility.' While thin forms of reason involve either purely instrumental calculations or the rule-observing consistency of an 'ethic of ultimate ends,' Weber defines the 'ethic of responsibility' in terms of a broad reason involving rational autonomy and requiring practical judgment (FMW, 120–2). Broad rationality involves the critical guidance of one's action towards considered ends, the ability to use one's understanding to achieve rational autonomy without relying on the morality of convention or the guidance of others. Weber's concept of rational autonomy, embodied here in broad reason and the ethic of responsibility, equates meaningfully human action with the capacity to provide an account of one's actions that relates to consciously chosen values as well as the circumstances of the material environment of action. Rational autonomy and broad reason thus combine both purposive- and value-rational action within the life praxis.

The archetypical institutional setting of reason as consistency is the rational bureaucratic organization. Concrete situations are assimilated to a uniform mode of treatment. Rules of conduct are formalized, cases are treated equally and impersonally. 'Consistency' alone is always a thin form of reason; as Weber illustrates in 'Politics as a Vocation,' action that exhibits a consistency vis-à-vis a particular rule or end is indifferent to human autonomy, for consistency takes no account of the possibility for unintended consequences, nor does it judge the applicability of the rule or end to a particular situation. The archetypical institutional setting of reason as instrumentalism is the capitalist market. Purposive-rational action is oriented to practical mastery and thus to means alone. Instrumentally rational action is indifferent to human autonomy for it is indifferent to whether humans or natural objects are used as means to ends. Institutional settings in which reason as instrumentalism predominates are founded upon discipline and hierarchy and individuals tend to be used in instrumental ways.

In the modern world, thin reason reinforces shallow-willing. In this social scenario, rationalization of material and social conditions directs people 'from the outside,' shaping their values according to the imperatives of consistency and instrumentalism. The thin rationality of modern political and economic structures fosters superficiality and discourages the development and preservation of deep-willing persons. Weber feared the modern world would be increasingly populated and run by shallow-willing persons: Fachmenschen 'who need "order" and nothing but order.' The formal legal rationality of economic and political structures of power contributes in a general way to the loss of value-oriented conduct in the public sphere by furthering 'the development of "rational matter-of-factness" and the personality type of the professional expert' (ES, 998). The 'rational matter-of-factness' encouraged by modern social arrangements induces what amounts to an ethic of adjustment, of 'adaptation to the possible' (MSS, 24). In shallow forms of purposive-rational conduct, Brubaker argues, '*given* wants guide the ... individual in his selection of ends'; by contrast, in value-rational orientations, '*chosen* ultimate values guide.'[14] This theme of shallow-willing and thin reason runs like a subterranean stream through Zygmunt Bauman's study of the Fachmenschen, the architects, engineers, and scientists who devised, built, and operated the concentrationary system of the Nazi empire of death.[15] Thin reason, involving the mastery of given problems through technical calculation in the sphere of economic activity and formal rule observance in the sphere of political conduct, promotes shallow forms of willing in individuals, an attitude of accommodation to the immediacy and heterogeneity of existing circumstances.

Weber more or less identifies modern social arrangements with thin rationality. Thus, he believes, any prospect for the substantive rationalization of ends, for the introduction of value-rationality into the 'iron cage,' must originate within individual actors, since modern institutions are by definition functional machines given over to the means-end mentality and not likely to be sources of newly emerging value. Yet the subsumption of ends under means and the fetishization of means in our culture lead to an inability of a growing number of people to live and work in accordance with goals that transcend the existing social order. The irony of modernity is that it represents an historical period in which individuals are least bound by prescriptive ethical custom and tradition, when they possess the greatest opportunity for self-realization, yet it is also a period with the most oppressive 'objective' culture.

Weber had no doubt about how far-reaching social change is likely to be brought about. It would originate in the value-oriented actions of individuals and small groups, and the more the values, ideals, or normative principles stand out in contrast to social reality and traditional patterns of social conduct, the more profound the changes these value-oriented actions initiate are likely to be. However, he feared that in the public sphere thin rationality would prevail and social arrangements would become immunized against visionary politics of any kind. One of the consequences of rationalization and routinization Weber feared most was the devitalization of politics, the reduction of the scope of the 'possible' to that which is in principle already realized, a process Mannheim describes as the 'transformation of all politics into problems of administration.'[16] As Weber argues, 'in a sense, successful political action is always the "art of the possible". Nonetheless, the possible is often reached only by striving to attain the impossible that lies beyond it' (MSS, 23–4). Weber adds, those qualities and achievements of our culture, which we all more or less esteem, were not achieved through adaptation to what the prevailing constellation of interests defined as 'possible.' The narrowing of the spectrum of the possible is evidenced in the mainstream politics of the West, where governments tend to stand or fall based on technical definitions of good economic management. The most absorbing political issue becomes one of balancing low inflation against high unemployment, and so forth. Even conflict between various mainstream political parties involves 'structured disagreement' that is never paradigm-challenging.

## 2. Weber's Political Response to the Modern Condition: Articulating the Limits of Formal Legal Rationality

Thin reason and shallow-willing are enormously significant in the modern world. They have transformed and continue to transform the West through the progressive subordination of social and natural processes to human purposes. But many of the most important problems of social life, even those with a technical dimension, are not purely technical problems of finding the most rational means to a pregiven or precisely determined end. It is difficult to overstress the importance of this point for Weber's social and political thought.

Whenever action is conceived by an actor as a means to some more or less defined end, this action can be understood as a technique (ES, 65). Every technique is subjectively rational, but techniques vary in their degree of objective rationality. The highest level of objective rationality can be obtained when techniques for achieving given ends are determined with scientific knowledge. Weber distinguishes between this technical point of view (weighing means for a fixed end) and an 'economic point of view' (weighing means and alternative ends as well as unintended but foreseeable consequences) (ES, 65–7). Objectively rational judgments can only be made from the technical point of view, for the economic point of view involves assessing the comparative importance of alternative possible ends or of balancing desirable ends against undesirable secondary consequences, and this cannot be done objectively. Technical rationality can be measured against an objective standard provided by the scientific knowledge of means-ends relations. But economic rationality is purely subjective: conscious calculations about the comparative value of ends, means, and secondary consequences cannot be assessed in terms of objective correctness.

As Weber points out, there may frequently seem to be 'general agreement about the self-evident character of certain goals,' for example, 'the concrete problems of social hygiene, poor-relief, factory inspection,' and so forth (MSS, 55–6). Yet, 'each individual understood something quite different by the ostensibly unambiguous end' (MSS, 12). The most pressing problems of social life, involving economic and social policy, 'cannot be resolved merely on the basis of purely technical considerations which assume already settled ends. Normative standards of value can and must be the objects of *dispute* in a discussion of a problem of social policy because the problem lies in the domain of general *cultural* values' (MSS, 56). Science can provide reliable empirical knowledge that can be used to formulate policy, but it cannot dictate solutions to problems that require decisions based on values rather than knowledge. 'Even such simple questions as to the extent to which an end should sanction unavoidable means, or the extent to which undesired repercussions should be taken into consideration ... are entirely matters of choice or compromise. There is no (rational or empirical) scientific procedure of any kind whatsoever which can provide us with a decision here' (MSS, 18–19).

Of course, Weber did not believe in the existence of any objective 'cultural values.' Influenced by Nietzsche, he argues that, in a post-traditional age, there is no ultimately legitimate foundation for values other than individual choice and consent. In other words, Weber argues for an 'individualist decisionism' as the basis of value-setting.[17]

Given the fundamental distinction between means-ends rationality and judgments of value that rationalism of modern social arrangements presume, it is possible to articulate the 'logical requirements' for the subordination of bureaucracy and formal legal rationality in general to an external form of value-setting. First, the formal rationality of rules presupposes the normative power of decision. This is the structural relationship between formal legal rationality and individual autonomy which has made such a significant contribution to modern experience of freedom. The rule-mechanism of bureaucracy inevitably makes room at its margins for the intervention of some kind of discretionary decision making, just as the rationalism of modern social arrangements eliminates ascriptive norms and releases the ends of social conduct to planful individual determination. By surpassing its 'proper' function bureaucratic rationality illegitimately colonizes or expropriates the function of end-setting. When this occurs, what managerial expertise purports to ground according to the dictates of technical calculation or rule-observance are in fact expressions of arbitrary but disguised will and preference.[18] Recalling the link between law and the rationality of modern social arrangements, the problem of inappropriate influence over value-setting is illustrated by the judicialization of social policy determination.

Second, bureaucracy and formal legal rationality in general must be subordinated to external value-setting because the attributes of efficiency, calculability, and predictability which they supply to modern social arrangements are in themselves moral concepts. Given the link between formal legal rationality and the promise of individual autonomy, the social attributes of efficiency, calculability, and predictability are not morally neutral features of the modern world. The early modern value-rational origins of modern rationalism illustrate that the formal legal rationality of modern social arrangements required a normative, moral context of value that could only by given culturally rather than instrumentally. Rather than attributing the formation of capitalism and the spread of bureaucracy solely to the importance of 'money' or 'order,' according to Weber, it would be more accurate to point to the cultural conditions of 'rationalization,' to the institutionalization of particular cultural values, as the appropriate explanation. In this view, the attributes of formal legal rational social arrangements (efficiency, calculability, and predictability) presuppose the a priori normative importance of individual autonomy – not to mention Enlightenment views about the relationship between rational control over social and natural processes and individual freedom.

Although philosophically, Weber was agnostic about the developmental direction of Western history, he believed that all the social 'weather vanes' of his own time pointed in the direction of increasing cultural predominance of allocative and authoritative practices employing thin forms of reason and social conduct oriented to the observance of rules or calculation of profit involving shallow forms of willing. Weber believed that bureaucracy was the salient edge of a process of rationalization and routinization that, if left unchecked, would eventually strangle the cultural development of the West, leading to a form of political and economic stagnation by destroying leadership qualities in politics and individual initiative in economic activities.[19]

Scope for individual assertion and the exercise of personal responsibility, according to Weber, could be maintained only at the head of large economic and political organizations, where individuals must not only make deliberate choices between conflicting value-possibilities but also have a clear understanding of the means and contingencies of acting in the real world. In this way the possibility for cultural innovation could be maintained through the deep-willing personalities of gifted political leaders and economic entrepreneurs. He wagered that the thin reason of modern social organizations could be successfully subordinated by the deep-willing personality of charismatic political leaders and entrepreneurs.

Weber's counterpositioning of deep-willing leaders and entrepreneurs against the thin rationality of social arrangements represents an attempt to maintain some scope for value-oriented conduct in social life, to supply some form of broad reason to the control and direction of the instrumentalities of government and economic enterprise. However, given the 'logical requirements' articulated above for the subordination of bureaucracy – and formal legal rationality in general – to an external form of end-setting, there is no necessity for the narrowness of his political formula for dealing with the problematic influence of shallow reason over the 'kingdom of cultural ends,' for his exclusive identification of political value-setting with the elite activity of virtuosi personalities. The non-necessity of virtuosi leadership is perfectly illustrated by the importance and immense influence of new social movements in the modern West, the environmental and feminist movements to name only two. As Ulrich Beck argues, this activation of subpolitics 'means shaping society from below.'[20]

## 2.1 Weber's Institutional Formula for Subordinating Legal Rationality and Resisting the Rationalization of Value-Setting

Weber's political theory is obviously connected with his critique of the German politics of his day. But it is also a logical extension of his sociological thought on modern society, specifically, the threat of the routinization of material interests created by a pattern of formally rational social arrangements. In general, Weber worried that the diminishing public relevance of the value-oriented action central to cultural innovation and the formation of autonomous moral 'personality' might eventuate in a form of social and cultural stagnation. In particular, he feared that the usurpation of political value-setting and end-determination by the thin reason of bureaucracy and economic processes might result in a form of political servitude.

The political questions Weber considered of paramount importance for his contemporaries remain relevant today. Are a rational bureaucratic administration and provision of services and the rational market allocation of economic resources to be the ultimate and the only values on which to decide the way in which our social affairs are managed (ES, 1403)? How can the power of modern institutions, the official's concern with administrative effectiveness, and the entrepreneur's concern with profit, be kept properly subordinated to the political function of defining the ends that power is to serve? What do we have to oppose to the machinery of these rational instrumentalities, Weber asks, 'in order to keep a remnant of humanity free from this fragmentation of the soul'? (GASS, 414).[21]

I will only discuss Weber's specific institutional formula for answering these political questions in a cursory manner. Weber argued that, because of a weak parliament, Germany in his day suffered from 'government by officials' (ES, 1381–4). All governments are, on a day-to-day basis, run by officials, especially modern governments, which employ a salaried, expert career officialdom to handle their large volume of routine administration. The power of bureaucracy lies in its superior knowledge and experience of routine matters, which inevitably exceeds that of elected politicians who come and go. What Weber criticized was the tendency for bureaucratic officials to assume the role of determining policy; political leadership was left to a civil service that was well-meaning but incapable of political leadership and far-sighted political judgment.

Corresponding to the distinction between thin- and deep-willing persons discussed above, Weber's critique of the German system of government relied on the distinction he drew between the roles of the bureaucratic official and the politician, the different character of their activities, and the personal qualities required of each in the performance of occupational duty. The official works within an organization and his or her role is to carry out the demands of the organization as efficiently as possible, either by issuing orders to subordinates or obeying instructions of superiors. The following of rules is paramount. The hallmarks of the bureaucratic official's activity are thus subordination and impersonality.

In contrast, the politician participates in an open struggle with other groups and other points of view in order to win a voluntary following. The decisive difference between these two types for Weber was that, whereas the official is responsible to a superior, works within an ordered hierarchy of command and obedience, and judges a situation by reference to rules and technical expertise, the politician is personally accountable for the policies he or she pursues and must work within a system of competition with other views and groups in order to recruit support. The ethos of the bureaucratic official is the disciplined performance of duty, while that of the politician is the assumption of personal responsibility.[22]

The contrast Weber draws between bureaucratic officials and politicians was shaped by his sociological conception of the struggle between charisma and routinization. His focus on a charismatic leader was a way of counteracting impersonal and disenchanted social life with a dynamic political culture, an attempt to provide some scope for the role of ideas and some possibility for the pursuit of goals that are far-reaching and not subject to everyday consideration. Thus, in Weber's view, bureaucracy could be limited to its proper function if control over the value-setting of its goals were placed in the hands of deep-willing individuals capable of exercising creative but responsible political judgment.

Weber sought an institutional blueprint that would allow the rise of charismatic leaders to influence and power within a framework of legal rule and bureaucratic authority. The institutional structure for supplying the kind of leadership capable of subordinating the bureaucratic machine to political value-setting, Weber argues, is a strong parliamentary institution within a constitutional framework of a plebiscitarian democracy (ES, 266–7; 1127–30). Such a parliament would offer a training ground for producing leaders capable of subordinating the state bureaucratic apparatus and providing effective political direction to the nation.

Weber also argues for the system of competitive market capitalism. Like the politician, the entrepreneur represents a model of individual initiative and personal responsibility, and the entrepreneur's struggle for economic existence leads to innovation and risk-taking. The institution of private property in the capitalist market guaranteed the individual property owner mastery over a sphere of independent activity. The control of large political or economic organizations, Weber believes, would provide scope for individual assertion and the exercise of personal responsibility. He was well-aware that capitalism was a general force behind the rationalization processes at work in modern society. Nevertheless, arguing for the importance of competing sources of power, he endorses the 'anarchy' of the competitive capitalist mar ket as a method of preserving opportunity for individual initiative. The competition between parties in parliament and capitalist firms in the economy, and that between the private economy and the state bureaucracy, would maintain countervailing and competing sources of power, thus thwarting the crystallization of social arrangements into a structure of total administration.

The issues generated by Weber's theory of leadership-democracy are legion. However, the critical point here is that, although Weber identifies, I believe correctly, the political problems of value-setting generated by the rational design of modern society, there is no logical necessity in the narrow gauge of the institutional solution he formulates.

Weber's conception of democracy is circumscribed by his conflation of charismatic leadership and charismatic domination: he tends to identify charisma too closely with genuine leadership of any kind. We may agree with Weber that the concept of charisma says something about the criteria of leadership in democratic systems. With the emergence of the universal franchise and the development of highly organized party machines, charismatic leadership-democracy is not simply a postulate but a reality of modern democracy. The old liberal parliament comprised of a group of elites who decided on matters of national interest by way of rational debate has long been replaced by party organizations, which have taken over the control of parliaments and the articulation of the political agenda. The electorate does not choose between political issues, but between political leaders who employ their charismatic capabilities via the mass media to convince the masses of the righteousness of their cause.

But though the concept of charisma may apply to the criteria of leadership in democratic systems, it has nothing to do with the legitimacy of such systems. Charisma may qualify a personality as a leader but it does not legitimize his or her authority. Although Weber's conception of leadership-democracy binds the leader to the rule of law and to the necessity of continual self-legitimation within the framework of the democratic electoral process, there is a need to distinguish more carefully than Weber did between charismatic leadership and charismatic domination. Weber simply did not give enough attention to the dangers of revolutionary dictatorship or the less extreme forms of 'caesaristic leadership' that can develop within the framework of mass democracy.

There is a second problem with Weber's political formula. Weber circumscribes the value-setting function of modern politics by formulating it as an elite activity reserved to special individuals at the head of large political organizations. Because of his emphasis on leadership, the bulk of the population is effectively deprived of any meaningful political agency. Given the dissolution of social distinctions based on birth and status and the formal equality of persons presupposed by the legal rationality of modern institutions, there is no basis for any form of suffrage short of universal. Despite this 'universal' participation in the electoral process, Weber contends that mass democracy would not eliminate oligarchy, or what he called the 'law of the small number,' but would merely modify the methods by which the few who ruled were selected and the kind of qualities they would have to possess to rule effectively. In other words, Weber considers the essence of democratic rule the principle of formally free selection of leadership. But even this formal freedom of selection, he believes, is subverted by the party machinery, which is capable of manufacturing a certain degree of assent.

In Weber's model of democratic politics the citizenry only becomes involved as a result of initiatives from above. It could be argued that the conception of what is 'possible' in Weber's political thought bears too much of the imprint of his sociological conception of the iron cage. Just as the thin reason of modern social arrangements cultivates shallow-willing individuals, so Weber's conception of democracy, instead of offering institutional devices for empowering the political agency of individuals against the excessive weight of the rational matrix of modern society, actually further interpolates the citizenry as a collection of shallow-willing individuals, incapable of any independent action and initiative. As Weber writes in a letter to Robert Michels, 'such notions as the "will of the people," the true will of the people, ceased to exist for me years ago; they are *fictions*. It is as if we were to speak of the will of the shoe buyer who has to decide what skills the shoemaker should employ. The shoe buyer knows, to be sure, *where* the shoe *pinches*, but he never knows how it could be made to fit.'[23]

As a result of the narrow conceptual framework in which Weber discusses democracy, the contribution that different groups can make to the decision-making process of politics is neglected. Treating the electorate as a 'mass' limits the people's role in politics to that of passive objects who respond to the leader's will. For instance, the plebiscitarian leadership of parties, Weber writes, 'entails the "soullessness" of the following, their intellectual proletarianization' (FMW, 113).

Weber seems willing to pay an extraordinary price in order to secure political direction by charismatic leaders. Many commentators have noted the peculiar tension between his political formulation, which emphasizes strong leadership, and his commitment to individual autonomy, the contradiction between the potential authoritarian implications of the principle of forming a gathering of followers on the basis of a charismatic gift for leadership and the equally important principle of individual self-determination.[24] The antinomy between the values of individual self-realization and strong leadership are for Weber reconciled from the perspective of the prescriptive idea that, under the rational social arrangements of modern political and economic structures, only strong leaders/entrepreneurs at the head of large organizations are capable of setting goals and objectives, which are then 'sold' to the people at large.

Perhaps, as Beetham has argued, Weber's assertions about the inevitability of oligarchy and the manufactured quality of the 'will of the people' are animated by a fear of what would happen if initiatives in politics did not stem from a few at the top.[25] But certainly, by relying on virtuosi leadership as a source of deep-willing, Weber ignores the possibility that the routinization of political and economic value-setting might be best resisted, and opportunity for creative political and economic action best ensured, through the extension rather than limitation of popular participation in a democratic, political process.

## 2.2 A Decisionist Ethic for the Politicization of Value-Setting

Despite its conceptual limitations, the strength of Weber's political thought lies in its definition of the problematic relationship between formal legal rationality and individual autonomy in terms of the former's capacity to subvert the value-setting function of politics and the value-setting capacity of individuals. Formal legal rationality is tied to individual autonomy in terms of the presumption of the normative power of intentionality and value-positivism. The countertendencies of rationalization reflect a subversion of this relationship between means and ends: either the capacity to will is weakened or the distinction between the rationality of means-ends calculation and the selection of ends is eroded.

At bottom, Weber's political thought is concerned with the reification of value-setting by the rational and routine character of modern social arrangements, the trivialization of politics through a growing collective inability to control the results of economic and technological rationalization, or even to imagine alternatives to the existing constellation of material interests. Weber's political thought is also about politicizing value-setting, that is, the question of the 'purposes' of social and economic power, while emphasizing at the same time the fundamental nonavailability of straightforward 'rational' solutions to age-old questions about 'how we ought to live.' Weber's specific political formula for a plebiscitarian leadership-democracy represents an institutional device for empowering the value-setting capacity of deep-willing individuals. Provision for responsible but visionary leadership at the helm of large political and economic organizations, in Weber's view, would help maintain a degree of constitutional value-indeterminacy to ensure some cultural innovation within the 'closed' orders of the rational, routine matrix of modern society. Although Weber's emphasis on leadership is objectionable for its authoritarian implications, the underlying principles of his political thought should be retained. Modern politics should be directed to empowering the capacity of individuals to participate in value-setting exercises, and this empowerment will not be achieved by the legalization of every feature of modern social life.

Weber more or less identified public life in modern society with thin reason and shallow-willing individualism. What concerned him was that the thin rationality of modern social arrangements, bureaucratic organizations, and market capitalism, where rule-observance and calculation of profit without regard for persons fosters formalism and instrumentalism, discourages the development of deep-willing orientations to public life. The modern world would perforce increasingly be run by shallow-willing persons.

According to Weber's account of modernity, the construction of modern social arrangements was directed by the value-orientations that deep-willing persons bestowed on the world. For their descendants who inhabit the modern world, however, these values are no longer chosen. In the arena of economic action, for example, Weber argues that, whereas the fulfilment of the vocational calling was once related to the highest spiritual and cultural values, today 'the individual generally abandons the attempt to justify it at all.' Instead of being fired by religious, ethical, and political ideals, such activity has become simply a response to 'economic compulsion' or to 'purely mundane passions' (PE, 182).

This is a classic example of reification: values developed by a people expressly to satisfy a psychological need lead them unwittingly to create new institutions which then impose the value on their progeny. As Weber writes, 'the Puritan wanted to work in a calling; we are forced to do so' (PE, 181). The deep-willing personality of the Puritans who shaped a society in conformance with the most far-reaching ideals is eventually replaced by a shallow-willing adaptation to the values enforced by modern social arrangements.

Bureaucracies and capitalist economies institutionalize thin forms of reason where the rationality of institutions, involving the coordination of individual activities through channels of consistency and instrumentality, conflicts with the broad reason of individual autonomy. As Weber's theory of personality argues, rational autonomy involves the development of one's capacity for self-guidance according to a consistent orientation towards deliberately chosen ends. People need to choose values in order to acquire a sense of meaningful autonomy. At the same time, however, the reduction of social conduct in public life to the calculation of effects and the observation of rules tends to destroy the public significance of value-oriented conduct. People continue to seek 'spiritual fulfilment' and 'salvation.' But such value-orientations towards the 'kingdom of ends' assume a highly personal, private form that has little impact on public norms at the workplace or in the shopping mall. They trivialize rather than intensify the notion of far-reaching ideals and as such they are the lubricant of a rational, orderly public life.

The crux of Weber's critique of modernity could be formulated as follows: the routine and thin reason of the modern matrix of social arrangements tends to negate the issue of value-contingency and trivialize the importance of choice and will in value-preference, thereby leading to superficial adaptive orientations and shallow expressions of personality. Modern social arrangements depoliticize value-setting by obscuring the fact that any valuation is occurring at all. Weber's political vision amounts to an attempt to counteract the effects of rationalization and routinization by (re)politicizing value-preference in disenchanted, post-traditional society. His decisionist political ethic derives from the attempt to subordinate thin forms of reason to human will. According to Weber's theory of value, all value-preferences are ultimately the product of human will; modernity is the epoch in which we become irreversibly aware of the unavoidability of choice, as premodern forms of legitimating norms (custom and revelation) become systematically disembedded and deracinated.

A fundamental premise of the whole decisionist framework of Weber's existential epistemology is that, to be truly human means, ultimately, to be free to choose. In the absence of God-willed authority, human beings must choose.[26] Weber argues, 'the fate of an epoch which has eaten of the tree of knowledge is that ... it must recognize that general views of life and the universe can never be the products of increasing empirical knowledge, and that the highest ideals, which move us most forcefully, are always formed only in the struggle with other ideals which are just as sacred to others as ours are to us' (MSS, 57).

The principle underlying Weber's political vision was the necessity of fighting against the belief in objective values in order to reserve values for individual choice.[27] To counteract the reification of value-setting that rationalization and routinization threaten, Weber emphasizes the contingent and conflictive character of values. Rather than attempting to overcome such a decisionist moment of choice with some notion of 'normative rationality,' he accentuates the agonistic, conflictive nature of personal value-preference in order to provide a counterbalance to the formal legality of bureaucratic administration and the instrumental calculation of profit in the capitalist economy. By emphasizing that scientific and technical understanding represent thin forms of reason with no inherent meaning, Weber hoped to clear a path for acts of authentic valuation within the social order.

Having identified public life in modern society with thin reason, shallow-willing, and excessive order and routine, Weber believed that the protection and promotion of individual autonomy under conditions of advanced capitalism had to be tied to limitations rather than extensions to the rationalization of economic and political structures of power. The 'fatefulness of reason' for Weber results from the way in which rationalization runs perpetually ahead of its subjects' collective capacity to make sense of, or to will, their own ends. In Löwith's interpretation, the implicit criterion by which Weber analyses the irrationality of modern social arrangements is the presupposition that the ultimate purpose of all institutions is not the institutions themselves but the human purposes they were meant to serve.[28] The autonomization of means, however, threatens to divorce the systematic forms of social action conducted within institutional settings from discernable human needs. In these terms, the capitalist economic system has become semi-autonomous of the substantive economic needs of a majority of people.

The key political question for Weber was how to maintain and enhance the freedom of the independent individual in relation to the excessive influence and weight of the rational, routine social arrangements of modern society. But if the thoughts and actions of individuals are becoming more confined within the narrow horizon of the technological order, then from where might the impetus and capacity to subordinate the rational institutions of public life come? The response Weber formulated involves resistance to the overformalization of life and rests on articulating possibilities for limiting the process of rationalization and maintaining opportunities for risk-taking and innovation, particularly at the head of large political organizations and economic enterprises. Specifically, of course, Weber advocated an institutional arrangement in which strong charismatic leadership could prevail.

While Weber's conception of democratic politics is unnecessarily truncated, the principle underlying it is valid: a counterbalance to the expropriation of the value-setting function of politics and consequent reification of values which the rationality of economic and political structures of power threatens must be obtained through some means that empowers the value-setting capacities of individuals. The main target of our criticism in Weber's political theory should be his unnecessarily narrow formulation of the value-setting function as an elite activity reserved to charismatic individuals at the head of large economic and political organizations.

Weber defines democracy as an 'anti-authoritarian reinterpretation of charismatic domination' (ES, 266–7). The connection he controversially posits between democracy and charismatic domination is usually explained in terms of the putative necessity of leadership. However, a deeper interpretation is possible. Unlike traditional domination, which adjusts to the possible in terms of what has always been, and legal domination, which adjusts to the possible in terms of the rule-governed present, democracy represents a constitutional form of value-indeterminacy.[29] In this view the specific character of democracy is more its contestational politics than its constitutionalism. As such, democracy embodies value-alterability vis-à-vis the rule machinery of legal domination. This indeterminacy contrasts with the structures of routine rule-observance without regard for persons in the formalized rationality of political structures of power, and the routine calculation of profit without regard for persons in the instrumentalized rationality of economic structures of power. The value-setting function of democratic politics, especially the 'sub-politics' of new social movements, provides a small foothold against the routinization of values and the surreptitious setting of values by thin forms of reason.[30] But William E. Scheuerman points out that the proliferation of subaltern social movements can be viewed in a less positive light: 'whatever their undeniable merits, these movements may *also* provide evidence for *worrisome* tendencies within contemporary representative democracy: precisely because the "centre" has gained exorbitant power in relation to the "periphery", extra-parliamentary social movements ... have emerged to fill the gap left by a formal political system increasingly dominated by ossified parties and organized vested interest.'[31]

Legal rationalization, while advancing the import of individual rights, has also further entrenched conceptions of the 'private' that function ideologically to limit the boundaries of the public sphere. Legal rationalization has shaped a public sphere that structurally inhibits informal contestation of actually existing democracy, depoliticizing the relationship between autonomous opinion formation and authoritative decision making, effectively creating a 'public in dormancy.'[32] As innovations in the institutions of democratic representation lag ever further behind developments in other institutional spheres of society, the vitality of civil society becomes increasingly jeopardized.

# Conclusion:
# In the Grip of Freedom

It is the possible, never the immediately existing, that contains locked up within itself a place for Utopia.[1]

Theodor W. Adorno, *Negative Dialectics*

To lack possibility means either that everything has become necessary or that everything has become trivial.[2]

Søren Kierkegaard, *The Sickness Unto Death*

In Weber's sociology of modernity, Löwith argues, the significance of '"rationality" is ambiguous precisely because it expresses the specific achievement of this world and at the same time the questionable character of this achievement.'[3] The point of Weber's emphasis on the impersonal, quasi-mechanical, and soulless quality of modern rational social arrangements is to illustrate that such arrangements, however formally or technically rational in terms of efficiency and productivity, are only a technical instrument of organization and production; they possess no inherent value, nor do they represent a substantively rational force in society. Weber emphasizes the 'precise, soulless and machine-like' character of bureaucracy so as to deny the bureaucratic apparatus the superior status or emotional mystique it held for many Germans of his day.

Similarly, we are accustomed to think of the 'Law' as a substantively rational force in modern society, perhaps even an institutional form of post-traditional 'normative rationality.' Weber's conception of modern law is salutary because it discourages overestimation of the ethical efficacy of legal rationality. Like other modern social arrangements, what is specific and peculiar to the rationalism of modern law is the formalism of its relations and functionings and the positive quality of its norms. The formal rationality of modern law has an important but only proximal relationship to the effectuation of justice. The modern legal order tends to function like a 'technically rational machine,' and this mode of functioning is both the heart of the freedom-guaranteeing capacity of modern law and the source of its tendency to acquire a life of its own.

Formal legal rationality is the structural concomitant of modern individual autonomy. The formal legal rationality of modern structures of power and authority promotes and protects individual autonomy. First, the legal rationality of social arrangements reduces the constraints on individual self-determination that arise from the concrete ascriptive norms of traditional structures of domination. In contrast to religiously revealed norms or the 'inviolable sacredness of age-old tradition,' the thread of meaning that unifies the structures of modern economic and political power is a rationalism premised on the fundamental tension between descriptions of fact and judgments of value, between an efficient means-ends calculus and the selection of ends in themselves. The legal rationalism of modern social arrangements represents a general *means* that indiscriminately facilitates a variety of substantive ends, providing a large scope for individuals to determine the ends of their social conduct according to personal choice and agreement. Values and norms are seen as artifacts of human volition rather than correspondents of some essential order in nature or the cosmos. The normative importance of choice and agreement is reflected in the legitimacy principle of modern law, which is based on correct enactment, and epitomized by the modern institution of purposive contracts, which facilitates planful association based on agreement.

Second, the corollary of the positivistic character of modern legal norms and the will-centred conception of personhood that they assume is the objectified and impersonal character of formal legal-rational social arrangements. Formal legal rationality means increased predictability of and control over social processes, which allows individuals to control their lives and pursue self-regarding aims in a purposive, planful manner. Thus, one might say that the substantive content of the legal guarantee of freedom has been about control over and distance from people and things. This control is achieved through the objectification and depersonalization of social relations and the elimination of evaluation and sentiment from 'public life.'

Weber's conception of modern law is also invaluable because it underscores the link between legal rationality and the countertendencies of modern rationalization. Weber's social reality was of the late nineteenth and early twentieth centuries.[4] Unlike Marx, he could study modernity in a more advanced stage, in its clearly unfolded rational complexity. The thematic congruencies between Weber's conception of rationalization and routinization and Marx's conception of alienation are striking.[5] The appearance of product as a power mastering and threatening the producer was a central problematic in Marx's thought; similarly Weber was concerned by the tendency of modern structures that support the experience of freedom to become independent and transformed into a power that restricts this very freedom.[6]

In Weber's view, the dominant developmental trend of our civilization is the increasing ascendance of processes of formalization and intellectualization, which reflect the increasing conscious and effective appropriation of the world and its processes. With the mass utilization of these rational structures of economic and political power, a practically indestructible form has come into being. Despite considerable political, economic, and cultural change, these structures continue operating unscathed. Weber had only to think of the state bureaucracy created by Bismarck which, while eliminating Bismarck, survived him and went on living a life of its own.[7]

The optimistic side of the liberal view of reason can be found in Kant's view that relations of power may be progressively transformed over time into relations of mutual recognition between rational, autonomous beings who are ends in themselves.[8] In his view, reason could replace power as a medium of political interaction. As reason extends into the public realm, politics becomes characterized less by coercive power and more by agreements between autonomous individuals. Thus power is supposed to recede as reason is progressively institutionalized. But Weber repudiated the Enlightenment expectation that reason and freedom reinforce one another: the extension of reason into the public sphere actually increases domination rather than producing rational autonomy.[9] For Weber, 'rational' institutions and social arrangements involve the most discipline and the most subordination of individually differentiated behaviour under the functional imperatives of the organization. As the scale of social and economic organization becomes more comprehensive, the realm of instrumental, routinized action is extended.

Weber believed that routinization destroys the incentives for autonomous action. Imagination as a social phenomenon becomes that much poorer because the imagination of what is real, and therefore believable, becomes tied to the verification of what is routinely experienced by the self. This is one manifestation of the loss of charisma. Modern society gives its shallow-willing inhabitants faith in the absolute reality of the concrete, the immediate moment, and in so doing inhibits their ability to express their will, to imagine that which is not in principle already 'realized.'

Wolfgang Schluchter argues that a major concern in Weber's social and political thought is the problem of determining the ethical way of life appropriate to modern society.[10] In the face of the 'naive optimism' of its practitioners and lay enthusiasts Weber demolished the myth that science (specifically the technique of mastering life that rests upon science) could teach us anything about 'the only important question for us: 'What shall we do and how shall we live' (FMW, 143). Similarly, a central proposition in Weber's discussion of legal-rational domination concerns the limits of its suitability to the resolution of questions that involve normative standards of value and problems that demand responsible judgment. His concern is linked to a more generalized anxiety about the dysfunctional possibility of 'regressive' de-differentiation of value-spheres: for example, the 'illegitimate' use of science, religious doxy, or art to supply determinate answers to political questions or existential needs. In a disenchanted world, Weber argues, these strategies can only constitute an attempt to disguise arbitrary will behind the fig-leaf of 'reason,' 'revelation,' or 'beauty,' or an abdication of will in the face of the primary necessity of individual choice.

According to Weber's positivistic theory of value, rational analysis cannot validate judgments of value. The correlate of this theory in his sociological writings is the proposition that rational social arrangements cannot create values, they can only function as a means to the furtherance of pregiven values. Weber believed that the most pressing problems of social life, even those economic and social policy issues that involve a technical dimension, are not purely problems of finding the most rational means to a predetermined end, but rather problems relating to general cultural values which must be objects of dispute and whose solutions must be posited (MSS, 56). Weber sought to politicize the problem of setting values in a post-traditional society precisely because the conflictive nature of value-preference and the agonistic character of value-choice are continually elided in the institutional sphere, by the routinization of thin forms of technical and purposive reasoning, and in the cultural sphere, by subjectivistic indulgence in forms of moral or aesthetic absolutism.

Moral, religious, and aesthetic ideals become redefined as private concerns in modernity because their general applicability can only be secured by universalistic criteria of justification that are no longer philosophically viable. The retreat of value into the pianissimo of personal preference is ironically a function of the legal-rational contribution to modern autonomy. In contrast to values deriving from habit or tradition, in the modern world the ends of social action are opened to individual determination, and individual choice and agreement assume a new moral importance. Individuals must heroically create weight and direction in their lives where none exists to begin with.

Thus, a core assumption in Weber's social and political thought is the individualistic mode by which values must be originated and energetically projected into the course of events. What worried Weber was that, given the modern cultural impetus to practical mastery over the world and the autonomous developmental logic of the capitalist economy, the consequent prestige of cognitive-instrumental modes of problem articulation and solution, and the premium placed on purposive-instrumental action orientations modern societies are constitutionally predisposed to approach the question of 'what shall we do and how shall we live' in terms of the thin reason of techno-managerial expertise. Issues of social life are resolved in terms of technical considerations even though such issues involve questions of value that have no one technically rational or correct solution. As Zygmunt Bauman writes, the 'organizing practices' of modernity have been animated by the belief in the possibility of 'a society free from irremovable contradictions, a society pointing the way, as logic does, to correct solutions only.'[11]

Legal domination draws its animus from the same ambition to institute legally correct recipes of social order. For example, Charter politics allows a post-traditional, pluralistic society like Canada to maintain the fantasy of objective value, that is, the promise of grounding values in reason, or, more specifically, resolving disputes via appeal to the 'truth' of a constitutional text. Canadian Charter adjudication represents a rationalization of the political process because, from a structural perspective, it depoliticizes aspects of the value-setting function of Canadian politics by redirecting acts of value-choice to judicial contexts, where issues like the subjectivity of value-preference and the contingency of value-setting are systematically obscured and marginalized by the rational processes of law-making and law-finding. With the legalization of politics, the logic of expertise dispenses with popular control over public policy. As the Arendtian theme of the 'decline of politics' argues, modern authoritative practices are founded less and less on collective communication and common deliberation.[12]

The impact of legal rationalization on modern politics is analogous to a more general tendency to subsume public life within the socioeconomic infrastructures, for example, the tendency to reduce politics to administration, or to allow the instrumental mechanisms of the capitalist market to assume the role of judge, opinion maker, and verifier of values. In terms of its impact on the political imaginary, Claus Offe compares the situation to that of a car without brakes: the running car stands for the functional efficiency of modern society, the lack of brakes symbolizes our incapacity to re-thematize its mode of running.[13] This metaphor relates to the effects of the cultural domination of economic imperatives and the resultant narrowing of the range of ideal interests which are permitted articulation in the political sphere. Official politics today is completely absorbed with the task of making the engine run more efficiently; the evaporation of critical debate about capitalism (say on increasing workplace democracy) demonstrates our inability to re-thematize the running of the car. Despite the substantive indeterminacy and transformative potential of the democratic project, its political import is continually threatened by the neutralizing impact of rationality and routine.[14]

As Weber argues, 'it is utterly ridiculous to suppose that it is an "inevitable" feature of our economic development under present-day advanced capitalism, as it has now been imported into Russia and as it exists in America, that it should have an elective affinity with "democracy" or indeed with "freedom" (in *any* sense of that word), when the only question to be asked is: how are all these things, in general and in the long term, *possible* where it prevails' (ST, 282)?

Just as there is no 'elective affinity' between capitalism and democracy, neither is there any between legal rationality and the experience of freedom. In order to free themselves from feudal custom and belief our ancestors created a vast technology of legal authority, replacing the rule of man by the rule of law and, more generally, eliminating unpredictable human sentiment from nonfamilial social relations. This was accomplished historically by objectifying the power structures in our societies in a manner that more or less identified freedom with economic mobility and the right to pursue personal economic interests. But tyranny today no longer derives from the centralized authority of the Church or the absolutist state. Perhaps we have now reached a stage of development at which the legal technologies of freedom through control simply reinforce our own authoritarian institutions: division of labour, the compulsory system of free wage labour, and so on.

Weber argues that the central issue of modern political organization must be expressed in terms of how best to subordinate the techno-managerial concern with administrative effectiveness to the political function of defining the ends that power is to serve. The question he posed to his fellow Germans is apropos of our political problematic today: is a rational provision of bureaucratic administration and allocation of economic resources to be the ultimate and the only value to decide how our affairs are managed? (ES, 1403). Behind Weber's dystopian image of the iron cage lies a question pertinent to the modern dyarchy of legal rules and legal rights: how is the relationship between legal rationality and politics to be conceived?

Notwithstanding the shortcomings of Weber's political thought, the lesson to be learned from his juxtapositioning of freedom and rationalization, democracy and bureaucracy, 'broad' and 'thin' reason, 'deep' and 'shallow-willing,' conflict and order, contestational struggle and rule-governance, charisma and routine, is that, from the standpoint of cultivating and supporting what appears to us as valuable in people, legal-rational domination should be limited within its proper function of implementing values set through a process of robust debate and discussion. As I argued in the previous chapter, although Weber's specific solution to the problem of modern politics is unacceptable – his theory of 'plebiscitarian leadership–democracy' amounts to recommendation of oligarchy – the underlying principle of his conception of modern political democracy should be retained. A counterbalance to the expropriation of the value-setting function of politics and consequent reification of values which the rationality of modern structures of power threatens must be obtained through some device that empowers the value-setting capacities of individuals and encourages meaningful political involvement in community life.

The routine and rational character of modern social arrangements, in combination with the prestige of shallow forms of reason, tend to negate the issue of value-contingency and trivialize the importance of choice and will in value-preference. As Schluchter points out, 'even more than by world flight Weber was repelled by unconscious world control, for it inevitably results in world adjustment – the typical attitude of the man of "law and order" (Ordnungsmensch).'[15] Within the rational order of modern society, liberal democracy preserves a sphere of value indeterminacy that maintains *possibilities* for cultural innovation nonidentical to routine order and the legal-rational rule fetish. But as Roy Boyne argues, 'market logics, technology logics, scientific logics, are controlling us – this is the abdication of both politics and social science because the risk is – massively – that we do not know where we are being taken.'[16] A sense of rational order can surround the most dismal situation, rendering its finality all the more eerie.

# Notes

## Introduction

1 An invaluable source for this new reception and interpretation of Weber's work can be found in a four-volume compendium, Peter Hamilton, ed., *Max Weber* (London, 1993). See also Sam Whimster and Scott Lash, eds., *Max Weber, Rationality and Modernity* (London, 1987) and Asher Horowitz and Terry Maley, eds., *The Barbarism of Reason: Max Weber and the Twilight of Enlightenment* (Toronto, 1994).

2 Important exceptions are Anthony Kronman, *Max Weber* (Jurists: Profiles in Legal Theory) (London, 1983) and Pt II of Jürgen Habermas, *The Theory of Communicative Action*, Vol. 1, *Reason and the Rationalization of Society,* trans. T. McCarthy (Boston, 1984).

3 Moreover, Weber's academic training was in jurisprudence and legal history (his first academic post was a lectureship in Roman, German, and commercial law at the University of Berlin). See Dirk Käsler, *Max Weber: An Introduction to His Life and Work*, trans. Philippa Hurd (Cambridge, 1988), 7.

4 Talcott Parsons, 'Value-freedom and Objectivity,' in O. Stammer, ed., *Max Weber and Sociology Today* (Oxford, 1971), 40.

5 Cf. Benjamin Nelson, 'Max Weber's "Author's Introduction" (1920): A Master Clue to His Main Aims,' *Sociological Inquiry* 44 (1974), 269–78; Wolfgang Mommsen, *The Age of Bureaucracy: Perspectives on the Sociology of Max Weber* (Oxford, 1974), 1–21; Stephen Kalberg, 'The Search for Thematic Orientations in a Fragmented Oeuvre: The Discussion of Max Weber in Recent German Sociological Literature,' *Sociology* 13 (1979), 127–39; Friedrich Tenbruck, 'The Problem of Thematic Unity in the Works of Max Weber,' *British Journal of Sociology* 31 (1980), 316–51; Wolfgang Schluchter, *The Rise of*

*Western Rationalism: Max Weber's Developmental History,* trans. G. Roth (London, 1981), 6–12; Wilhelm Hennis, 'Max Weber's "Central Question,"' *Economy and Society* 12 (1983), 135–80; Rogers Brubaker, *The Limits of Rationality: An Essay on the Social and Moral Thought of Max Weber* (London, 1984), 1–7; and Steven Seidman, 'The Main Aims and Thematic Structures of Max Weber's Sociology,' *Canadian Journal of Sociology* 9 (1984), 381–404.

6 It is certainly a testament to the depth and complexity of Weber's work that such divergent schools of thought and programs of research as Talcott Parsons's structural functionalism, Karl Jaspers's existential philosophy, or even Wilhelm Hennis's neo-Aristotelian critique of modernity could all claim some degree of provenance to Weber.

7 In linking Weber's legal thought with the rest of his work, it is essential to remember that the substantive sense of his sociology of law is far more extensive than the chapter in *Economy and Society,* which was formally packaged and labelled such by his widow Marianne (see Guenther Roth's comments in his 'Introduction' (ES, n.85). For instance, the role of law in the formation of modern economic arrangements is already a central concern of Weber's doctoral research, in which he studied the late-medieval development of legal instruments for sharing risk and profit between individuals in business organizations.

8 Cf. Christian Joerges and David Trubek, eds., *Critical Legal Thought: A German-American Debate* (Baden-Baden, 1989).

9 Habermas, *Theory of Communicative Action,* Vol. 1, 243–71.

10 Wolfgang Mommsen, 'Max Weber's Political Sociology and His Philosophy of World History,' *International Social Science Journal* 17 (1965), 23–45 at 41).

11 Brubaker, *The Limits of Rationality,* 1–2.

12 Kronman, *Max Weber,* 20–2.

13 A weakness in Kronman's approach is that there is some dispute over the degree to which Weber's methodological writings are representative of his 'mature' substantive interpretation of modernity. Cf. Tenbruck, *Problem of Thematic Unity,* 326–8.

14 See, for example, Weber's 'Author's Introduction' (PE, 13–31), 'Intermediate Reflections' (FMW, 323–59), and 'Science as a Vocation' (FMW, 129–56).

15 Mommsen, *The Age of Bureaucracy,* 95–115.

16 Habermas, *Theory of Communicative Action,* Vol. 1, 253.

17 The discussion and analysis of legal rights and legal rules tends to be bifurcated into separate disciplinary discourses. The problems posed by the intersection of rights-oriented individualism and 'community,' issues which relate to what I call the positivization of norms, have been addressed traditionally by political theorists, e.g., the liberal-communitarian debate

(see Michael Walzer, 'The Communitarian Critique of Liberalism,' *Political Theory* 18 (1990), 6–23; for a liberal critique of communitarianism see Will Kymlicka, 'Liberalism and Communitarianism,' *Philosophy and Public Affairs* 18 (1988), 181–204). Conversely, the problems posed by the organizational features of modern society, issues which relate to the formalization of social relations, have been addressed by sociologists, e.g., the German juridification debate of the 1980s (see Gunther Teubner, 'Juridification: Concepts, Aspects, Limits, Solutions,' in Teubner, ed., *Juridification of Social Spheres* (Berlin, 1987), 3–48). The problem is that, because of this division of academic labour, the legal integument binding the subjective and objective moments of individual autonomy and social order into the same structure of legal domination lies, as it were, in a penumbra between the focal lines of the two discourses.

18 David Trubek, 'Reconstructing Max Weber's Sociology of Law,' *Stanford Law Review* 37 (1985), 919–36.

19 This Weberian theme of the 'iron cage' destroying meaningful social community often appears in the 'communitarian' analysis of North American political life. Cf. Charles Taylor, 'Alternative Futures: Legitimacy, Identity and Alienation in Late Twentieth Century Canada,' in A. Cairns and C. Williams, eds., *Constitutionalism, Citizenship and Society in Canada* (Toronto, 1985), 183–229, and Michael J. Sandel, 'The Political Theory of the Procedural Republic,' in A. Hutchinson and Monahan, eds., *The Rule of Law: Ideal or Ideology* (Toronto, 1987), 96.

20 Cf. Peter Wagner, *A Sociology of Modernity: Liberty and Discipline* (London, 1994), 154–74, and Nikolas Rose, 'Governing "Advanced" Liberal Democracies,' in A. Barry, T. Osborne and N. Rose, eds., *Foucault and Political Reason* (Chicago, 1996).

21 See Russel Keat and Nicholas Abercrombie, eds., *Enterprise Culture* (London, 1991).

22 Cf. David Kettler, 'Sociological Classics and the Contemporary State of the Law,' *Canadian Journal of Sociology* 9 (1984), 447–58.

23 Alan Hunt, for example, stresses the value of individual rights in contradistinction to the utility of litigation ('Rights and Social Movements: Counter-Hegemonic Strategies,' *Journal of Law and Society* 17 (1990), 309–28 at 309).

## Chapter One: The 'Specific and Peculiar Rationalism of Western Culture'

1 Although Weber calls this latter type of social action 'value-rational,' he ranks it as a lesser form of rationalism. Hence I have subsumed it under the category of 'evaluative' action. With value-rational action, for instance,

objectives are considered valuable in themselves, regardless of the costs incurred by their pursuit or achievement; thus, this type of social action frequently produces decisively 'irrational' consequences.

2 Also *GEH*, 92–114, 275–8. Cf. Karl Polanyi, *The Great Transformation* (Boston, 1944).

3 Max Weber, 'Developmental Tendencies in the Situation of East Elbian Rural Labourers,' in Keith Tribe, ed. and trans., *Reading Weber* (London, 1989), 158–87.

4 Anthony Giddens defines 'disembedding' as 'the lifting-out of social relations from local contexts of interaction and their restructuring across indefinite spans of time-space' (*The Consequences of Modernity* (Cambridge, 1990), 21). As we will see in Chapters 2 and 3, in the development of the West, legal rationalization has been a primary mechanism for disembedding social relations.

5 Cf. Randall Collins, 'Weber's Last Theory of Capitalism: A Systematization,' *American Sociological Review* 45 (1980), 925–42.

6 Of course, Weber notes, 'the development of these sciences and the technology based on them has been, and still is, given a decisive impetus by the capitalist opportunities which reward their economic application' (ST, 338–9).

7 Weber, 'Anticritical Last Word on *The Spirit of Capitalism*,' *American Journal of Sociology* 83 (1978), 1105–31 at 1128–9.

8 Cf. Anthony T. Kronman, *Max Weber* (Jurists: Profiles in Legal Theory) (London, 1983), 36.

9 J. Weiss, 'Max Weber: Die Entzauberung der Welt,' in J. Speck, ed., *Grundproblem der grossen Philosophen* (Philosophie der Gegenwart IV) (Göttingen, 1981), 14; quoted in Hubert Treiber, 'Criticism as a Vocation-Theory and Practice in a Disenchanted World: A Review Essay,' *Contemporary Crises* 9 (1985), 375–86 at 377.

10 Robert Bellah, *Beyond Belief: Essays on Religion in a Post-Traditional World* (London, 1970), 40.

11 Karl Löwith, *Max Weber and Karl Marx*, trans. T. Bottomore and W. Outhwaite (London, 1993), 61.

12 Cf. Wolfgang Mommsen, *The Age of Bureaucracy: Perspectives on the Sociology of Max Weber* (Oxford, 1974), 19. *In the Grip of Freedom* is itself 'like a *utopia* [or dystopia] which has been arrived at by the analytical accentation of certain elements of reality' (MSS, 90).

13 Kronman, *Max Weber*, 19.

14 Ibid.

15 Weber's value-positivism has been labelled (with varying degrees of hostil-

ity) a 'nihilistic doctrine of value' (Leo Strauss), 'emotivism' (Alasdair MacIntyre), and 'decisionism' (Jürgen Habermas). All of these labels are in some sense apposite. However, they possess pejorative sting only if one affirms the possibility of 'objective value' or 'normative rationality.' See Leo Strauss, *Natural Right and History* (Chicago, 1953), 42; Alasdair MacIntyre, *After Virtue: A Study in Moral Theory* (London, 1985), 26; and Jürgen Habermas, 'Discussion on Value-freedom and Objectivity,' in Otto Stammer, ed., Kathleen Morris, trans., *Max Weber and Sociology Today* (Oxford, 1971).

16 Cf. E.B.F. Midgley, *The Ideology of Max Weber: A Thomist Critique* (Totowa, N.J., 1983), 122.

17 Cf. Rogers Brubaker, *The Limits of Rationality: An Essay on the Social and Moral Thought of Max Weber* (London, 1984), 92.

18 See Wolfgang Mommsen, 'Max Weber's Political Sociology and His Philosophy of World History,' *International Social Science Journal* 17 (1965), 23–45 and E.B. Portis, 'Max Weber's Theory of Personality,' *Sociological Inquiry* 48 (1978), 113–20.

19 Cf. Martin Albrow, *Max Weber's Construction of Social Theory* (London, 1990), 34–45.

20 The Kantian formula is 'Man as *noumenon* is free' and 'Man as *phenomenon* is part of the causal order of nature' (S. Körner, *Kant* (London, 1955), 153).

21 This process of objectification elucidates both the character of sociological inquiry and the nature of 'personality': just as the sociologist attempts to construe social phenomena through the heuristic device of deliberately constructed ideal-types, so our conceptions of ourselves as distinct personalities are dependent upon volitional reference to values. Cf. Portis, 'Max Weber's Theory of Personality,' 115.

22 Kronman, *Max Weber*, 20.

23 This is a central deficiency in Kronman's interpretation of Weber's theory of value: the logical non-availability of objective standards of choice does not mean that individual value choices must be founded ultimately upon irrational suppositions – the 'decisionism' which Weber's critics so often vilify.

24 To speak of an inherent human moral capacity to make substantively rational choices is not to deny the significance of society in the development of such moral capacity. Obviously society through various processes of socialization promotes morally regulated behaviour and discourages the opposite; the heuristic value of Weber's formulation is that it avoids identification of morality with social regulation. But theorization of these issues involves extrapolations which carry us away from Weber's work itself. For

a development of these ideas see Zygmunt Bauman, 'Towards a Sociological Theory of Morality,' in *Modernity and the Holocaust* (Cambridge, 1988), 169–200.

25  Löwith, *Max Weber and Karl Marx*, 61.
26  Brubaker, *Limits of Rationality*, 37.

## Chapter Two: The 'Specific and Peculiar Rationalism' of Modern Authority

1  Among various efforts to explicate Weber's typology of legal rationality, the most thoroughgoing can be found in Reinhard Bendix, *Max Weber: An Intellectual Portrait* (London, 1966), 398–400; David Trubek, 'Max Weber on Law and the Rise of Capitalism,' *Wisconsin Law Review* 3 (1972), 720–53 at 727–31; Wolfgang Schluchter, *The Rise of Western Rationalism: Max Weber's Developmental History*, trans. G. Roth (London, 1981), 87–9; and Anthony Kronman, *Max Weber* (Jurists: Profiles in Legal Theory) (London, 1983), 72–95.

2  Kronman, *Max Weber*, 87.

3  Cf. John O'Neill, 'The Disciplinary Society: From Weber to Foucault,' *British Journal of Sociology* 37 (1986), 42–60; Nikolas Rose, 'Governing "Advanced" Liberal Democracies,' in Andrew Barry, Thomas Osborne, Nikolas Rose, eds., *Foucault and Political Reason: Liberalism, Neo-liberalism and Rationalities of Government* (Chicago, 1996), 37–64.

4  Roberto Unger, *Law in Modern Society* (London, 1977), 49.

5  New norms could emerge through explicit imposition, but, as Weber argues, 'this could happen in one way only, viz., through a new charismatic revelation which could ... indicate what was right in an individual case ... [or] point to a general norm for all future similar cases' (ES, 761).

6  An example of the 'shattering' effect of the appearance of positive law and its erosion of the normative power of the actual was evidenced in the anxiety of German jurists in the nineteenth century over the rising tide of enacted positive law. See the discussion in Roger Cotterrell, *The Sociology of Law: An Introduction* (London, 1992), 16–43. Even today, the validation of English common law remains, according to Weber's typology of legitimacy, 'traditional' in mode. Although the legal norms of the common law tradition have been codified through adjudication on a case-by-case basis, as we will see in Chapter 5, their self-conception of legitimacy harbours an idea of 'common sense' which allegedly has been spontaneously generated over the centuries by everyday English social life. Such legal norms are thus supposedly just descriptive of prepolitical and 'natural' human relationships.

7  Unger, *Law in Modern Society*, 52–3.

8  Ibid., 67.
9  Ibid., 54.
10 The French Civil Code (proclaimed 21 March 1804) states in Art. 1134: 'Les conventions légalement formées tiennant lieu de loi à ceux qui les ont faites'; quoted by Weber (ES, fn. 3, 877–8).
11 In 'Politics as a Vocation,' and in the 'Social Psychology of the World Religions,' Weber elaborates only three ideal-types of legitimation: charismatic, traditional, and legal (see FMW, 78–9 and 295–9). However, in *Economy and Society* and in the 'Sociology of Law' Weber describes a fourth basis of legitimacy, 'value-rational authority,' which historically corresponds with eighteenth-century natural law conceptions (ES, 36). I will return to this issue in Chapter 3, in the context of Weber's account of the developmental history of Western law in terms of formal rationalization and the demise of the 'metaphysical dignity of law.'
12 Lawrence Friedman, *The Republic of Choice: Law, Authority, and Culture* (London, 1990), 38–9.
13 Jürgen Habermas, *The Theory of Communicative Action*, Vol. 1, *Reason and the Rationalization of Society*, trans. T. McCarthy (Boston, 1984), 260 and 163.
14 Karl Löwith, *Max Weber and Karl Marx*, trans. T. Bottomore and W. Outhwaite (London, 1993), 61.
15 Reinhard Bendix, *Max Weber: An Intellectual Portrait* (London, 1966), 422; emphasis added.
16 Regarding the problem of modernity's self-legitimation, see Jürgen Habermas, *The Philosophical Discourse of Modernity*, trans. Frederick Lawrence (Cambridge, Mass., 1987), 42.
17 Alasdair MacIntyre, *After Virtue: A Study in Moral Theory* (London, 1985), 51–9.
18 Roberto Unger makes an analogous argument about 'liberalism' as a cultural system which presumes value-positivism and intentionality (*Knowledge and Politics* (London, 1975), 31–6).
19 Weber's characterization of formal legal rationality was influenced by ideas developed earlier by his friend Georg Simmel. See Simmel's *The Philosophy of Money*, trans. Tom Bottomore and David Frisby (London, 1978), 227. On the relationship between Weber and Simmel see Jim Faught, 'Neglected Affinities: Max Weber and Georg Simmel,' *British Journal of Sociology* 36 (1985), 155–74; and Lawrence A. Scaff, *Fleeing the Iron Cage: Culture, Politics, and Modernity in the Thought of Max Weber* (London, 1989), 193–201.
20 Behind the impersonal, rule-guided transactions that suffuse the formalized everyday interaction of strangers lies the ethos of the Protestant inner-worldly ascetic: 'the person who lives as a worldly ascetic is a rationalist,

not only in the sense that he rationally systematizes his own conduct, but also in his rejection of everything that is ethically irrational, aesthetic, or dependent upon his own emotional reactions to the world and its institutions' (ES, 544).

21 For instance, Herbert Marcuse complains that 'Weber's analysis of capitalism was not value-free enough, in that it imported values and norms specific to capitalism into the "pure" definitions of formal rationality ... The concept of technical reason is perhaps itself ideology,' ('Industrialization and Capitalism,' in O. Stammer, ed., Kathleen Morris, trans., *Max Weber and Sociology Today* (Oxford, 1971), 149).

22 As David Trubek remarks, if Weber's commitment to an ideal of individual autonomy had constrained his depiction of modernity to an apologetic defence of the formal legal rationality of modern social arrangements, then Weber's sociology would represent a precursor of the kind of 'free-market theology' one finds in the work of Friedrich Hayek (Trubek, 'Reconstructing Max Weber's Sociology of Law,' *Stanford Law Review* 37 (1985), 919–36 at 932). For example, see Friedrich Hayek, *Law, Legislation and Liberty*, Vol. 1, *Rules and Order* (Chicago, 1973).

23 See Wolfgang Mommsen, *The Age of Bureaucracy: Perspectives on the Sociology of Max Weber* (Oxford, 1974), 65–71; David Beetham, *Max Weber and the Theory of Modern Politics* (Cambridge, 1985), 273–5; and Rogers Brubaker, *The Limits of Rationality: An Essay on the Social and Moral Thought of Max Weber* (London, 1984), 38–43.

24 Cf. the tension between formal and substantive rationality with the liberal antinomies of the 'universal' (e.g., theory, reason, rules, etc.) versus the 'particular' (e.g., facts, desire, values, etc.) described by Unger, *Knowledge and Politics*, 138.

25 'Major calls for "capitalism with a conscience",' *The Guardian* (15 November 1994).

26 Unger, *Law in Modern Society*, 86.

27 Joseph Raz, *The Morality of Freedom* (London, 1986), 369.

28 Cf. Unger, *Law in Modern Society*, 103.

29 MacIntyre, *After Virtue*, 68.

30 Of particular interest see J.M. Finnis, 'On "Positivism" and "Legal Rational Authority,"' *Oxford Journal of Legal Studies* 5 (1985), 74–90; Jürgen Habermas, *Legitimation Crisis*, trans. T. McCarthy (Boston, 1975), 95–102 and *Theory of Communicative Action*, Vol. 1, 243–71; Leo Strauss, *Natural Right and History* (Chicago, 1953), 35–80.

In general, see Arnold Brecht, *Political Theory: The Foundations of Twentieth-Century Political Thought* (Princeton, 1959), 207–60; Alexander

D'Entrèves, 'Legality and Legitimacy,' *Review of Metaphysics* 16 (1963), 687–702; Robert Grafstein, 'The Failure of Weber's Conception of Legitimacy: Its Causes and Implications,' *Journal of Politics* 43 (1981), 456–72; John Keane, 'Power, Legitimacy, and the Fate of Liberal Contract Theory,' *Praxis International* 2 (1982), 284–96; Roger Cotterrell, 'Legality and Political Legitimacy in the Sociology of Max Weber,' in David Sugarman, ed., *Law, State and Society Series: 'Legality, Ideology and the State'* (London, 1983), 69–93; H.L.A. Hart, *Essays in Jurisprudence and Philosophy* (Oxford, 1983), 49–87; Alan Hyde, 'The Concept of Legitimation in the Sociology of Law,' *Wisconsin Law Review* 17 (1983), 379–426; David Campbell, 'Truth Claims and Value-Freedom in the Treatment of Legitimacy: The Case of Weber,' *Journal of Law and Society* 13 (1986), 207–24; and Sheldon S. Wolin, 'Max Weber: Legitimation, Method, and the Politics of Theory,' in A. Horowitz and T. Maley, eds., *The Barbarism of Reason: Max Weber and the Twilight of the Enlightenment* (Toronto, 1994), 287–309.

31  The idea that 'legality,' meaning 'conformity with actually existing law,' might be able to 'summon up the force of legitimacy,' is not an original observation in Weber's work. In the words of Michel de Montaigne, that inimitable voice of sixteenth-century wisdom, 'the laws maintain their credit, not because they are just, but because they are laws. This is the mystical basis of their authority; they have no other. And this serves them well' (*Essays*, trans. J.M. Cohen (London, 1958), 353).

32  Habermas, *Theory of Communicative Action*, Vol. 1, 259.

33  Nancy Schwartz, 'Max Weber's Philosophy,' *Yale Law Journal* 93 (1984), 1386–98 at 1396.

34  In *Korematsu v. U.S.*, 323 U.S. 214 (1945), the U.S. Supreme Court upheld the constitutionality of the internment of Japanese-Americans; in *Dred Scott v. Sandford*, 60 United States (19 How.) 396 (1856), the court upheld the constitutionality of slavery.

35  Compare with Tracey B. Strong's interpretation of the import of Nietzsche's 'death of God' thesis, in '"What Have We to do with Morals"; Nietzsche and Weber on History and Ethics,' *History of the Human Sciences* 5 (1992), 9–18 at 11.

36  The idea of Weber's 'disillusioned realism' in his analysis of formal legal rationality derives from David Kettler and Volker Meja, 'Legal Formalism and Disillusioned Realism in Max Weber,' *Polity* 18 (1996), 307–31 at 321–2. Cf. Mommsen's assessment of Weber as a 'liberal in despair,' in *The Age of Bureaucracy*, 95–115.

37  Cf. Wolin, 'Max Weber,' 298–9. Of course, this process of 'forcing' relies extensively on possibility of educating individuals to make informed and responsible choices.

38 See Primo Levi's reflections on the Nazi concentrationary system (*The Drowned and the Saved*, trans. Raymond Rosenthal (London, 1988)). As Zygmunt Bauman argues in his provocative interpretation of the Holocaust, 'immanently and irretrievably, the process of rationalization facilitates behaviour that is inhuman and cruel in its consequences, if not in its intentions. *The more rational is the organization of action, the easier it is to cause suffering* – and remain at peace with oneself'; with the rationalization of modern structures of political and economic power (in the present day, rationalization in the name of efficiency and profit accumulation), 'the causal links in co-ordinated actions are masked, and the very fact of being masked is a most powerful factor of their effectiveness' (Zygmunt Bauman, *Modernity and the Holocaust* (Cambridge, 1988), 155, 163).

## Chapter Three: The Developmental History of Modern Law

1 In general, see Peter Hamilton, ed., *Max Weber* (London, 1993); on the sociology of law in particular, see David M. Trubek, John Esser, and Laurel Munger, *Preliminary, Eclectic, Unannotated Working Bibliography for the Study of Max Weber's 'Sociology of Law'* (Madison, Wis., 1986).
2 On contradictions in Weber's model of legal rationalization, see Anthony Kronman, *Max Weber* (Jurists: Profiles in Legal Theory) (London, 1983), 185; Jürgen Habermas, *The Theory of Communicative Action*, Vol. 1, *Reason and the Rationalization of Society*, trans. T. McCarthy (Boston, 1984), 253; David Trubek, 'Max Weber's Tragic Modernism and the Study of Law in Society,' *Law and Society Review* 20 (1986), 573–98 at 575. For criticism of Weber's conception of legal-rational authority see Leo Strauss, *Natural Right and History* (Chicago, 1953), 42; Jürgen Habermas, *Legitimation Crisis*, trans. T. McCarthy (Boston, 1975), 101; and Alasdair MacIntyre, *After Virtue: A Study in Moral Theory* (London, 1985), 26.
3 For example, see Jürgen Habermas, *Between Facts and Norms: Contributions to a Discourse Theory of Law and Democracy*, trans. William Rehg (Cambridge, Mass., 1996), 67–74.
4 As Trubek explains, legal thought of this type is 'logical' to the extent that rules or principles are consciously constructed by specialized modes of legal thought that rely on a highly logical systematization, and to the extent that decisions of specific cases are reached by processes of specialized deductive logic proceeding from previously established rules or principles. David M. Trubek, 'Max Weber on Law and the Rise of Capitalism,' *Wisconsin Law Review* 3 (1972), 720–53 at 730.
5 The contradistinction of 'logically' and 'extrinsically' formal legal-rational

thought follows the terminology of Stephen M. Feldman, 'An Interpretation of Max Weber's Theory of Law: Metaphysics, Economics, and the Iron
Cage of Constitutional Law,' *Law and Social Inquiry* 16 (1991), 205–48 at 218.

This distinction between the two topics of investigation can be discerned,
for example, in Weber's discussion of the transposition of Roman legal
thought of antiquity into the entirely alien circumstances of medieval
Europe. Weber writes, 'the task of "construing" the situation in a logically
impeccable way became almost the exclusive task [of jurists]. In this way
that conception of law which still prevails today and which sees in law a
logically consistent and gapless complex of "norms" waiting to be
"applied" became the decisive conception for legal thought. Practical
needs, like those of the bourgeoisie, for a "calculable" law, which were decisive in the tendency towards a *formal law as such*, did not play any considerable role in this particular process' (ES, 855; emphasis added).

6  Sally Ewing, 'Formal Justice and the Spirit of Capitalism: Max Weber's
Sociology of Law,' *Law and Society Review* 21 (1987), 487–512.

7  Weber's characterization of the way English legal training shapes an
'empirical' mode of legal thought is not out of date. See P. Smith and S.
Bailey, *The Modern English Legal System* (London, 1984), 92–131.

8  The logical formal rationality of such legal thought was often criticized as
too remote from the needs of everyday life: 'it took some effort, for instance,
to prevent the incorporation into the German Civil Code of the principle
that a lease is terminated by the sale of the land. That principle had originated in the distribution of social power in Antiquity. However, the plan of
taking it over into the new Code was entirely due to a blind desire for logical consistency' (ES, 789).

9  For detailed discussions of the 'English-problem' see Trubek, 'Max Weber
on Law and the Rise of Capitalism,' 746–8; Paul Walton, 'Max Weber's Sociology of Law: A Critique,' in P. Carlen, ed., *The Sociology of Law*, Sociological
Review Monograph 23 (Keele, 1976), 16–17; and Alan Hunt, *The Sociological
Movement in Law* (London, 1978), 122–8.

10 Trubek 'Max Weber on Law and the Rise of Capitalism,' 746–7.

11 This avenue of interpretation was initiated by Max Rheinstein, who argues,
correctly, that 'the categories of legal thought are obviously conceived
along lines parallel to the categories of economic conduct'; but Rheinstein
then continues, 'the logically formal rationality of legal thought is the coun-
terpart to the purposive rationality of economic conduct' ('Introduction,'
*Max Weber on Law in Economy and Society* (New York, 1954), i). Yet, as Rheinstein acknowledges, Weber nowhere explicitly equated logically formal
rational legal thought and purposive-rational economic conduct. Following

Rheinstein, Trubek argues erroneously that Weber 'stressed that *only* logical formal rationality, the autonomous legal system with universal and general rules' could guarantee the legal security required by capitalistic transactions. Trubek, 'Max Weber on Law and the Rise of Capitalism,' 746; my emphasis.

12 See Ewing, 'Formal Justice and the Spirit of Capitalism,' 499; and Hubert Treiber, 'Criticism as a Vocation – Theory and Practice in a Disenchanted World: A Review Essay,' *Contemporary Crises* 9 (1985), 375–86 at 382.

13 Cf. Hubert Treiber, '"Elective Affinities" between Weber's Sociology of Religion and Sociology of Law,' 14 *Theory and Society* (1985), 809–61 at 834–61.

14 Friedrich Tenbruck has influentially argued this significance of Weber's comparative historical sociology of the world religions. See, 'The Problem of Thematic Unity in the Works of Max Weber,' *British Journal of Sociology* 31 (1980), 316–51.

15 Ibid., 341.

16 Of course, Weber rejects the teleological and nomothetic implications of evolutionary theories of history (MSS, 102–3/203–5). His developmental models constitute ideal-type generalizations, a 'scaffolding' that must not be 'confused with reality' nor should these models be viewed as universal evolutionary stages through which all history progresses from one level to the next (see Stephen Kalberg, *Max Weber's Comparative-Historical Sociology* (Cambridge, 1993), 118). But, as Guenther Roth argues, Weber's account of Western legal rationalization does reveal a certain pattern and a direction ('Rationalization in Max Weber's Developmental History,' in S. Whimster and S. Lash, eds., *Max Weber, Rationality and Modernity* (London, 1987), 80–7).

17 Treiber, '"Elective Affinities",' 845.

18 Treiber worries that the natural law idea cannot provide an 'inner logic' of legal rationalization because, unlike the theodicy problematic, the idea of natural law is not universal to all societies and thus does not form a functional analogy with the problem of theodicy (ibid., 845). But as Harold Berman's historical research indicates, this specificity of natural law does not mean its logical dissimilarity to theodicy; on the contrary, natural law represents the secular condensate of a particular solution to theodicy, one in which the secular order was differentiated from the sacred, but never fully divorced from its Judeo-Christian roots (*Law and Revolution: The Formation of the Western Legal Tradition* (Cambridge, Mass., 1983), 558).

19 Roberto Unger, *Law in Modern Society* (New York, 1976), 79.

20 Ibid., 79–80.

21  See Wolfgang Schluchter, 'The Paradox of Rationalization,' in G. Roth and W. Schluchter, eds., *Max Weber's Vision of History: Ethics and Methods* (Berkeley, 1979), 11–59.

22  See Kalberg, *Max Weber's Comparative-Historical Sociology*, 102–17.

23  See David M. Trubek, 'Max Weber on Law and the Rise of Capitalism,' *Wisconsin Law Review* 3 (1972), 720–53 at 727–31, and esp. Kronman, 72–95.

24  Cf. Unger, *Law in Modern Society*, 68.

25  Ibid., 69.

26  Rogers Brubaker, *The Limits of Rationality: An Essay on the Social and Moral Thought of Max Weber* (London, 1984), 37.

27  This point is reinforced by the legal historian Harold Berman, who argues that the invention of legal institutes (such as corporation, contract, and property law, and principles of constitutional law) which contribute to the normative securities upon which capitalist economic conduct depends, occurred in Western Europe from the twelfth to the fifteenth centuries, long before the economic and political changes of the nineteenth century associated with the development of modern capitalism (*Law and Revolution*, 43; cf. ES, 1464, fn.14).

28  See Stephen Kalberg, 'The Search for Thematic Orientations in a Fragmented Oeuvre: The Discussion of Max Weber in Recent German Sociological Literature,' *Sociology* 13 (1979), 127–39 at 132.

29  Habermas, *Legitimation Crisis*, 95–102; *Theory of Communicative Action*, Vol. 1, 243–71; and *Between Facts and Norms*, 66–73.

30  See Habermas, *Theory of Communicative Action*, Vol. 1, 253.

31  Cf. Schluchter, 'The Paradox of Rationalization,' 32–59.

32  Habermas, *Theory of Communicative Action*, Vol. 1, 230.

33  Jürgen Habermas, *The Theory of Communicative Action*, Vol. 2, *The Critique of Functionalist Reason*, trans. T. McCarthy (Boston, 1987), 309–10.

34  Ibid., 357–8.

35  Jürgen Habermas, 'Law as Medium and Law as Institution,' Iain Fraser and Constance Meldrum, trans., in G. Teubner, ed., *Dilemmas of Law in the Welfare State* (Berlin, 1988), 204.

36  Cf. Zygmunt Bauman, *Freedom* (Concepts in the Social Sciences) (Milton Keynes, 1988), 44–8.

37  Habermas, *Theory of Communicative Action*, Vol. 2, 154.

38  Habermas, 'Law as Medium,' 213.

39  Cf. Habermas, 'Law as Medium,' 212–15 and *Between Facts and Norms*, 66–81.

40  Habermas, *Between Facts and Norms*, 447–50.

41  Habermas, *Theory of Communicative Action*, Vol. 2, 361.

42  Ibid., 210.
43  Alan Hunt and John Tweedy, 'The Future of the Welfare State and Social
    Rights: Reflections on Habermas,' *Journal of Law and Society* 21 (1994),
    288–316 at 308.
44  Habermas, *Theory of Communicative Action*, Vol. 1, 259; *Between Facts and
    Norms*, 72.
45  Habermas, *Theory of Communicative Action*, Vol. 1, 261.
46  Habermas, 'Law as Medium,' 212.
47  Habermas, *Theory of Communicative Action*, Vol. 2, 368.
48  Or, to phrase Habermas's Weberian problematic more precisely: how do
    we institutionalize a 'broad' form of collective reasoning, say, 'communi-
    cative action,' when the structural grammar of modern institutionaliza-
    tion, relying as it does on the 'thin' reason of 'systems' rationality, is
    fundamentally alien to nurturing the kind of discursive mutuality and
    experimentation which such action requires (cf. Fred Dallmayr, 'Max
    Weber and the Modern State,' in A. Horowitz and T. Maley, eds., *The Bar-
    barism of Reason: Max Weber and the Twilight of Enlightenment* (Toronto, 1994
    62–3).
49  For example, David Kettler and Meja Volker, 'Legal Formalism and Disillu-
    sioned Realism in Max Weber,' *Polity* 18 (1996), 307–31.
50  Feldman, 'An Interpretation of Max Weber's Theory of Law', 205–48; Allan
    C. Hutchinson, *Waiting for Coraf: A Critique of Law and Rights* (Toronto,
    1995); Joel Bakan, *Just Words: Constitutional Rights and Social Wrongs* (Tor-
    onto, 1997).
51  Roosevelt considered an Economic Bill of Rights crucial for the postwar
    resumption of the 'New Deal' program of social and economic reform. See
    Arthur A. Ekirch, *Ideologies and Utopias: The Impact of the New Deal on Ameri-
    can Thought* (Chicago, 1969), 245–66.
52  See Russel Keat and Nicholas Abercrombie, *Enterprise Culture* (London,
    1991); Peter Wagner, *A Sociology of Modernity: Liberty and Discipline* (London,
    1994), esp. 154–74.

**Chapter Four: The 'Dynamic' of Legal Rationalization**

1  As discussed in Chapter 3, the process of legal rationalization involves the
   'juridification' of social relations. See Jürgen Habermas, 'Law as Medium
   and Law as Institution,' Iain Fraser and Constance Meldrum, trans., in
   G. Teubner, ed., *Dilemmas of Law in the Welfare State* (Berlin, 1988), 203–20; a
   substantially similar version of this article can be found also in *The Theory of*

*Communicative Action*, Vol. 2, *The Critique of Functionalist Reason*, trans. T. McCarthy (Boston, 1987), 356–73.

2 Zygmunt Bauman, *Postmodern Ethics* (Oxford, 1993), 126.

3 Georg Simmel, *The Philosophy of Money*, trans. T. Bottomore and D. Frisby (London, 1978), 296.

4 Theodore J. Lowi, 'The Welfare State, The New Regulation, and the Rule of Law,' in A. Hutchinson and Monahan, eds., *The Rule of Law: Ideal or Ideology* (Toronto, 1987), 17–58.

5 Regarding the relations between the development of capitalism and changes in American law, see Morton Horwitz, *The Transformation of American Law, 1780–1860* (Cambridge, Mass., 1977).

6 Lowi, 'The Welfare State,' 25.

7 Ibid., 36.

8 Lawrence M. Friedman, 'Legal Culture and the Welfare State,' in G. Teubner, ed., *Dilemmas of Law in the Welfare State* (Berlin, 1988), 19.

9 Ibid., 23.

10 Christopher D. Stone, *Should Trees Have Standing? Toward Legal Rights for Natural Objects* (Palo Alto, Calif., 1988), 3–10.

11 Maxwell Cohen, 'Human Rights: Programme or Catchall? A Canadian Rationale,' 46 *Canadian Bar Review* (1968), 554–64 at 557.

12 Rogers Brubaker, *The Limits of Rationality: An Essay on the Social and Moral Thought of Max Weber* (London, 1984), 65; emphasis added.

13 For example, see Charles Taylor, 'Alternative Futures: Legitimacy, Identity and Alienation in Late Twentieth Century Canada,' in A. Cairns and C. Williams, eds., *Constitutionalism, Citizenship and Society in Canada* (Toronto, 1985), 183–229.

14 David M. Engel, 'The Oven Bird's Song: Insiders, Outsiders, and Personal Injuries in an American Community,' *Law and Society Review* 18 (1984), 551–82.

15 Ibid., 551–9.

16 Michael J. Sandel, 'The Political Theory of the Procedural Republic,' in Hutchinson and Monahan, eds., *The Rule of Law*, 89.

17 Taylor, 'Alternative Futures,' 210 and 211.

18 Sandel, 'Political Theory of the Procedural Republic,' 93.

19 Ibid., 95.

20 Lawrence M. Friedman, *The Republic of Choice: Law, Authority, and Culture* (London, 1990), 15.

21 Anthony Giddens, *The Transformation of Intimacy: Sexuality, Love and Eroticism in Modern Societies* (Cambridge, 1992).

22  Cf. Alan Hunt, *Explorations in Law and Society: Toward a Constitutive Theory of Law* (London, 1993), 301–33.
23  Lawrence Stone, *Road to Divorce: England, 1530–1987* (Oxford, 1990).
24  Bauman, *Postmodern Ethics*, 107.
25  Giddens, *Transformation of Intimacy*, 58.
26  Taylor, 'Alternative Futures,' 212–13.
27  Wolfgang Mommsen, 'Max Weber's Political Sociology and His Philoso-phy of World History,' *International Social Science Journal* 17 (1965), 23–45 at 41.
28  Zygmunt Bauman, *Freedom* (Concepts in the Social Sciences) (Milton Key-nes, 1988), 49–70; and Mike Featherstone, *Consumer Culture and Postmodern-ism* (London, 1991).
29  Habermas, 'Law as Medium,' 209.
30  Sandel, 'Political Theory of the Procedural Republic,' 96.

**Chapter Five: The Constitutionalization of Individual Rights in Canada**

1  Cf. Jürgen Habermas, *The Theory of Communicative Action*, Vol. 1; *Reason and the Rationalization of Society*, trans. T. McCarthy (Boston, 1984), 26–67. The continuing relevance of Weber's depiction of the regulatory-administrative features of modernity in terms of formal legal rationality is also revealed, for instance, in Stewart R. Clegg's overview of current approaches in orga-nizational studies, *Modern Organizations: Organization Studies in the Post-modern World* (London, 1990), 1–24.
2  David Kettler and Volker Meja, 'Legal Formalism and Disillusioned Real-ism in Max Weber,' *Polity* 18 (1996), 307–31 at 310; see also David Kettler, 'Sociological Classics and the Contemporary State of the Law,' *Canadian Journal of Sociology* 9 (1984), 447–58 at 457.
3  Cf. Phillip Nonet and Philip Selznick, *Law and Society in Transition* (London, 1978); Theodore S. Lowi, *The End of Liberalism: The Second Republic of the United States* (New York, 1979); and Gunther Teubner, ed., *Dilemmas of Law in the Welfare State* (Berlin, 1988).
4  The application of Weber's sociology of modern law to problems of con-temporary constitutional adjudication is not without precedent. Cf. Stephen M. Feldman's use of Weber to elucidate issues of jurisprudence within American constitutional law, 'An Interpretation of Max Weber's Theory of Law: Metaphysics, Economics, and the Iron Cage of Constitu-tional Law,' *Law and Social Inquiry* 16 (1991), 205–48.
5  Charles Taylor, 'Alternative Futures; Legitimacy, Identity and Alienation in Late Twentieth Century Canada,' in A. Cairns and C. Williams, eds., *Consti-tutionalism, Citizenship and Society in Canada* (Toronto, 1985), 211.

6 Cf. Patrick Fitzgerald and King McShane, *Looking at Law: Canada's Legal System* (Ottawa, 1985), 21–32.

7 H.J. Glasbeek, 'A No-Frills Look at the Charter of Rights and Freedoms or How Politicians and Lawyers Hide Reality,' *Windsor Yearbook of Access to Justice* 9 (1989), 293–352 at 299.

8 Cf. Andrew Petter, 'Canada's Charter Flight: Soaring Backwards into the Future,' *Journal of Law and Society* 16 (1989), 151–65 at 160.

9 This typology is adapted from Joel Bakan's discussion. See, 'Constitutional Arguments: Interpretation and Legitimacy in Canadian Constitutional Thought,' *Osgoode Hall Law Journal* 27 (1989), 123–93.

10 *Reference Re Public Service Employee Relations Act (Alta.)*, [1987] 1 S.C.R. 313; *R. v. Big M Drug Mart*, [1985] 1 S.C.R. 295; *Edwards Books and Art v. R.* [1986] 2 S.C.R. 713; *Société des Acadiens v. Association of Parents, Etc.* (1986), 27 D.L.R. (4th) 406.

11 *Hunter v. Southam Inc.*, [1985] 1 S.C.R. 145; *R. v. Morgentaler*, [1988] 1 S.C.R. 30; *Operation Dismantle v. R.*, [1985] 1 S.C.R. 441.

12 *Dolphin Delivery Ltd. v. Retail, Wholesale & Department Store Union*, [1986] 2 S.C.R. 573.

13 Cf. Chief Justice Dickson's comments in *Edwards Books and Art*, 779.

14 See J.A.G. Griffith, *The Politics of the Judiciary* (London, 1985), 198.

15 Justice Bertha Wilson, 'The Making of a Constitution: Approaches to Judicial Interpretation,' *Public Law* (1988), 370–84 at 372.

16 *R. v. Morgentaler*, 39.

17 Peter H. Russell, 'Canada's Charter of Rights and Freedoms: A Political Report,' *Public Law* (1988), 385–401 at 395.

18 John H. Ely, *Democracy and Distrust: A Theory of Judicial Review* (Cambridge, Mass., 1980).

19 J. Skelly Wright, 'The Judicial Right and the Rhetoric of Restraint: A Defense of Judicial Activism in an Age of Conservative Judges,' *Hastings Constitutional Law Quarterly* 14 (1987), 487–523 at 502.

20 *The Charter of Rights and Freedoms: A Guide for Canadians* (Ottawa, 1987), 5; emphasis added.

21 *R. v. Oakes*, [1986] 1 S.C.R. 103.

22 Ibid., 105, 106.

23 Bakan, 'Constitutional Arguments,' 165.

24 *Edwards Books and Art*, 744, 748.

25 See Sidney Peck, 'An Analytical Framework for the Application of the Canadian Charter of Rights and Freedoms,' *Osgoode Hall Law Journal* 25 (1987), 1–85.

26 Justice B. Wilson, 'The Making of a Constitution,' 379–80.

27  For instance, Lynn Smith argues that adjudication of s. 15 equality provisions has on the whole 'improved the legal position of women, persons with disabilities, non-citizens in Canada, gays and lesbians, and other disadvantaged groups' ('Have the Equality Rights Made Any Difference?,' in Philip Bryden, Steven Davis, and John Russel, eds., *Protecting Rights and Freedoms: Essays on the Charter's Place in Canada's Political, Legal, and Intellectual Life* (Toronto, 1994), 72). But these improvements, however laudable, still fit within the larger pattern of liberal individualism that is structurally congruent with the 'dynamic' of legal rationalization discussed previously.

28  For particularly incisive analyses of *Dolphin Delivery* see David Beatty, 'Constitutional Conceit: The Coercive Authority of Courts,' *University of Toronto Law Journal* 50 (1987), 183–92; Allan C. Hutchinson and Andrew Petter, 'Private Rights/ Public Wrongs: The Liberal Lie of the Charter,' *University of Toronto Law Journal* 38 (1988), 278–97; and Michael Mandel, *The Charter of Rights and the Legalization of Politics in Canada* (Toronto, 1992).

29  *Coke on Littleton*, Bk 3, Chap. 3, s. 283, 183b: see Roger Cotterrell, *The Politics of Jurisprudence: A Critical Introduction to Legal Philosophy* (London, 1989), 24–9.

30  See Cotterrell regarding the role of politics in the development of common law (ibid., 27–32).

31  Cf. Morton J. Horowitz, 'The History of the Public/Private Distinction,' *University of Pennsylvania Law Review* 130 (1982), 1423–8.

32  *A.G. Quebec v. Irwin Toy*, [1989] 1 S.C.R. 927.

33  *The Alberta Labour Reference; Public Service Alliance of Canada v. R.*, [1987] 1 S.C.R. 424; *Saskatchewan v. Retail, Wholesale and Dept. Store Union*, [1987] 1 S.C.R. 460.

34  Justice Le Dain, *Alberta Labour Reference*, 391.

35  Chief Justice Dickson, ibid., 366.

36  See Russell, 'Canada's Charter of Rights and Freedoms,' 387; Beatty, 'Constitutional Conceit'; and Leo Panitch and Donald Swartz, *The Assault on Trade Union Freedoms* (Toronto, 1988).

37  *Edwards Books and Art*.

38  *Re Lavigne and Ontario Public Service Employees Union* (1986), 29 D.L.R. (4th) 327; *Re Lavigne and Ontario Public Service Employees Union et al. (No. 2)* (1987), 41 D.L.R. (4th) 86.

39  *Andrews v. Law Society of British Columbia*, [1989] 1 S.C.R. 172.

40  *Edwards Books and Art Ltd., supra; The Queen v. Canadian Newspapers Company Ltd.*, [1988] 2 S.C.R. 122; and *Lavigne*.

41  Lars Osberg, *Economic Inequality in Canada* (Toronto, 1981). Statistics on income distribution are notoriously subject to political manipulation. For

the sake of comparison, in a study published by the C.D. Howe Institute, W. Irwin Gillespie's research shows that 'the poorest 20 percent of family units had 4.4 percent of total income in 1951 and 4.7 percent in 1994. The richest 20 percent had 42.8 percent in 1951 and 43.6 percent in 1994; the richest 5 percent had 17.9 percent in 1951 and 16.0 percent in 1994' (W. Irwin Gillespie, 'The Deficit- and Debt-Reduction Challenge and the Distribution of Income in Canada,' in William B.P. Robson and William M. Scarth, eds., *Equality and Prosperity: Finding Common Ground* (Ottawa, 1994), 54).

42 Historically it has been the nature of the judiciary to bolster the rights of property owners. These 'rights' are always infringed upon by 'public' regulation of the economy. See Mandel, 'The Charter of Rights,' 7, and, in the American context, Russell Galloway, *The Rich and the Poor in Supreme Court History, 1790–1982* (Greenbrae, Calif., 1982), 146.

43 *Black v. Law Society of Alberta* (1986), 27 D.L.R. (4th) 527 (Alta. C.A.).

44 *Hunter v. Southam.*

45 *Bastile v. Attorney General of Nova Scotia* (1984–85), 11 D.L.R. (4th) 219 (N.S.C.A.).

46 *Wilson and Maxson v. Medical Services Commission of B.C.* (1988), 30 B.C.L.R. (2nd) 1 (B.C.C.A.).

47 *Ford v. Attorney General of Quebec*, [1988] 2 S.C.R. 712.

48 See Mandel, 'The Charter of Rights,' 213.

49 *Re Shechuk and Richard* (1986), 28 D.L.R. (4th) 429 (B.C.C.A.); *R. v. Seaboyer*, [1991] 2 S.C.R. 577; *R. v. Canadian Newspapers Company; Schachter v. R.* (1988), 9 *Canadian Human Rights Reporter* D/5320 (F.C.T.D.); *Andrews v. Law Society of British Columbia.*

50 Petter, 'Private Rights, Public Wrongs,' 156–7.

51 Taylor, 'Alternative Futures,' 209.

## Chapter Six: The Limits of Formal Legal Rationality

1 'Loss of meaning' and 'loss of freedom' are Jürgen Habermas's terminology (*The Theory of Communicative Action*, Vol. 1, *Reason and the Rationalization of Society*, trans. T. McCarthy (Boston, 1984), 243).

2 Edward A. Shils, 'Charisma, Order and Status,' *American Sociological Review* 30 (1965), 199–213.

3 Cf. Weber's 'switchmen' metaphor regarding the nexus of ideal and material interests (FMW, 280).

4 Benjamin Nelson, 'Civilizational Complexes and Intercivilizational Encounters,' *Sociological Analysis* 34 (1973), 79–105.

5 Georg Simmel, *On Individuality and Social Forms* (Chicago, 1971), 133.

6 There is some dispute about the relationship between the dynamic of charisma and routinization and Weber's developmental history of the West.
In older parts of *Economy and Society* Weber frequently suggests that, with
disenchantment and rationalization, in the modern West charisma disap-
pears in toto (ES, 1111–56). However, in chronologically more recent parts
of ES, the dynamic of charisma and routinization emerges as a synchronic
model of social change, rather than a description of 'actual' historical
events (ES, 241–54). For a discussion of this problem see Wolfgang Mommsen, *The Political and Social Theory of Max Weber* (Cambridge, 1989), 145–
65.

7 Cf. Zygmunt Bauman, *Freedom* (Concepts in the Social Sciences) (Milton
Keynes, 1988), 49–70.

8 See Wilhelm Hennis, 'Max Weber's "Central Question",' *Economy and Society* 12 (1983), 135–80.

9 Quoted after Hubert Treiber, 'Criticism as a Vocation – Theory and Practice
in a Disenchanted World: A Review Essay,' *Contemporary Crises* 9 (1985),
375–86 at 379.

10 Quoted after David Beetham, *Max Weber and the Theory of Modern Politics*
(Cambridge, 1985), 79.

11 See David Beetham, 'Max Weber and the Liberal Political Tradition,' in A.
Horowitz and T. Maley, eds., *The Barbarism of Reason: Max Weber and the Twilight of Enlightenment* (Toronto, 1994), 105.

12 Joan Tronto, 'Law and Modernity: The Significance of Max Weber's *Sociology of Law*,' *Texas Law Review* 63 (1984), 565–77 at 570.

13 Mark E. Warren, 'Nietzsche and Weber: When Does Reason Become
Power?,' in Horowitz and Maley, eds., *The Barbarism of Reason*, 70–4.

14 Rogers Brubaker, *The Limits of Rationality: An Essay on the Social and Moral
Thought of Max Weber* (London, 1984), 105.

15 Zygmunt Bauman, *Modernity and the Holocaust* (Cambridge, 1988).

16 Karl Mannheim, *Ideology and Utopia*, trans. Louis Wirth and Edward Shils
(New York, 1936), 105.

17 Wolfgang Mommsen, *The Age of Bureaucracy: Perspectives on the Political
Sociology of Max Weber* (Oxford, 1974), 7. Cf. Jürgen Habermas, 'Discussion on Value-freedom and Objectivity,' in Otto Stammer, ed., Kathleen
Morris, trans., *Max Weber and Sociology Today* (Oxford, 1971), 64. Of
course, as noted earlier, a deficiency in Weber's liberal thought is the
excessive emphasis on value-setting as a purely individual process.
Indeed, choice and consent ultimately rest in the hands of the individual.
But, as Habermas rightly points out, Weber ignores the sociological significance of intersubjective dialogue in the formation of informed choice and
consent.

18 Cf. Alasdair MacIntyre, *After Virtue: A Study in Moral Theory* (London, 1985), 107.

19 Some critics argue that Weber was not always so careful to distinguish those features of Wilhelmine German experience which could be universalized from those which were more context specific (cf. Beetham, *Max Weber*, 88). However, despite these problems I am in agreement with Fred Dallmayr's assessment that, in broad outlines, Weber's theory of bureaucracy 'has been largely predictive of twentieth-century developments' ('Max Weber and the Modern State,' in Horowitz and Maley, *The Barbarism of Reason*, 49).

20 Ulrich Beck, 'The Reinvention of Politics,' in Ulrich Beck, Anthony Giddens, and Scott Lash, eds., *Reflexive Modernization: Politics, Tradition and Aesthetics in the Modern Social Order* (Stanford, 1994), 23.

21 Quoted after Karl Löwith, *Max Weber and Karl Marx*, trans. T. Bottomore and W. Outhwaite (London, 1993), 75; translation modified.

22 Beetham, *Max Weber*, 51.

23 See Weber's 'Letter to Robert Michels of 4 August 1908'; quoted in Wolfgang Mommsen, *Max Weber and German Politics, 1890–1920*, trans. Michael S. Steinberg (London, 1984), 395.

24 Anthony Kronman, *Max Weber* (Jurists: Profiles in Legal Theory) (London, 1983), 187; Beetham, *Max Weber*, 114; and Mommsen, *The Political and Social Theory of Max Weber*, 31–2.

25 Beetham, *Max Weber*, 111.

26 Cf. Sheldon S. Wolin, 'Max Weber: Legitimation, Method, and the Politics of Theory,' in Horowitz and Maley, eds., *The Barbarism of Reason*, 298–9.

27 Löwith, *Max Weber and Karl Marx*, 122.

28 Ibid., 70.

29 Cf. Claude Lefort's more recent reflections on democratic society as 'the historical society par excellence, a society which, in its very form, accepts and preserves indeterminacy' (*Essais sur le politique* (Paris, 1986), 25; also, *Democracy and Political Theory* (Cambridge, 1988).

30 Cf. Beck, 'The Reinvention of Politics,' 19.

31 William E. Scheuerman, 'Between radicalism and resignation: democratic theory in Habermas's *Between Facts and Norms*,' in Peter Dews, ed., *Habermas: A Critical Reader* (Oxford, 1999), 166–7.

32 See Nancy Fraser, 'Rethinking the Public Sphere: A Contribution to the Critique of Actually Existing Democracy,' in Craig Calhoun, ed., *Habermas and the Public Sphere* (Cambridge, Mass., 1992), 109–42. Habermas refers to a 'public sphere at rest' [öffentlickeit im Ruhezustand] (*Between Facts and Norms: Contributions to a Discourse Theory of Law and Democracy*, trans. William Rehg (Cambridge, Mass., 1996), 379).

## Conclusion: In the Grip of Freedom

1 Theodor W. Adorno, *Negative Dialectics*, trans. E.B. Ashton (New York, 1987), 56–7; translation amended by David Held: see *Introduction to Critical Theory: Horkheimer to Habermas* (Berkeley and Los Angeles, 1980), 221–2.

2 Søren Kierkegaard, *The Sickness unto Death*, trans. Alastair Hannay (London, 1989), 70.

3 Karl Löwith, *Max Weber and Karl Marx*, trans. T. Bottomore and W. Outhwaite (London, 1993), 71.

4 In Eric Hobsbawm's periodization, the nineteenth century did not draw to a close until the First World War, well into Weber's middle age, and just years before his sudden death in 1920 (*The Age of Empire, 1870–1914* (London, 1987)).

5 Cf. Löwith, *Max Weber and Karl Marx*, 49.

6 Cf. ibid., 68–9.

7 Cf. A.J.P. Taylor, *The Course of German History* (London, 1961), 157–9.

8 Cf. Michel Foucault's discussion of Kant's 1784 article, 'What Is Enlightenment?' in Paul Rabinow, ed., *The Foucault Reader* (New York, 1984), 34–5.

9 Cf. William Connolly, *Political Theory and Modernity* (Oxford, 1988).

10 Wolfgang Schluchter, 'The Paradox of Rationalization,' in G. Roth and W. Schluchter, *Max Weber's Vision of History: Ethics and Methods* (London, 1979), 54–5.

11 Zygmunt Bauman, *Postmodern Ethics* (Oxford, 1993), 9.

12 See Seyla Benhabib, *Situating the Self: Gender, Community and Postmodernism in Contemporary Ethics* (Cambridge, 1992), 89–120.

13 Claus Offe and Helmut Wiesenthal, 'Two Logics of Collective Action,' *Political Power and Social Theory* 1 (1980), 67–115.

14 The reduction in the meaning and scope of democratic institutions indicates the rigidification of the democratic project, the neutralization of its substantive import, which might be defined in terms like the 'institutionalization of autonomy' (Castoriadis) or the 'institutional recognition of indeterminacy' (Lefort). See Cornelius Castoriadis, trans. Kathleen Blamey, *The Imaginary Institution of Society* (Cambridge: Mass., 1987); and Claude Lefort, trans. David Macey, *Democracy and Political Theory* (Cambridge, 1988).

15 Schluchter, 'The Paradox of Rationalization,' 53–4.

16 Roy Boyne, 'The Politics of Risk Society,' *History of the Human Sciences* 11 (1998), 126.

# Bibliography

Adorno, Theodor W. *Negative Dialectics*. Trans. E.B. Ashton. New York, 1987.

Albrow, Martin. *Bureaucracy*. London, 1970.

– *Max Weber's Construction of Social Theory*. London, 1990.

Bakan, Joel. 'Constitutional Arguments: Interpretation and Legitimacy in Canadian Constitutional Thought.' *Osgoode Hall Law Journal* 27 (1989), 123–93.

– *Just Words: Constitutional Rights and Social Wrongs*. Toronto, 1997.

Bauman, Zygmunt. *Freedom* (Concepts in the Social Sciences). Milton Keynes, 1988.

– *Modernity and the Holocaust*. Cambridge, 1988.

– *Postmodern Ethics*. Oxford, 1993.

Beatty, David. 'Constitutional Conceit: The Coercive Authority of the Courts.' *University of Toronto Law Journal* (1987), 37 183–92.

Beck, Ulrich. 'The Reinvention of Politics.' In Ulrich Beck, Anthony Giddens, and Scott Lash, eds., *Reflexive Modernization: Politics, Tradition and Aesthetics in the Modern Social Order*. Stanford, 1994.

Beetham, David. *Max Weber and the Theory of Modern Politics*. Cambridge, 1985.

– 'Max Weber and the Liberal Political Tradition.' In A. Horowitz and T. Maley, eds., *The Barbarism of Reason: Max Weber and the Twilight of Enlightenment*. Toronto, 1994.

Bellah, Robert. *Beyond Belief: Essays on Religion in a Post-Traditional World*. London, 1970.

Bendix, Reinhard. *Max Weber: An Intellectual Portrait*. London, 1966.

Benhabib, Seyla. *Situating the Self: Gender, Community and Postmodernism in Contemporary Ethics*. Cambridge, 1992.

Berman, Harold. *Law and Revolution: The Formation of the Western Legal Tradition.*
Cambridge, Mass., 1983.
– 'Some False Premises of Max Weber's Sociology of Law.' *Washington University Law Quarterly* 65 (1987) 758–70.
Boyne, Roy. 'The Politics of Risk Society.' *History of the Human Sciences* 11
(1998), 125–30.
Brecht, Arnold. *Political Theory: The Foundations of Twentieth-Century Political Thought.* Princeton, 1959.
Brubaker, Rogers. *The Limits of Rationality: An Essay on the Social and Moral Thought of Max Weber.* London, 1984.
Campbell, David. 'Truth Claims and Value-Freedom in the Treatment of Legitimacy: The Case of Weber.' *Journal of Law and Society* 13 (1986), 207–24.
Camus, Albert. *The Fall.* Trans. Justin O'Brien. New York, 1956.
Canada. *The Charter of Rights and Freedoms: A Guide for Canadians.* Ottawa, 1987.
Castoriadis, Cornelius. *The Imaginary Institution of Society.* Trans. Kathleen Blamey. Cambridge, Mass., 1987.
Clegg, Stewart R. *Modern Organizations: Organization Studies in the Postmodern World.* London, 1990.
Cohen, Maxwell. 'Human Rights: Programme or Catchall? A Canadian Rationale.' *Canadian Bar Review* 46 (1968), 554–64.
Collins, Randall. 'Weber's Last Theory of Capitalism: A Systematization.' *American Sociological Review* 45 (1980), 925–42.
Connolly, William. *Political Theory and Modernity.* Oxford, 1988.
Cotterrell, Roger. 'Legality and Political Legitimacy in The Sociology of Max Weber.' In David Sugarman, ed., *Law, State and Society Series: 'Legality, Ideology and the State,'* 69–93. London, 1983.
– *The Politics of Jurisprudence: A Critical Introduction to Legal Philosophy.* London, 1989.
– *The Sociology of Law: An Introduction.* London, 1992.
Dallmayr, Fred. 'Max Weber and the Modern State.' In A. Horowitz and T. Maley, eds., *The Barbarism of Reason: Max Weber and the Twilight of Enlightenment.* Toronto, 1994.
D'Entrèves, Alexander P. 'Legality and Legitimacy.' *Review of Metaphysics* 16 (1963), 687–702.
Ekirch, Arthur A. *Ideologies and Utopias: The Impact of the New Deal on American Thought.* Chicago, 1969.
Ely, John H. *Democracy and Distrust: A Theory of Judicial Review.* Cambridge, Mass., 1980.
Engel, David M. 'The Oven Bird's Song: Insiders, Outsiders, and Personal Injuries in an American Community.' *Law and Society Review* 18 (1984), 551–82.

Ewing, Sally. 'Formal Justice and the Spirit of Capitalism: Max Weber's Sociology of Law.' *Law and Society Review* 21 (1987), 487–512.

Faught, Jim. 'Neglected affinities: Max Weber and Georg Simmel.' *British Journal of Sociology* 36 (1985), 155–74.

Featherstone, Mike. *Consumer Culture and Postmodernism*. London, 1991.

Feldman, Stephen M. 'An Interpretation of Max Weber's Theory of Law: Metaphysics, Economics, and the Iron Cage of Constitutional Law.' *Law and Social Inquiry* 16 (1991), 205–48.

Finnis, J.M. 'On "Positivism" and "Legal Rational Authority".' *Oxford Journal of Legal Studies* 5 (1985), 74–90.

Fitzgerald, Patrick and King McShane. *Looking at Law: Canada's Legal System*. Ottawa, 1985.

Foucault, Michel. 'What Is Enlightenment?' In Paul Rabinow, ed., *The Foucault Reader*. New York, 1984.

Fraser, Nancy. 'Rethinking the Public Sphere: A Contribution to the Critique of Actually Existing Democracy.' In Craig Calhoun, ed., *Habermas and the Public Sphere*. Cambridge, Mass., 1992.

Friedman, Lawrence. 'Legal Culture and the Welfare State.' In G. Teubner, ed., *Dilemmas of Law in the Welfare State*. Berlin, 1988.

– *The Republic of Choice: Law, Authority, and Culture*. London, 1990.

Galloway, Russell. *The Rich and the Poor in Supreme Court History 1790–1982*. Greenbrae, Calif., 1982.

Giddens, Anthony. *Capitalism and Modern Social Theory*. Cambridge, 1971.

– *The Consequences of Modernity*. Cambridge, 1990.

– *The Transformation of Intimacy: Sexuality, Love and Eroticism in Modern Societies*. Cambridge, 1992.

Gillespie, W. Irwin. 'The Deficit- and Debt-Reduction Challenge and the Distribution of Income in Canada.' In William B.P. Robson and William M. Scarth, eds., *Equality and Prosperity: Finding Common Ground*. Ottawa, 1994.

Glasbeek, H.J. 'A No-Frills Look at the Charter of Rights and Freedoms or How Politicians and Lawyers Hide Reality.' *Windsor Yearbook of Access to Justice* 9 (1989), 293–352.

Grafstein, Robert. 'The Failure of Weber's Conception of Legitimacy: Its Causes and Implications.' *Journal of Politics* 43 (1981), 456–72.

Griffith, J.A.G. *The Politics of the Judiciary*. London, 1985.

Habermas, Jürgen. 'Discussion on Value-freedom and Objectivity.' In Otto Stammer, ed., Kathleen Morris (trans.), *Max Weber and Sociology Today*. Oxford, 1971.

– *Legitimation Crisis*. Trans. T. McCarthy. Boston, 1975.

- *Communication and the Evolution of Society.* Trans. and intro. T. McCarthy. Boston, 1979.
- *The Theory of Communicative Action,* Vol. 1. *Reason and the Rationalization of Society.* Trans. T. McCarthy. London, 1984.
- *The Philosophical Discourse of Modernity.* Trans. F. Lawrence. Cambridge, Mass., 1987.
- *The Theory of Communicative Action,* Vol. 2. *The Critique of Functionalist Reason.* Trans. T. McCarthy. Boston, 1987.
- 'Law as Medium and Law as Institution.' In G. Teubner, ed., Iain Fraser and Constance Meldrum, trans., *Dilemmas of Law in the Welfare State.* Berlin, 1988.
- *Between Facts and Norms: Contributions to a Discourse Theory of Law and Democracy.* Trans. William Rehg. Cambridge, Mass., 1996.

Hamilton, Peter, ed. *Max Weber.* London, 1993.

Hart, H.L.A. *Essays in Jurisprudence and Philosophy.* Oxford, 1983.

Hayek, Friedrich. *Law, Legislation and Liberty,* Vol. 1. *Rules and Order.* Chicago, 1973.

Held, David. *Introduction to Critical Theory: Horkheimer to Habermas.* Berkeley and Los Angeles, 1980.

Hennis, Wilhelm. 'Max Weber's "Central Question".' *Economy and Society* 12 (1983), 135–80.

Hobsbawm, Eric. *The Age of Empire, 1870–1914.* London, 1987.

Holton, Robert J., and Bryan S. Turner. *Max Weber on Economy and Society.* London, 1989.

Horowitz, Morton J. 'The History of the Public/ Private Distinction.' *University of Pennsylvania Law Review* 130 (1982), 1423–8.

Horwitz, Morton J. *The Transformation of American Law, 1780–1860.* Cambridge, Mass., 1977.

Hunt, Alan. *The Sociological Movement in Law.* London, 1978.

- 'Rights and Social Movements: Counter-Hegemonic Strategies.' *Journal of Law and Society* 17 (1990), 309–28.
- *Explorations in Law and Society: Toward a Constitutive Theory of Law.* London, 1993.

Hunt, Alan, and John Tweedy. 'The Future of the Welfare State and Social Rights: Reflections on Habermas.' *Journal of Law and Society* 21 (1994), 288–316.

Hutchinson, Allan. *Waiting for Coraf: A Critique of Law and Rights.* Toronto, 1995.

Hutchinson, Allan C., and Andrew Petter. 'Private Rights/Public Wrongs: The Liberal Lie of the Charter.' *University of Toronto Law Journal* 38 (1988), 278–97.

Hyde, Alan. 'The Concept of Legitimation in the Sociology of Law.' *Wisconsin Law Review* 17 (1983), 379–426.

Joerges, Christian, and David Trubek, eds., *Critical Legal Thought: A German–American Debate*. Baden-Baden, 1989.

Kalberg, Stephen. 'The Search for Thematic Orientations in a Fragmented Oeuvre: The Discussion of Max Weber in Recent German Sociological Literature.' *Sociology* 13 (1979), 127–39.

– 'Max Weber's Types of Rationality: Cornerstones for the Analysis of Rationalization Processes in History.' *American Journal of Sociology* 85 (1980), 1145–79.

– 'The Role of Ideal Interests in Max Weber's Comparative Historical Sociology.' In Robert Antonio and Ronald Glassman, eds., *A Weber–Marx Dialogue*. Lawrence, Kansas, 1985.

– *Max Weber's Comparative-Historical Sociology*. Cambridge, 1993.

Käsler, Dirk. *Max Weber: An Introduction to his Life and Work*. Trans. Philippa Hurd. Cambridge, 1988.

Keane, John. 'Power, Legitimacy, and the Fate of Liberal Contract Theory.' *Praxis International* 2 (1982), 284–96.

Keat, Russel, and Nicholas Abercrombie, eds. *Enterprise Culture*. London, 1991.

Kennedy, Duncan. 'Legal Formality.' *Journal of Legal Studies* 2 (1973), 351–98.

Kettler, David. 'Sociological Classics and the Contemporary State of the Law.' *Canadian Journal of Sociology* 9 (1984), 447–58.

Kettler, David, and Volker Meja. 'Legal Formalism and Disillusioned Realism in Max Weber.' *Polity* 18 (1996), 307–31.

Kierkegaard, Søren. *The Sickness Unto Death*. Trans. Alastair Hannay. London, 1989.

Kinsey, Richard. 'Marxism and the Law: Preliminary Analyses.' *British Journal of Law and Society* 5 (1978), 202–27.

Körner, S. *Kant*. London, 1955.

Kronman, Anthony T. *Max Weber* (Jurists: Profiles in Legal Theory). London, 1983.

Kymlicka, Will. 'Liberalism and Communitarianism.' *Philosophy and Public Affairs* 18 (1988), 181–204.

Lefort, Claude. *Essais sur le politique*. Paris, 1986.

– *Democracy and Political Theory*. Trans. David Macey. Cambridge, 1988.

Levi, Primo. *The Drowned and the Saved*. Trans. Raymond Rosenthal. London, 1988.

Levine, Donald N. 'Rationality and Freedom: Weber and Beyond.' *Sociological Inquiry* 51 (1981), 5–25.

Lowi, Theodore J. *The End of Liberalism: The Second Republic of the United States*. New York, 1979.

– 'The Welfare State, The New Regulation, and the Rule of Law.' In A. Hutchinson and P. Monahan, eds., *The Rule of Law: Ideal or Ideology*. Toronto, 1987.

Löwith, Karl. *Max Weber and Karl Marx*. Trans. T. Bottomore and W. Outhwaite. London, 1993.

MacIntyre, Alasdair. *After Virtue: A Study in Moral Theory*. London, 1985.

Mandel, Michael. *The Charter of Rights and the Legalization of Politics in Canada*. Toronto, 1992.

Mannheim, Karl. *Ideology and Utopia*. Trans. Louis Worth and Edward Shils. New York, 1936.

Marcuse, Herbert. 'Industrialization and Capitalism.' In O. Stammer, ed., Kathleen Morris, trans., *Max Weber and Sociology Today*. Oxford, 1971.

Midgley, E.B.F. *The Ideology of Max Weber: A Thomist Critique*. Totowa, N.J., 1983.

Mommsen, Wolfgang. 'Max Weber's Political Sociology and His Philosophy of World History.' *International Social Science Journal* 17 (1965), 23–45.

– *The Age of Bureaucracy: Perspectives on the Sociology of Max Weber*. Oxford, 1974.

– *Max Weber and German Politics, 1890–1920*. Trans. Michael S. Steinburg. London, 1984.

– *The Political and Social Theory of Max Weber*. Cambridge, 1989.

Montaigne, Michel de. *Essays*. Trans. J.M. Cohen. London, 1958.

Nelson, Benjamin. 'Civilizational Complexes and Intercivilizational Encounters.' *Sociological Analysis* 34 (1973), 79–105.

– 'Max Weber's "Author's Introduction" (1920): A Master Clue to His Main Aims.' *Sociological Inquiry* 44 (1974), 269–78.

Nonet, Phillip, and Philip Selznick. *Law and Society in Transition*. London, 1978.

Offe, Claus, and Helmut Wiesenthal. 'Two Logics of Collective Action.' *Political Power and Social Theory* 1 (1980), 67–115.

O'Neill, John. 'The Disciplinary Society: From Weber to Foucault,' *British Journal of Sociology* 37 (1986), 42–60.

Osberg, Lars. *Economic Inequality in Canada*. Toronto, 1981.

Panitch, Leo, and Donald Swartz. *The Assault on Trade Union Freedoms*. Toronto, 1988.

Parsons, Talcott. 'Value-freedom and Objectivity.' In O. Stammer, ed., *Max Weber and Sociology Today*. Oxford, 1971.

Peck, Sidney. 'An Analytical Framework for the Application of the Canadian Charter of Rights and Freedoms.' *Osgoode Hall Law Journal* 25 (1987), 1–85.

Petter, Andrew. 'Canada's Charter Flight: Soaring Backwards into the Future.' *Journal of Law and Society* 16 (1989), 151–65.

Polanyi, Karl. *The Great Transformation*. Boston, 1944.

Portis, E.B. 'Max Weber's Theory of Personality.' *Sociological Inquiry* 48 (1978), 113–20.

Raz, Joseph. *The Morality of Freedom*. London, 1986.

Rheinstein, Max. 'Introduction.' *Max Weber on Law in Economy and Society*. New York, 1954.

Rose, Nikolas. 'Governing "advanced" Liberal Democracies.' In A. Barry, T. Osborne, and N. Rose, eds., *Foucault and Political Reason: Liberalism, Neo-Liberalism and Rationalities of Government*. Chicago, 1996.

Roth, Guenther. 'Introduction.' In Max Weber *Economy and Society: An Outline of Interpretive Sociology*. Berkeley, 1978.

– 'Rationalization in Max Weber's Developmental History.' In Sam Whimster and Scott Lash, eds., *Max Weber, Rationality and Modernity*. London, 1987.

Roth, Guenther, and Wolfgang Schluchter. *Max Weber's Vision of History: Ethics and Methods*. Berkeley, 1979.

Russell, Peter H. 'Canada's Charter of Rights and Freedoms: A Political Report.' *Public Law* (1988), 385–401.

Sandel, Michael J. 'The Political Theory of the Procedural Republic.' In A. Hutchinson and P. Monahan, eds., *The Rule of Law: Ideal or Ideology*. Toronto, 1987.

Scaff, Lawrence A. *Fleeing the Iron Cage: Culture, Politics, and Modernity in the Thought of Max Weber*. London, 1989.

Schluchter, Wolfgang. 'The Paradox of Rationalization.' In G. Roth and W. Schluchter, *Max Weber's Vision of History: Ethics and Methods*. Berkeley, 1979.

– *The Rise of Western Rationalism: Max Weber's Developmental History*. Trans. G. Roth. London, 1981.

Scheuerman, William E. 'Between radicalism and resignation: democratic theory in Habermans's *Between Facts and Norms*. In Peter Dews, ed., *Habermas: A Critical Reader*. Oxford, 1999.

Schwartz, Nancy. 'Max Weber's Philosophy.' *Yale Law Journal* 93 (1984), 1386–98.

Seidman, Steven. 'Modernity, Meaning and Cultural Pessimism in Max Weber.' *Sociological Analysis* 44 (1983), 267–78.

– 'The Main Aims and Thematic Structures of Max Weber's Sociology.' *Canadian Journal of Sociology* 9 (1984), 381–404.

Shils, Edward A. 'Charisma, Order and Status.' *American Sociological Review* 30 (1965), 199–213.

Simmel, Georg. *On Individuality and Social Forms*, ed. Donald N. Levine. Chicago, 1971.

– *The Philosophy of Money*. Trans. T. Bottomore and D. Frisby. London, 1978.

Simmonds, N.E. *Central Issues in Jurisprudence: Justice, Law and Rights*. London, 1986.

Smith, Lynn. 'Have the Equality Rights Made Any Difference?.' In Philip Bryden, Steven Davis, and John Russell, eds., *Protecting Rights and Freedoms: Essays on the Charter's Place in Canada's Political, Legal, and Intellectual Life*. Toronto, 1994.

Smith, P., and S. Bailey. *The Modern English Legal System*. London, 1984.

Spitzer, Steven. 'Marxist Perspectives in the Sociology of Law.' *Annual Review of Sociology* 9 (1983), 103–24.

Stone, Christopher D. *Should Trees Have Standing? Toward Legal Rights for Natural Objects*. Palo Alto, Cal., 1988.

Stone, Lawrence. *Road to Divorce: England 1530 to 1987*. Oxford, 1990.

Strauss, Leo. *Natural Right and History*. Chicago, 1953.

Strong, Tracey B. '"What Have We to Do with Morals": Nietzsche and Weber on History and Ethics.' *History of the Human Sciences* 5 (1992), 9–18.

Sugarman, D. *Weber, Modernity and 'The Peculiarities of the English': The Rationality and Irrationality of Law, State and Society in Modern Britain*. Working Paper Series. Madison Wis., 1986.

Taylor, A.J.P. *The Course of German History*. London, 1961.

Taylor, Charles. 'Alternative Futures: Legitimacy, Identity and Alienation in Late Twentieth Century Canada.' In A. Cairns and C. Williams, eds., *Constitutionalism, Citizenship and Society in Canada*. Toronto, 1985.

Tenbruck, Friedrich. 'The Problem of Thematic Unity in the Works of Max Weber.' *British Journal of Sociology* 31 (1980), 316–51.

Teubner, Gunther. 'Substantive and Reflexive Elements in Modern Law.' *Law and Society Review* 17 (1983), 239–85.

– 'Juridification: Concepts, Aspects, Limits, Solutions.' In G. Teubner, ed., *Juridification of Social Spheres*. Berlin, 1987.

– ed., *Dilemmas of Law in the Welfare State*. Berlin, 1988.

Thompson, E.P. *Whigs and Hunters: The Origin of the Black Act*. London, 1975.

Treiber, Hubert. 'Criticism as a Vocation – Theory and Practice in a Disenchanted World: A Review Essay.' *Contemporary Crises* 9 (1985), 375–86.

– '"Elective Affinities" between Weber's Sociology of Religion and Sociology of Law.' *Theory and Society* 14 (1985), 809–61.

Tronto, Joan. 'Law and Modernity: The Significance of Max Weber's *Sociology of Law*.' *Texas Law Review* 63 (1984), 565–77.

Trubek, David. 'Max Weber on Law and the Rise of Capitalism.' *Wisconsin Law Review* 3 (1972), 720–53.

– 'Reconstructing Max Weber's Sociology of Law.' *Stanford Law Review* 37 (1985), 919–36.

- 'Max Weber's Tragic Modernism and the Study of Law in Society,' *Law and Society Review* 20 (1986), 573–98.
Trubek, David, John Esser, and Laurel Munger. *Preliminary, Eclectic, Unannotated Working Bibliography for the Study of Max Weber's 'Sociology of Law.'* Madison, Wis., 1986.
Turner, Stephen P., and Regis A. Factor. *Max Weber and the Dispute Over Reason and Value: A Study in Philosophy, Ethics, and Politics.* London, 1984.
- 'Decisionism and Politics: Weber as Constitutional Theorist.' In Sam Whimster and Scott Lash, eds., *Max Weber, Rationality and Modernity.* London, 1987.
- *Max Weber: The Lawyer as Social Thinker.* London, 1994.
Unger, Roberto. *Knowledge and Politics.* London, 1975.
- *Law in Modern Society.* London, 1977.
Wagner, Peter. *A Sociology of Modernity: Liberty and Discipline.* London, 1994.
Walton, Paul. 'Max Weber's Sociology of Law: A Critique.' In P. Carlen, ed., *The Sociology of Law.* Sociological Review Monograph 23 (Keele, 1976).
Walzer, Michael. 'The Communitarian Critique of Liberalism.' *Political Theory* 18 (1990), 6–23.
Warren, Mark E. 'Max Weber's Liberalism for a Nietzschean World.' *American Political Science Review* 82 (1988), 31–50.
- 'Nietzsche and Weber: When Does Reason Become Power?' In A. Horowitz and T. Maley, eds., *The Barbarism of Reason: Max Weber and the Twilight of Enlightenment.* Toronto, 1994.
Weber, Marianne. *Max Weber: A Biography.* Trans. Harry Zohn. New Brunswick, N.J., 1988.
Weber, Max. *The Protestant Ethic and the Spirit of Capitalism.* Trans. Talcott Parsons. London, 1930.
- *From Max Weber: Essays in Sociology.* Trans. and ed. H.H. Gerth and C. Wright Mills. London, 1948.
- *The Methodology of the Social Sciences.* Trans. and ed. Edward A. Shils and Henry A. Finch. New York, 1949.
- *The Religion of China.* Trans. and ed. Hans Gerth. New York, 1951.
- *Ancient Judaism.* Trans. and ed. Hans Gerth and Don Martindale. New York, 1952.
- *Max Weber on Law in Economy and Society.* New York, 1954.
- *The Religion of India.* Trans. and ed. Hans Gerth and Don Martindale. New York, 1958.
- *Max Weber: The Interpretation of Social Reality.* Ed. J.E.T. Eldridge. London, 1972.
- *The Agrarian Sociology of Ancient Civilizations.* Trans. R.I. Frank. London, 1976.
- 'Anticritical Last Word on *The Spirit of Capitalism.*' Trans and intro. by Wallace M. Davis. *American Journal of Sociology* 83 (1978), 1105–31.

- *Economy and Society: An Outline of Interpretive Sociology,* Ed. Guenther Roth and Claus Wittich. London, 1978.
- *General Economic History.* Trans. Frank H. Knight. New Brunswick, N.J., 1981.
- 'Developmental Tendencies in the Situation of East Elbian Rural Labourers.' In Keith Tribe, ed. and trans., *Reading Weber.* London, 1989.

Whimster, Sam, and Scott Lash. 'Introduction.' In *Max Weber, Rationality and Modernity.* London, 1987.

Wilson, Justice Bertha. 'The Making of a Constitution: Approaches to Judicial Interpretation.' *Public Law* (1988), 370–84.

Wolin, Sheldon. 'Max Weber: Legitimation, Method, and the Politics of Theory.' In A. Horowitz and T. Maley, eds., *The Barbarism of Reason: Max Weber and the Twilight of the Enlightenment.* Toronto, 1994.

Wright, J. Skelly. 'The Judicial Right and the Rhetoric of Restraint: A Defense of Judicial Activism in an Age of Conservative Judges.' *Hastings Constitutional Law Quarterly* 14 (1987), 487–523.

# Legal Cases

(All cases are Canadian except *Korematsu* and *Dred Scott*).

*A.G. Quebec v. Irwin Toy*, [1989] 1 S.C.R. 927.

*Andrews v. Law Society of British Columbia*, [1989] 1 S.C.R. 143.

*Bastile v. A.G. Nova Scotia* (1984–5), 11 D.L.R. (4th) 219 (N.S.C.A.).

*Black v. Law Society of Alberta* (1986), 27 D.L.R. (4th) 527 (Alta. C.A.).

*Dolphin Delivery v. Retail, Wholesale and Department Store Union*, [1986] 2 S.C.R. 573.

*Dred Scott v. Sandford*, 60 United States (19 How.) 396 (1856).

*Edwards Books and Art v. R.*, [1986] 2 S.C.R. 713.

*Ford v. A.G. Quebec*, [1988] 2 S.C.R. 712.

*Hunter v. Southam*, [1985] 1 S.C.R. 145.

*Korematsu v. United States*, 323 U.S. 214 (1945).

*Operation Dismantle v. R.*, [1985] 1 S.C.R. 441.

*Public Service Alliance of Canada v. R.*, [1987] 1 S.C.R. 424.

*R. v. Big M Drug Mart*, [1985] 1 S.C.R. 295.

*R. v. Canadian Newspapers Company*, [1988] 2 S.C.R. 122.

*R. v. Morgentaler*, [1988] 1 S.C.R. 30.

*R. v. Oakes*, [1986] 1 S.C.R. 103.

*R. v. Seaboyer*, [1991] 2 S.C.R. 577.

*Re Lavigne and Ontario Public Service Employees Union* (1986), 29 D.L.R. (4th) 327; *Re Lavigne and Ontario Public Service Employees Union (No. 2)* (1987), 41 D.L.R. (4th) 86.

*Re Shechuk and Richard* (1986), 28 D.L.R. (4th) 429 (B.C.C.A.).

*Reference Re Public Service Employee Relations Act (Alta.)*, [1987] 1 S.C.R. 313.

*Saskatchewan v. Retail, Wholesale and Dept. Store Union*, [1987] 1 S.C.R. 460.

*Schachter v. R.* (1988), 9 Canadian Human Rights Reporter D/5320 (F.C.T.D.).

*Société des Acadiens v. Association of Parents* (1986), 27 D.L.R. (4th) 406.

*Wilson and Maxson v. Medical and Services Commission of B.C.* (1988), 30 B.C.L.R. (2nd) 1 (B.C.C.A.).

# Index

action: basic types, 20, 194n. 1. *See also* purposive-rational action
Adorno, Theodor W., 182
*Andrews* v. *Law Society of British Columbia*, 148, 152
Arendt, Hannah, 187
*A.G. Quebec* v. *Irwin Toy*, 147
authority. *See* legal-rational authority, traditional authority
autonomy. *See* freedom

Bakan, Joel, 140, 141
Bauman, Zygmunt, 109, 125, 167, 186, 200n. 38
Beetham, David, 176
Bellah, Robert, 31
Bendix, Reinhard, 57
Bismarck, Otto von, 184
Boyne, Roy, 189
Brubaker, Rogers, 8, 40, 92, 120, 167
bureaucracy, 26–9, 157–9; formal rationality of, 27; and government, 172; as indispensable to democracy, 158–9; and shallow-willing, 163–5, 172

calculability of action: in bureaucracy, 28, 39–40; in capitalist economy, 23–4; in modern legal system, 51, 90, 110; in personal relationships, 125–6; in relation to constitutional adjudication, 144, 153; in relation to freedom, 125–6
Camus, Albert, v
Canadian Charter of Rights and Freedoms, 14; and adjudication, 16; and applicability to common law, 146; and depoliticization of values, 133, 144, 154, 186–7; and formal legal rationality, 132, 135, 142–3; and freedom, 149–52, 153–4; and legal rationalization, 153–5; and judicial review, 132, 134–5 (legitimacy of) 135–9; and restrictions on governments, 132, 133–5, 136, 146–51. *See also* Charter adjudication, legitimacy
capitalism: development of, 11; formal rationality of, 23–6; and freedom, 159; and law, 26; and legal rationalization, 83–6, 92–4, 96, 111–14; and legal regulation,